T0353432

Neural Networks for Natural Language Processing

Sumathi S.
St. Joseph's College of Engineering, India

Janani M.
St. Joseph's College of Engineering, India

A volume in the Advances
in Computer and Electrical
Engineering (ACEE) Book Series

Published in the United States of America by
    IGI Global
    Engineering Science Reference (an imprint of IGI Global)
    701 E. Chocolate Avenue
    Hershey PA, USA 17033
    Tel: 717-533-8845
    Fax: 717-533-8661
    E-mail: cust@igi-global.com
    Web site: http://www.igi-global.com

Library of Congress Cataloging-in-Publication Data

Names: S., Sumathi, 1979- editor. | M., Janani, 1988- editor.
Title: Neural networks for natural language processing / Sumathi S, Janani
  M, editors.
Description: Hershey PA : Engineering Science Reference, [2020] | Includes
  bibliographical references and index. | Summary: "This book examines
  natural language processing models and algorithms using traditional
  symbolic and more recent statistical approaches"-- Provided by
  publisher.
Identifiers: LCCN 2019025554 (print) | LCCN 2019025555 (ebook) | ISBN
  9781799811596 (h/c) | ISBN 9781799811602 (s/c) | ISBN 9781799811619
  (ebook)
Subjects: LCSH: Natural language processing (Computer science) | Neural
  networks (Computer science)
Classification: LCC QA76.9.N38 N4785 2020 (print) | LCC QA76.9.N38
  (ebook) | DDC 006.3/2--dc23
LC record available at https://lccn.loc.gov/2019025554
LC ebook record available at https://lccn.loc.gov/2019025555

This book is published in the IGI Global book series Advances in Computer and Electrical Engineering (ACEE) (ISSN: 2327-039X; eISSN: 2327-0403)

British Cataloguing in Publication Data
A Cataloguing in Publication record for this book is available from the British Library.

For electronic access to this publication, please contact: eresources@igi-global.com.

Advances in Computer and Electrical Engineering (ACEE) Book Series

ISSN:2327-039X
EISSN:2327-0403

Editor-in-Chief: Srikanta Patnaik, SOA University, India

MISSION

The fields of computer engineering and electrical engineering encompass a broad range of interdisciplinary topics allowing for expansive research developments across multiple fields. Research in these areas continues to develop and become increasingly important as computer and electrical systems have become an integral part of everyday life.

The **Advances in Computer and Electrical Engineering (ACEE) Book Series** aims to publish research on diverse topics pertaining to computer engineering and electrical engineering. **ACEE** encourages scholarly discourse on the latest applications, tools, and methodologies being implemented in the field for the design and development of computer and electrical systems.

COVERAGE

- Applied Electromagnetics
- Digital Electronics
- Computer Architecture
- Programming
- Microprocessor Design
- Computer Science
- Sensor Technologies
- Analog Electronics
- Circuit Analysis
- VLSI Design

IGI Global is currently accepting manuscripts for publication within this series. To submit a proposal for a volume in this series, please contact our Acquisition Editors at Acquisitions@igi-global.com or visit: http://www.igi-global.com/publish/.

Titles in this Series

For a list of additional titles in this series, please visit:
https://www.igi-global.com/book-series/advances-computer-electrical-engineering/73675

Electrical Insulation Breakdown and Its Theory, Process, and Prevention Emerging Research and Opportunities
Boxue Du (Tianjin University, China)
Engineering Science Reference • copyright 2020 • 230pp • H/C (ISBN: 9781522588856)
• US $215.00 (our price)

Challenges and Applications for Implementing Machine Learning in Computer Vision
Ramgopal Kashyap (Amity University Chhattisgarh, India) and A.V. Senthil Kumar (Hindusthan College of Arts and Science, India)
Engineering Science Reference • copyright 2020 • 300pp • H/C (ISBN: 9781799801825)
• US $195.00 (our price)

Handbook of Research on Recent Developments in Electrical and Mechanical Engineering
Jamal Zbitou (University of Hassan 1st, Morocco) Catalin Iulian Pruncu (Imperial College London, UK) and Ahmed Errkik (University of Hassan 1st, Morocco)
Engineering Science Reference • copyright 2020 • 553pp • H/C (ISBN: 9781799801177)
• US $255.00 (our price)

Architecture and Security Issues in Fog Computing Applications
Sam Goundar (The University of the South Pacific, Fiji) S. Bharath Bhushan (Sree Vidyanikethan Engineering College, India) and Praveen Kumar Rayani (National Institute of Technology, Durgapur, India)
Engineering Science Reference • copyright 2020 • 205pp • H/C (ISBN: 9781799801948)
• US $215.00 (our price)

Handbook of Research on Advanced Applications of Graph Theory in Modern Society
Madhumangal Pal (Vidyasagar University, India) Sovan Samanta (Tamralipta Mahavidyalaya, India) and Anita Pal (National Institute of Technology Durgapur, India)
Engineering Science Reference • copyright 2020 • 591pp • H/C (ISBN: 9781522593805)
• US $245.00 (our price)

For an entire list of titles in this series, please visit:
https://www.igi-global.com/book-series/advances-computer-electrical-engineering/73675

701 East Chocolate Avenue, Hershey, PA 17033, USA
Tel: 717-533-8845 x100 • Fax: 717-533-8661
E-Mail: cust@igi-global.com • www.igi-global.com

Table of Contents

Detailed Table of Contents

Artificial intelligence (AI) is defined as a machine that can do everything a human being can do and produce better results. Means AI enlightening that data can produce a solution for its own results. Inside the AI ellipsoidal, Machine learning (ML) has a wide variety of algorithms produce more accurate results. As a result of technology, improvement increasing amounts of data are available. But with ML and AI, it is very difficult to extract such high-level, abstract features from raw data, moreover hard to know what feature should be extracted. Finally, we now have deep learning; these algorithms are modeled based on how human brains process the data. Deep learning is a particular kind of machine learning that provides flexibility and great power, with its attempts to learn in multiple levels of representation with the operations of multiple layers. Deep learning brief overview, platforms, Models, Autoencoders, CNN, RNN, and Appliances are described appropriately. Deep learning will have many more successes in the near future because it requires very little engineering by hand.

Chapter 2

The chapter is about deep learning fundaments and its recent trends. The chapter mentions many advanced applications and deep learning models and networks to easily solve those applications in a very smart way. Discussion of some techniques for computer vision problem and how to solve with deep learning approach are included. After taking fundamental knowledge of the background theory, one can create or solve applications. The current state-of-the-art of deep learning for education, healthcare, agriculture, industrial, organizations, and research and development applications are very fast growing. The chapter is about types of learning in a deep learning approach, what kind of data set one can be required, and what kind of hardware facility is required for the particular complex problem. For unsupervised learning problems, Deep learning algorithms have been designed, but in the same way Deep learning is also solving the supervised learning problems for a wide variety of tasks.

Chapter 3

    Chitra A. Dhawale, P. R. Pote College of Engineering and Management, India
    Krtika Dhawale, Indian Institute of Information Technology, Nagpur, India

Artificial Intelligence (AI) is going through its golden era by playing an important role in various real-time applications. Most AI applications are using Machine learning and it represents the most promising path to strong AI. On the other hand, Deep Learning (DL), which is itself a kind of Machine Learning (ML), is becoming more and more popular and successful at different use cases, and is at the peak of developments. Hence, DL is becoming a leader in this domain. To foster the growth of the DL community to a greater extent, many open source frameworks are available which implemented DL algorithms. Each framework is based on an algorithm with specific applications. This chapter provides a brief qualitative review of the most popular and comprehensive DL frameworks, and informs end users of trends in DL Frameworks. This helps them make an informed decision to choose the best DL framework that suits their needs, resources, and applications so they choose a proper career.

Chapter 4

    Revathi A., SASTRA University, India
    Sasikaladevi N., SASTRA University, India

This chapter on multi speaker independent emotion recognition encompasses the use of perceptual features with filters spaced in Equivalent rectangular bandwidth (ERB) and BARK scale and vector quantization (VQ) classifier for classifying groups and artificial neural network with back propagation algorithm for emotion classification in a group. Performance can be improved by using the large amount of data in a pertinent emotion to adequately train the system. With the limited set of data, this proposed system has provided consistently better accuracy for the perceptual feature with critical band analysis done in ERB scale.

Chapter 5

Neural networks are like the models of the brain and nervous system. It is highly parallel and processes information much more like the brain than a serial computer. It is very useful in learning information, using and executing very simple and complex behaviors, applications like powerful problem solvers and biological models. There are different types of neural networks like Biological, Feed Forward, Recurrent, and Elman. Biological Neural Networks require some biological data to predict information. In Feed Forward Networks, information flows in one way. In Recurrent Networks, information flows in multiple directions. Elman Networks feature Partial re-currency with a sense of time.

Chapter 6

Question Classification(QC) mainly deals with syntactic parsing for finding the similarity. To improve the accuracy of classification, a semantic similarity approach of a question along with the question dataset is calculated. The semantic similarity of the question is initially achieved by syntactic parsing to extract the noun, verb, adverb, and adjective. However, adjectives and adverbs do give sentences an exact meaning that should also be considered for computing the semantic similarity. The proposed RLQC (Register Linear and Question Classification) model for semantic similarity of questions uses HSO (Hirst and St. Onge) measure with Gloss based measure to enhance the semantic similarity relatedness by considering the Noun, Verb, Adverb and Adjective. The semantic similarity of the question pairs for RLQC is 0.2% higher compared to HSO model. The highest semantic similarity of the proposed model achieves a better accuracy.

Chapter 7

Anjali Daisy, SASTRA University, India

Nowadays, as computer systems are expected to be intelligent, techniques that help modern applications to understand human languages are in much demand. Amongst all the techniques, the latent semantic models are the most important. They exploit the latent semantics of lexicons and concepts of human languages and transform them into tractable and machine-understandable numerical representations. Without that, languages are nothing but combinations of meaningless symbols for the machine. To provide such learning representation, embedding models for knowledge graphs have attracted much attention in recent years since they intuitively transform important concepts and entities in human languages into vector representations, and realize relational inferences among them via simple vector calculation. Such novel techniques have effectively resolved a few tasks like knowledge graph completion and link prediction, and show the great potential to be incorporated into more natural language processing (NLP) applications.

Chapter 8

Anumeera Balamurali, St.Joseph's College of Engineering, India
Balamurali Ananthanarayanan, Tamilnadu Agriculture Department,
India

A Bag-of-Words model is widely used to extract the features from text, which is given as input to machine learning algorithm like MLP, neural network. The dataset considered is movie reviews with both positive and negative comments further converted to Bag-of-Words model. Then the Bag-of-Word model of the dataset is converted into vector representation which corresponds to a number of words in the vocabulary. Each word in the review documents is assigned with a score and the scores are later represented in vector representation which is later fed as input to neural model. In the Kera's deep learning library, the neural models will be simple feedforward network models with fully connected layers called 'Dense'. Bigram language models are developed to classify encoded documents as either positive or negative. At first, reviews are converted to lines of token and then encoded to bag-of-words model. Finally, a neural model is developed to score bigram of words with word scoring modes.

Chapter 9

Kayalvizhi S., SSN College of Engineering, India
Thenmozhi D., SSN College of Engineering, India

Catch phrases are the important phrases that precisely explain the document. They represent the context of the whole document. They can also be used to retrieve relevant prior cases by the judges and lawyers for assuring justice in the domain of law. Currently, catch phrases are extracted using statistical methods, machine learning techniques, and deep learning techniques. The authors propose a sequence to sequence (Seq2Seq) deep neural network to extract catch phrases from legal documents. They have employed several layers, namely embedding layer, encoder-decoder layer, projection layer, and loss layer to build the deep neural network. The methodology is evaluated on IRLeD@FIRE-2017 dataset and the method has obtained 0.787 and 0.607 as mean average precision and recall scores respectively. Results show that the proposed method outperforms the existing systems.

Chapter 10

Arunmozhi Mourougappane, St.Joseph's College of Engineering, India
Suresh Jaganathan, SSN College of Engineering, India

Sentiment Analysis and classification becomes a key trend in the human world in analyzing the nature and quality of the product, people's emotion, inference about products, and movies. Sentiment Analysis is the process of classification as it classifies the inference or review into positive or negative. Since the data that are labeled are very expensive and difficult to gather, it is hard. Also, the sarcastic data and homonyms are difficult to be identified. Hence the assumption of reviews will be wrong. The solution to identify the sarcastic words and the words with different meanings happens with the help of Recurrent Neural Networks.

Chapter 11

Sumathi S., St.Joseph's College of Engineering, India
Rajkumar S., HCL Technologies Ltd., India
Indumathi S., Jerusalem College of Engineering, India

Lease abstraction is the method of compartmentalization of key data from a lease document. Lease document for a property contains key business, money, and legal data about a property. A lease abstract report contains details concerning the property location and basic lease details, price schedules, key events, terms and conditions, automobile parking arrangements, and landowner and tenant obligations. Abstracting a true estate contract into electronic type facilitates easy access to key data, exchanging the tedious method of reading the whole contents of the contract every time. Language process may be used for data extraction and abstraction of knowledge from lease documents.

Chapter 12
Brian Tuan Khieu, San Jose State University, USA
Melody Moh, San Jose State University, USA

This chapter presents a literature survey of the current state of hate speech detection models with a focus on neural network applications in the area. The growth and freedom of social media has facilitated the dissemination of positive and negative ideas. Proponents of hate speech are one of the key abusers of the privileges allotted by social media, and the companies behind these networks have a vested interest in identifying such speech. Manual moderation is too cumbersome and slow to deal with the torrent of content generation on these social media sites, which is why many have turned to machine learning. Neural network applications in this area have been very promising and yielded positive results. However, there are newly discovered and unaddressed problems with the current state of hate speech detection. Authors' survey identifies the key techniques and methods used in identifying hate speech, and they discuss promising new directions for the field as well as newly identified issues.

Foreword

A few years ago, I got acquainted with Machine Learning. Computational linguistics motivated me towards this path. Since then, the field has progressed heights. However, the core ideas behind linguistics and its computation remains the same. When I founded Phosphene AI, it was no surprise, our first product was also based on Natural Language Processing (NLP). Our R&D strives towards quality research on NLP. But, with the advent of new technology, new challenges accompany us. Deep Learning has transformed this field so much that, even as an AI company, we struggle to keep up with nouvelle research and techniques. Its natural for beginners to the industry and new researchers, to feel overwhelmed by how much the industry has changed with time. This book "Neural Networks for Natural Language Processing" gives the reader a concise, yet highly relevant and application focused content to allow them to quickly grasp and understand the ideas that are highly important in this data-driven Deep Learning era. The book also quickly dives into the most important applications of Natural Language Processing directly in chapter four, which is quite rare. At the same time, it doesn't abstract the core mathematical ideas as well which is crucial for any deep learning practitioner or researcher.

This is what makes books like these so valuable; the quick impact they have on the readers. The industry is evolving faster than ever. This book will serve as a guide to that exciting future that NLP will offer for us.

Arockia Praveen J. B.
Phosphene AI, India

Preface

Natural language processing (NLP) is a component of Artificial Intelligence (AI) and it can be defined as the ability of a computer program to understand human language as it is spoken. Basically Natural Language Processing (NLP) is taking raw language input and using linguistics and neural network algorithms to transform or enrich the text in such a way that it delivers greater value.

The book focuses on addressing the practical applications of Neural Networks for Natural Language Processing (NLP) in Deep Learning to three categories of users: Beginners, Intermediates and Sophisticated Users, by not only discussing the research issues in Natural Language Processing (NLP) but also to solve those problems with the help of Deep Learning.

The book provides an introduction to statistical methods for NLP and a decent foundation to comprehend new NLP methods and support the creation of NLP tools. Mathematical and linguistic foundations, plus statistical methods, are equally represented in a way that supports readers in creating language processing applications.

Through this book an attempt has been made to provide NLP practitioners as well as newcomers with the basic background, tools, and methodologies that will allow them to understand the principles behind neural network models for language, and apply them in their own work.

Since artificial neural networks allow modeling of nonlinear processes, they have turned into a very popular and useful tool for solving many problems such as classification, clustering, regression, pattern recognition, dimension reduction, structured prediction, machine translation, anomaly detection, decision making, visualization, computer vision, and others. This wide range of abilities makes it possible to use artificial neural networks in many areas. Through this book, we discuss applications of artificial neural networks in Natural Language Processing tasks (NLP).

Neural networks have many applications in Natural Language Processing (NLP) such as text classification, information extraction, semantic parsing, question answering, paraphrase detection, language generation, multi-document summarization, machine translation, and speech and character recognition. In many cases, neural networks methods outperform other methods.

The intended audience includes:

- Faculties Working in Universities and Technical Institutions
- Research Scholars
- Academics
- R&D People
- Industrialists
- Developers
- Professionals
- Data Analyst
- Technology Specialist
- Post-Graduate Students and
- People Who Are Interested in Using Machine Learning and Deep Learning for Natural Language Processing.

Another projected audience is the researchers and academicians who identify methodologies, concepts, tools, and applications through reference citations, literature reviews, quantitative/qualitative results, and discussions.

Also, the book is designed to be first choice reference at university libraries, academic institutions, research and development centers, information technology centers, and any institutions interested in using, design, modeling, and analyzing Natural Language Processing. The book is designed to be used as a textbook for courses teaching machine learning and modelling for under/post graduate students in the area of NLP.

1. DEEP LEARNING NETWORK: DEEP NEURAL NETWORKS

Artificial intelligence (AI) is defined as a machine has the ability to doing everything a human being can do and produce better results. Means AI enlightening that data can produce a solution for its own results. Inside the AI ellipsoidal, Machine learning (ML) has a wide variety of algorithms produce more accurate results. As a result of technology improvement increasing amounts of data is available. But with ML and AI it is very difficult to extract such high level, abstract features from raw data moreover hard to know what feature should be extracted. Finally, we now have deep learning; these algorithms are modeled based on how human brains processing the data. Deep learning is a particular kind of machine learning that provides flexibility and great power, its attempts to learn in multiple levels of representation with the operations of multiple layers. Deep learning brief overview, platforms, Models, Autoencoders, CNN, RNN, Appliances are described appropriately. Deep learning will have many more successes in the near future because it requires very little engineering by hand.

2. A JOURNEY FROM NEURAL NETWORKS TO DEEP NETWORKS: COMPREHENSIVE UNDERSTANDING FOR DEEP LEARNING

The chapter is about deep learning fundaments and its recent trends. The chapter has mention many advanced applications and deep learning models and networks to solve those applications easily in a very smart way. Discussion of some technics for computer vision problem and how to solve with deep learning approach fall into the chapter. After taking fundamental knowledge of the background theory one can create or solve applications. The current state-of-the-art of deep learning for education, healthcare, agriculture, industrial, organizations, research and development applications are very fast growing. The chapter is about types of learning in a deep learning approach, what kind of data set one can be required, what kind of hardware facility is required for the particular complex problem. For unsupervised learning problems, Deep learning algorithms have been designed, but same way Deep learning is also solving the supervised learning problems for a wide variety of tasks.

- Learning Types
- Building deep networks
- Advanced techniques
- Resent Research going on Deep learning
- Motivation on deep learning
- Why care about deep learning

3. CURRENT TRENDS IN DEEP LEARNING FRAMEWORKS WITH OPPORTUNITIES AND FUTURE PROSPECTUS

Now a days Artificial Intelligence (AI) is going through its golden era by playing an important role in various real time applications. Most AI applications are indeed using Machine learning and it currently represents the most promising path to strong AI. On the other hand, Deep Learning (DL), which is itself a kind of Machine Learning (ML) is becoming more and more popular and successful at different use cases and is at the peak of developments hence DL is becoming a leader in this domain. To foster the growth of the DL community to more and more extent, many open source frameworks are available which implemented DL algorithms. Each framework is based on some algorithm with some specific applications. The objective of this chapter is to provide a brief qualitative review of most popular and comprehensive DL frameworks and to make aware to the end users regarding the current trends in DL Frameworks. This can be helpful for them to make an informed decision to choose the best DL framework that suits their needs, resources, applications and choose proper career.

4. EMOTION RECOGNITION FROM SPEECH USING PERCEPTUAL FILTER AND NEURAL NETWORK

This chapter on multi speaker independent emotion recognition encompasses the use of perceptual features with filters spaced in Equivalent rectangular bandwidth (ERB) and BARK scale and vector quantization (VQ) classifier for classifying groups and artificial neural network with back propagation algorithm for emotion classification in a group. Performance can be improved by using the large amount of data in a pertinent emotion to adequately train the system. With the limited set of data, this proposed system has provided consistently better accuracy for the perceptual feature with critical band analysis done in ERB scale.

5. ONTOLOGY CREATION

This chapter discusses on the ONTOLOGY Creation. Ontology is closely connected to Natural Language Processing (NLP) - a field of artificial intelligence, computer science and linguistics. As such, NLP is related to the area of human–computer interaction. Ontologies and Natural Language Processing (NLP) can often be seen as two sides of the same coin. An Ontology Model is the classification of entities and modeling the relationships between those entities. The purpose of NLP is the identification of entities, understanding the relationship between those entities. NLP- Driven Ontology modeling means we're using natural language processing techniques to drive semantic models from unstructured data. Using Ontologies with NLP allows an enterprise to turn data into knowledge.

6. SEMANTIC SIMILARITY USING REGISTER LINEAR QUESTION CLASSIFICATION (RLQC) FOR QUESTION CLASSIFICATION

Question Classification(QC) mainly deals with syntactic parsing for finding the similarity. To improve the accuracy of classification, a semantic similarity approach of a question along with the question dataset is calculated. The semantic similarity of the question is initially achieved by syntactic parsing to extract the noun, verb, adverb and adjective. However, adjectives and adverbs do give sentences an exact meaning that should also be considered for computing the semantic similarity. The proposed RLQC (Register Linear and Question Classification) model for semantic similarity of questions uses HSO measure with Gloss based measure to enhance the semantic similarity relatedness by considering the Noun, Verb, Adverb and Adjective. The semantic similarity of the question pairs for RLQC is 0.2% higher compared to HSO model. The highest semantic similarity of the proposed model achieves a better accuracy.

7. KNOWLEDGE GRAPH GENERATION

Nowadays, as computer systems are expected to be intelligent, techniques that help modern applications to understand human languages are in much demand. Amongst all the techniques, the latent semantic models are the most important, they exploit the latent semantics of lexicons and concepts of human languages and transform them into tractable and machine understandable numerical representations. Without which, languages are nothing but combinations of meaningless symbols for the machine. To provide such learning representation, in recent years, embedding models for knowledge graphs have attracted much attention, since they intuitively transform important concepts and entities in human languages into vector representations, and realize relational inferences among them via simple vector calculation. Such novel techniques have effective resolved a few tasks like knowledge graph completion and link prediction, and show the great potential to be incorporated into more natural language processing (NLP) applications.

8. DEVELOP A NEURAL MODEL TO SCORE BIGRAM OF WORDS USING BAG-OF-WORDS MODEL FOR SENTIMENT ANALYSIS

Natural Language Processing is a subset of computer science and artificial intelligence, which is concerned about the interaction between the human and the computer that analyse natural human data. When NLP is linked with deep learning, large amount of natural language human data is considered to develop a model that analyse the given big data and predicts the reply for that questions from the data. And then the neural model is developed for the NLP model which takes large amount of data to analyse the meaning of the context. Basic neural network model is considered in this project which works as natural language processing model that uses many pre-processing tools. Bag-of-word is one of the technique used here, that consider the words of same meaning from the sentence as a bag.

9. DEEP LEARNING APPROACH FOR EXTRACTING CATCH PHRASES FROM LEGAL DOCUMENTS

In legal domain, the important keywords that describe the motivation of whole documents are known as catch phrases. Generally, the legal practitioners will make an extensive search of prior case documents in order to ensure justice. Thus, extracting the catch phrases from the legal documents seems to have a great advantage in the legal domain to make the search easier. Many traditional methods have been used to extract the catch phrase from the legal documents. Making use of a deep learning approach to extract the same is done in this chapter. There are several deep learning methods such as RNN, CNN, Deep Neural networks, etc. Among these Long-Short Term Memory (LSTM) are made use since they learn the long term dependencies among the sequences.

10. ENHANCED SENTIMENT CLASSIFICATION USING RECURRENT NEURAL NETWORKS

Sentiment Analysis is an interesting area because analysis of text that is available online is advantageous and used from top to bottom in everyday lives from online shopping to movie reviews, business perspectives, etc., . But it is a measurable source of information with many applications and this process of identifying and extracting subjective information from raw data is known as Sentiment Analysis. Sentiment Analysis plays the major role in identifying the best of things such as products and movies reviews. The identification of sarcastic words and homonyms are very difficult. Hence, it involves Recurrent Neural Network to classify based on the context of the sentences. This network classifies the statement into positive or negative. These type of classification are much needed by the people since it exhibits dynamic timely response. RNN improves the efficiency of classification.

11. NATURAL LANGUAGE PROCESSING-BASED INFORMATION EXTRACTION AND ABSTRACTION FOR LEASE DOCUMENTS

Text classification is that the method of assignment tags or classes to text consistent with its content. It's one amongst the elemental tasks in language process (NLP) with broad applications like sentiment analysis, topic labeling, spam detection, and intent detection. This chapter have four level process such as text classification to differentiate the types of lease documents, Topic modeling to find the best topic from multiple documents, information extraction to identify the important information from the lease documents and abstraction of data to identify the data such as basic information, financial information, retail and miscellaneous such as monthly parking fees and storage fees.

12. NEURAL NETWORK APPLICATIONS IN HATE SPEECH DETECTION

The chapter "Neural Networks in Hate Speech Detection" presents a literature survey of the current state of hate speech detection models, with a focus on neural network (NN) applications in the area. The growth and freedom of social media has facilitated both the dissemination of positive and negative ideas. While manual moderation is too cumbersome and slow to deal with the torrent of content generation on these social media sites which is why many have turned to machine learning, NN applications in this area have been very promising and yielded positive results. The survey presented in this chapter identifies the key techniques and methods used in identifying hate speech, and discuss promising new directions for the field as well as newly identified issues.

Natural language processing (NLP) is a subfield of computer science, information engineering, and artificial intelligence concerned with the interactions between computers and human (natural) languages, in particular how to program computers to process and analyze large amounts of natural language data.

Though natural language processing tasks are closely intertwined, they are frequently subdivided into categories for convenience such as Grammar induction, Lemmatization, Morphological segmentation, Part-of-speech tagging, Parsing, sentence boundary disambiguation, Stemming, Word segmentation, Terminology extraction, Lexical semantics, Machine translation, Named entity recognition (NER), Natural language generation, Natural language understanding, Optical character recognition (OCR), Question answering, Recognizing Textual entailment, Relationship extraction, Sentiment analysis, Topic segmentation and recognition, Word sense disambiguation, Automatic summarization, Coreference resolution, Discourse analysis.

In all these cases, the overarching goal is to take raw language input and use linguistics and neural network algorithms to transform or enrich the text in such a way that it delivers greater value.

Acknowledgment

I am very much happy and thankful to IGI Global Inc., USA for giving me the opportunity to produce my first book on Handbook of Research on Neural Networks for Natural Language Processing, which is very much necessary in the present data driven internet world.

I express a deep sense of gratitude to the Ms. Josie Dadeboe and other members of IGI Global Inc., USA who supported either directly or indirectly during book project development.

I am thankful to all authors who have contributed their valuable efforts and ideas in the form of chapters in the book. I would like to express my sincere thanks to all my reviewers for their continuous supports, guidance and encouragements in bringing this book project into successful one.

We express our gratitude in thanking our Chairman, Managing Director, Director, Principal and other faculty members of St. Joseph's College of Engineering, Chennai, and Tamilnadu, India for their great support and kindness in completing this book.

I am very much thankful to my family members for their support and encouragement in achieving this target goal in my academic career.

Finally, I am dedicating this work to my Husband, Mr. K.C. Tamilselvan, and to my lovely sons, T.S. Guru and T.S. Balaa.

Chapter 1
Deep Learning Network:
Deep Neural Networks

Bhanu Chander
https://orcid.org/0000-0003-0057-7662
Pondicherry University, India

ABSTRACT

Artificial intelligence (AI) is defined as a machine that can do everything a human being can do and produce better results. Means AI enlightening that data can produce a solution for its own results. Inside the AI ellipsoidal, Machine learning (ML) has a wide variety of algorithms produce more accurate results. As a result of technology, improvement increasing amounts of data are available. But with ML and AI, it is very difficult to extract such high-level, abstract features from raw data, moreover hard to know what feature should be extracted. Finally, we now have deep learning; these algorithms are modeled based on how human brains process the data. Deep learning is a particular kind of machine learning that provides flexibility and great power, with its attempts to learn in multiple levels of representation with the operations of multiple layers. Deep learning brief overview, platforms, Models, Autoencoders, CNN, RNN, and Appliances are described appropriately. Deep learning will have many more successes in the near future because it requires very little engineering by hand.

INTRODUCTION

At present most of the modern artificial intelligence (AI) appliances build based on the deep neural networks. Because of the improvement results in speech and image recognition involvement of deep neural networks in various appliances enlarged like

DOI: 10.4018/978-1-7998-1159-6.ch001

as self-driving cars, playing complex games and detecting cancer and in many more domains deep neural networks surpass human precision. Artificial intelligence (AI) is the reproduction of human intelligence by machine and computer systems. This evolution of reproduction done by *learning* - rules to use information, *reasoning* - rules to reach suitable execution and *self-correction* – take appropriate actions based on learning, reasoning procedure. Machine learning (ML) is made use of computational methods to get better machinery performances by detecting influential patterns and inconsistency information. ML makes decisions based on what they memorize/learn from data. Deep learning (DL) is the nature of machine learning; solves the problems that were insoluble with ML. Deep learning uses neural networks, learns through an artificial neural network that acts very much like a human brain to increase computational work and provide accurate results. Machine learning has great accuracy results when it has pre-processed data but in real-time applications, it is not so easy to get pre-processed data. Deep learning has multiple neural layers where each layer describes hidden information from real world raw data (William et al., 2018; Vivienniesze et al., 2017; Mehadi., et al 2017; Russakousky et al., 2012).

Nowadays Deep neural networks (DNNs) are most extensively used in multimedia appliances such as computer vision- teaching machines to automate tasks performed by human visual systems classification, object detection, image restoration, and image segmentation and even can be recognized, speech recognition. Healthcare- including patients' records, medical reports and insurance records for best results. Automatic text generation- handwritten digits. Image recognition- identifies an image and creates a reasoned caption. Wireless sensor networks- weather forecasting and detecting unusual events. Sounds - voice generation and music composition. Business and finance - to improve customer experience and fraud detection, trading, risk evaluation. Computer games- Deep Reinforcement learning to teach a computer to play sports games itself and robotics - takes care of pretty sophisticated tasks.

Deep learning (DL) basically involves feeding a computer system by a lot of data, which it can use to make decisions about other data, simply input raw data acts as fuel to DL methods. Many appliances can profit from Deep neural networks (DNNs) ranging from multimedia to medical space. In this chapter, we will discuss real-time example areas where DNNs are currently making an impact, hope to make an impact in the future emanate areas (William et al., 2018; Vivienniesze et al., 2017; Russakousky et al., 2012).

BACKGROUND

Artificial intelligence (AI) is defined as a machine has the ability to doing everything a human being can do and produce better results. Means AI enlightening that data can produce a solution for its own results. Inside the AI ellipsoidal, Machine learning (ML) has a wide variety of algorithms produce more accurate results. In fact, ML is a branch of statistics whereby the algorithms learn from the data as it is input into the system. Machine learning from last two decades stands as one of the greatest development in information technology. As a result of technology improvement constantly increasing amounts of data is available, so there is a need for a good reason to believe and smart data analysis becomes a necessary ingredient for technological progress. Machine learning methods give a boost to many aspects of modern society from content filtering to object recognition which growing interestingly in modern computers, Smartphone's. Performance of machine learning technique highly depending on the representation of data given to them. Many AI, ML techniques solve tasks by designing feature sets which examining and extracting useful information which designed meaning full for that task, but it is very difficult to extract such high level, abstract features from raw data moreover hard to know what feature should be extracted.

Artificial neural networks are modeled on how the human brain and neurons process information. ANN consists of numerous numbers of layers working as unison, connected with interconnected links which have weights. By properly adjusting these weights ANN can learn prior assumptions with a small number of inputs. ANN typically has one input layer, one output layer and depending on networks any number of hidden layers. It useful where algorithms or rules to solve problems difficult to express or unknown. ANN produces good results but it suffers from design and computational complexity.

Finally, we now have deep learning; these algorithms are modeled based on how human brains processing the data. Deep learning is a particular kind of machine learning that provides flexibility and great power, its attempts to learn in multiple levels of representation with the operations of multiple layers. If you provide a large number of statistics or information to the system it starts to analyze it and give its response in a useful way. It will have many more successes in the near future because it requires very little engineering by hand, so it can easily take advantage of increases in the amount of available computation and data.

ARTIFICIAL INTELLIGENCE

Artificial Intelligence (AI) is the ability of system, system-controlled machines perform special tasks based on human base intelligence with the help of learning, reasoning, and problem-solving. Learning deals with possession of information along with principle rules for using the information, reasoning utilizes the learning rules to achieve suitable conclusion about information. Finally, problem solving or self-correction makes an immediate reaction on the bases of learning and reasoning. Father of Artificial intelligence (AI) is John McCarthy describes aspects of learning, he makes a machine to simulate them, makes them use abstractions, concepts, and languages. Marin Minsky cofounder of AI labs in MIT describes the perfect definition of intelligence "intelligence is just a word people use to describe how our brains solve problems we call hard. But whenever you learn a new skill yourself, you are less impressed when other people do the same. This is why the meaning of intelligence is elusive" simply it is the ability to acquire and apply skills (Mehdi et al., 2017; Goodfelow et al., 2018).

Various type learning's could be applied on artificial intelligence like trial and error, simple computer algorithm to solve mate try to move randomly in one class chess until it finds a mate in opposition, algorithm saves the step with a solution so if the algorithm encountered with the same step it will recall the stored solution. As we described in the above paragraph reasoning describe the hypothesis to the solution. The hypothesis will describe in inductive or deductive formation. Inductive-provides truths to the hypothesis provide support to the conclusion exclusive of prior guarantee whereas in Deductive- the precision of the hypothesis guarantees the truth of the conclusion. Artificial intelligence shows massive impact on Gaming-by using heuristic search machine can able to predict or think multiple possible steps in strategic games such as tic-tac-toe, chess etc. speech recognition- some systems that can possibly understand the language and talk like human even they can understand background noise, slag etc. natural language processing- able to communicate and understand the human-based languages to machine, computers. Handwriting recognition- text is written on paper, screen by pen able to read by some software, it will also change font style and make it as editable text. Expert systems- the main purpose of programming, thinking's of AI used in the expert system. Visual system-these systems understand, grasp visual input on the computer such as drones, spy planes. Robots status will stand and takes the first row in best creations by humans; they can complete most critical tasks within in time (Bengio., et al 2009; Bengio., et al 2013; Lecun 2015).

MACHINE LEARNING

Machine learning (ML) introduced as a technique for Artificial Intelligence. Machine learning is a procedure with the purpose of automatically learns out of possession of trained data furthermore perform without being specifically programmed. Simply applying computational methods to improve machine performance by detecting and describing the inconsistency in the available data. ML concepts are learning iteratively in training, extracts output of the trained model. In training procedure size of data separated into train, test and mostly makes a validation data set. ML takes care of training data and attempts to learn some representations like a set of decision positioned on the contribution of one-by-one feature besides this validation set apply as a reference set to validate the effectiveness of training method, results applied to tune learning or training parameters in order to increase final accuracy. Then test set applied on newly collected data to determine the final accuracy (Bengio., et al 2013; Lecun 2015; Arnold et al., 2011; Mehdi et al., 2017).

ML techniques make calculation process with higher proficient, consistent and cost-effective. The potentiality of ML is inherent ability toward providing comprehensive solutions via a structural design that can learn to progress achievements. From last decade ML techniques most widely used in classification, density estimation, regression, clustering in a mixture of appliances like as fraud detection, marketing & sales, transportation, computer vision, bioinformatics, healthcare, big data, and social media. In general, ML consist trilogy type of learning's those are supervised, unsupervised and semi-supervised learning. In *supervised learning* - we already have a test as well as train data here first regular classifier trained with previously labeled data and applied towards test data such as Decision trees, Bayesian networks. *Unsupervised learning*- we only have train data here there is no need for dissimilarities accompanied by test datasets as well as train datasets such as Principal component analysis. *Semi-supervised learning* where set-up utilizes both training and testing data sets where training data must enclose only with normal data such as neural networks. But here important question will rise with all these dissimilar algorithms in ML, how we select the best-suited technique to our problem. If we want to expect or forecast a destination value we can go with a supervised learning algorithm like neural networks, you try to fit our data into some discrete groups we should look at clustering, if we need to put some numerical estimation how much it will suit to each group we should look into a density estimation techniques (Deng et al., 2013; He et al., 2016; Barabasi et al., 2016; Russakousky et al., 2012).

Many machine learning techniques become extremely difficult when train data dimensioning is high. With the help of unchanging training samples, extrapolative power of ML will first increase but increase features dimensions will decrease ML performance. Most machine learning algorithms use manually designed features means features of real-world data must be identified, processed by human beings then only it will provide the best accuracy results. Moreover, ML has time-consuming in design and validation, takes incomplete information, ML application cannot be generalized easily to other applications, and handcrafted features are a costly and complex procedure.

DEEP LEARNING OVERVIEW

Father of deep learning *Geoffrey Hinton* computer scientist & researcher at Google back propagation restricted Boltzmann machines, Alex nets, and Capsules. Machine learning is an operation/learning where computational methods adopted to improve machinery performances by detecting and relating the stability, inequality in testing/training data sets. Simply if you train an algorithm what to do with collected data/information it will do it automatically without being explicitly programmed. Deep leaning attempts to learn a large number of representations through a hierarchy of multiple layers and it begin to understand and respond in a useful way. DL provides more flexibility and great power by learning than ML techniques. ML incorporates a wide variety of techniques but mostly no one of them which show classification performance as Deep learning. Statistical, Bayesian algorithms, as well as functions approximations such as linear, logistic, decision trees, are powerful ML techniques although restricted in specific appliance behavior, the capability to trained key features from extremely complex data representation. Deep learning progressed from cognitive with information theories, reproduce learning from human brain moreover generate a tricky interrelated neuron structure. Human brain posse great pre-processing capabilities every day we relieve numerous data from the existent world under multifaceted atmosphere large amount of raw data collected by our sense organs then our brain extracts main characteristics from raw data and make a decision on it. Exactly the same operation applied on neural networks extracts hidden important information layer by layer. In DL there is no solitary formation in favor of every appliance; on behalf of a frequently applicable model, all appliances are employed. As results regarding advance developments in industrial, computing and scientific domains, implementation of a large collection of neurons are possible. DL uses learns from multiple levels of features to learn rich hierarchical features automatically. Hierarchical representation learns high levels of abstraction where each layer is trainable with non-linear feature term. Deep learning techniques with increasing availability data/information, considerable improvement in computing, auto-extraction will increase new representation learning, deep learning process flexible enough to address broad range applications (Goodfellow et al., 2018; Deng et al., 2013; He et al., 2016).

History

First neural network emerges in the 1940s after that multiple neurons appeared in 1980s with handwritten digit recognition which is widely used in numerous real-life applications like image pixel and ATM digit recognition. Hardware for shallow neural nets from Intel Corporation started from the 1990s. Nonetheless, blossoming of DNNs applications boosted early on the 2010s with best-part equivalent as Microsoft-speech-realization method in 2011 moreover AlexNet scheme for image identification in 2012. From 2014 onwards an era for deep learning based system research takes to rise and it grows continuously. There are some notable reasons which influence the development of deep learning successes: Amount of available data to train networks, rather than handcrafted representation in-order to learn a powerful representation we need a huge amount of training information. Semiconductor and as the result of development in computer architectures have continued and increased to offer computing competence, which requires in favor of mutually inference and training in DNN be able to be performed in the authentic quantity of time. As a result of success in DNN applications and available frameworks inspire researchers, scientists to develop, use and explore DNNs (Vivienne et al., 2017; Krizhevsky et al., 2012; He et al., 2016).

DEEP LEARNING TAXONOMY

Deep learning taxonomy divides into supervised, unsupervised and reinforcement learning. Mostly learning algorithms classify based on the nature of input data/ information that they function (William et al., 2018; Fadullah et al., 2017).

Supervised Learning

In supervised learning what-ever, the need about data requirement is already explored clearly so that outcome data classified correct or incorrect. Most of the supervised algorithms applied as a predictive method where some part of data trained, another part of the data used to validate the trained model. Here accuracy is a most important metric for measurements like recall, F1 score, LOC curve, and precision these are utilized to check the capacity of skilled form to generalization toward innovative data/information (William et al., 2018; Fadullah et al., 2017).

Classification

In classification first, we build a classifier model based/trained on available one class trained data then applied to classify unseen/new data. The output of the learning model is a fixed set of classes. That could be obtained a form of binary categorization of two classes. Multiclass classification resulting acquire as one-class out of a set of three or further total classes like multiple label classifications (Hatchula et al., 2017).

Regression

Regression is a statistical measurement to determine the strength of relationship among one dependent variable and continuous other variables. The productivity of regression knowledge method is single or additional continuous-valued members. Regression applied to various applications like image object recognition (William et al., 2018; Nguyen et al., 2017).

Unsupervised Learning

Un-supervised learning as the name suggests no labeled data provided as input for ML but any-way it conclude accurate or inaccurate end result. As a replacement for find a boarder goal, it will find a method that has the capability to discover an impressive result that effortlessly human-noticeable or else it will endow with a statistical method to extract promised value. For example, density estimation determines part of the evaluation that can or cannot suitable for the desired data set. Autoencoders decrease data set dimensionality as well as compression. However, the capacity to pull-out compacted demonstration perfectly might still need suitability performance (William et al., 2018; Fadullah et al., 2017).

Density Estimation

Density estimation is statistical estimation to extract data distribution like extraction of densities, subgroups of data distribution, correlations or approximate data distribution as a whole (Marquardt et al., 2017; Yeshwanth et al., 2017; Arulkumaran et al., 2017).

Dimensionality Reduction

Dimensionality reduction employing a mixture of behavior such as component and discriminated analysis. Auto-encoders renovate input data into a compact or encoded output for the purposes of data firmness or storage space diminution (Arsa et al., 2016; Silver et al., 2016, William et al., 2018).

Clustering

Clustering is nothing but divides data points into separate groups where each group data point is similar to its own group data points and completely different from other group data points moreover simply clustering statistically groups data. This will occurs through an alternating selection of cluster centroids, memberships. K-means and fuzzy c means algorithm make use of least mean square error among cluster and centroids. Fuzzy uses membership of data from multiple cluster centroids, making edges of cluster fuzzy. Gaussian mixture model and Euclidean distance as mean to select the cluster. Self-organizing feature map, beep belief networks fuzzy systems are some deep learning implementation for cluster analysis (William et al., 2018; Zhang et al., 2017; Ge et al., 2017; Cominetti et al., 2010).

Reinforcement Learning

In reinforcement learning instead of data labeling, remuneration was endowed upon the execution of an act. Most interestingly reinforcement learning interrelates with atmosphere directly means an alteration in the adjoining atmosphere returns an explicit remuneration. The main objective for reinforcement learning structure is maximizing remuneration function for every-state transmission as a result of learning the most excellent actions to receive each given state. This process will run for infinite time or can be applied in the session's in-order to learn to make the best use of the outcome of every session.

Value Function

Value function techniques run by expectation revisit of the given state, attempt to choose the best strategy that will maximize the estimated value in all actions for a prearranged state. This strategy can be enhanced through iterative evaluations furthermore keep update value-function estimation. For instance, sate-action-value-function which also known as the quality function is the foundation for q-learning. Q learning and deep learning techniques provide a state of art improvement in extracting data points and score reward functionalities (Arulkumaran et al., 2017; Bonarini et al., 2009).

DEEP LEARNING PLATFORMS

Matlab Neural Network Toolkit

Matlab neural network toolkit contains the most important popular deep learning algorithms like convolution neural networks, recurrent neural networks, deep belief networks, artificial neural networks, and auto-encoders. Each input layer takes raw data and hidden layer performs various actions like pooling, extracting, convolutions and ReLU function upon input raw data. Convolution filters applied upon raw data to extract certain features from the input, pooling operation performs non-linear operations upon the output of convolution filters which in-turn reduce computation complexity and dimension reduction. ReLU map negatives to zero in order to make positive values and improve training efficiency. After repeating all these functions in hidden layers finally specific features extracted for the classification purpose. Based on these features output layer perform classification (William et al., 2018).

Microsoft Cognitive Toolkit

Development of Microsoft cognitive toolkit or also acknowledged as CNTK started in the middle of 2015. CNTK has a special feature added as a library to python, C++ moreover C# or it can exploit as unrelated with its owned script language. CNTK is made easy to use and production ready to use on large scale data, supported on Linux, Windows. It can run models from Java as well as from other programming languages. CNTK has a most emerging powerful tool to machine learning with similar skills to other platforms (Microsoft 2017; Shi 2016)

Theano

It is an open source python library that can allow the abuser to define, optimize and evaluate mathematical expressions. With the help of Theano abuser can implement and train a neural network on fast concurrent graphical processing unit architectures (Theano 2017).

WILL

WILL is created by Hongkong base prevision limited company. It is an open-source neural network toolkit which can support pooling, fully connected layers, convolution functions and also performs Tanh, softmax, sigmoid.

Tensorflow

Tensorflow is developed by Google brain team, it is open-source, written in CUDA, Python, C++ and supported by Windows, Linux, macOS, and android systems. It is originally developed for deep learning and machine learning techniques and representation of graph where node indicates mathematical operations, an edge indicates connection among nodes. It is flexible, flow-based programming model and capable of making other kind implementations (Shi 2016).

Caffe

As the name suggests convolution architecture for fast feature embedding it supports CNN, RNN, RCNN, and LSTM with fully connected neural networks and operates wide-variety functions like pooling, logistic unit, convolution, inner units, element-wise operations, normalization, and hinge. It is an open source software tool implemented by the Berkeley lab. (Jia 2014; Caffe 2017).

Torch

Torch implemented in C and derives its own script language. The Torch is a scientific computing framework and its main functionalities focus on the graphical processing unit. Most part of Torch documentation along with the implementation of different algorithms is derived and placed on GitHub. It mainly supported on Ubuntu and MacOS whereas windows implementation will not so support well (Shi 2016; Torch 2017).

Keras

Keras initiates a high-level API that incorporates with tensor-flow, Caffe and Theano. Keras operates on both CPUs as well as GPUs, developer-friendly, supports CNN, RNN and integrates with other popular machine learning packages. The command of Keras is capacity to speedily prototype deep learning to intend with user-friendly, flexible as well as extensible interference (Keras 2017, 2018).

AUTO-ENCODER

Auto-encoders are one type of deep neural networks which produce or simply copy input to the output means auto-encoder discovers representations of features from raw data which can form training data. Auto-encoders internally have hidden layer h that describes the special code to represent input data to output. It has two components encoder: mapping input data to hidden code, decoder: which mapping data from hidden code to reconstruction output. But if an auto-encoders simply successful to learn copy input to output it is not so useful. Instead of this is designed in a specific way where it will copy appropriately means copy input data which only look a lot like training data, for these auto-encoders strictly forced to prioritize about specific data and then learns useful information from that data (Bengio et al., 2013; Tie Luo et al., 2018; Goodfellow et al., 2018).

Modern auto-encoders are valuable in dimensionality reduction and feature extraction process. Recent innovative connections in auto-encoders with latent variable models have brought auto-encoders to the made front line for designing generative model. Here, in some special situation, we can consider auto-encoders as feed-forward neural networks, apply the entire trained sample same as feedforward networks. Auto-encoders traditionally applied on image recognition and spacecraft made data analysis which will have a well-organized test and train data sets. In artificial neural networks (ANN) collection of interconnected neurons form a specified network to show some desired output. Auto-encoders are special kind neural networks which will perform reconstruct input instead of proceeding target variables. While reconstructing input auto-encoders tries to learn a special or useful representation of input data. Generally, auto-encoder consists with an input layer, an output layer and one or more hidden layers (it depends on the application or user mostly one hidden layer is capable to represent any kind of data) (Goodfellow et al., 2018; Bengio et al., 2013). Figure 1. General Structure of Auto-encoders.

Input Layer

An N-dimension vector to facilitate characterize input signals, symbolize by $x = (x 1, x 2... xM)$, it could be image pixels or a number of characters.

Output Layer

In auto-encoders input has the same dimension as output dimension used for the objective of reconstructing the creative input moreover automatically we get our preparation samples by reversing operations for this reason it called as unsupervised learning models. Output is symbolize as $x = (\hat{x} 1, \hat{x} 2, ..., \hat{x} M)$.

Hidden Layer

Hidden layer placed among input and output layers and aims to learn patterns in the raw input data so as to encode essential information. L indicates a total number of layers in Auto-encoder.

Activation Functions and Hyperparameters

Each and every neuron of L layers will present with activation function such as sigmoid, Tanh, ReLU. Weight W and Bias b are hyper-parameters where W is interconnection from node j in layer l to layer I in layer l+1 and bias allied by node i in layer l + 1.

Under-Complete Auto-Encoder

If an auto-encoder copy input data to output data it is no way of use in any application. One simple method to acquire the most important information from auto-encoders is making a hidden code dimension smaller than input data dimension. Whose code dimensionality smaller than input dimension that auto-encoder is named as under-complete auto-encoder. Learning under-complete representation learns most silent features from auto-encoder. Learning process determined easily as minimize loss functions like $L(x, g(f(x)))$ where L is loss function imprisoning output different from input data. But one drawback if we provide more capacity to encoder or decoder, auto-encoder cannot learn to achieve copying task without functional information about the distribution of data (Bengio et al., 2013; Goodfellow et al., 2018; Andrew et al., 2012).

Over-Complete Auto-Encoder

In over-complete auto-encoder code, dimension is similar or equal to input dimension. Basically, any structural designs of auto-encoder learn effectively by prefer code dimension, the capacity of encoder and decoder based on complication of distribution to be modeled. Over-complete auto-encoders utilizes loss function which can encourage the model to perform well formation such as adding scarcity penalty, robustness, missing or noised values besides its capability to reproduction its input to output. Sparse auto-encoders, denoising auto-encoder are some notable over-complete auto-encoders. In *sparse auto-encoders*, on code layer h small scarcity penalty is added along with loss function. Most of the sparse auto-encoders used to select feature for a different assignment such as taxonomy, clustering. Auto-encoder which regularized with scarcity penalty must react with some statistical features of data set that has been trained or simply acts as an identity function. In *Denoising auto-encoder*, corrupted data points are taken as input and try to portend the uncorrupted data point as its output. In this reconstruction, progression was employed which performs conditional distribution on corrupted data points. *Contractive auto-encoder*, which implement definite regularizer on hidden code h, for supporting derivatives of encoder element (f) as small as possible. There is light differential or relation among contractive with denoising auto-encoders; denoising rebuilding error is the same as a contractive penalty on reconstruction function that maps input into reconstruction output. It optimistic in mapping neighborhood input points to a miniature neighborhood of output points. *Predictive sparse decomposition*, as the name suggests predictive sparse decomposition is a combination of sparse coding and parametric auto-encoders. It is widely used in image, video recognition and unsupervised learning procedure (Bengio et al., 2013; Goodfellow et al., 2018; Andrew et al., 2012; Sarah et al., 2016; Alain et al., 2013).

Figure 1.

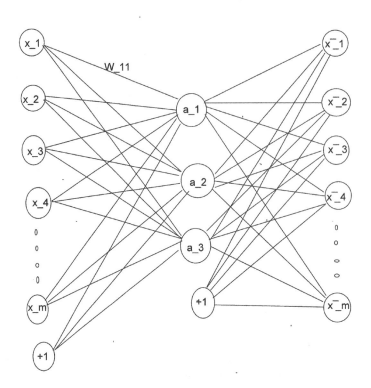

CONVOLUTION NEURAL NETWORK

Convolution neural network performs a special kind of linear mathematical operation called convolution. Generally, traditional neural networks perform matrix multiplication in their layers, coming to convolution neural networks convolution operations performed in any one of its layers. In general idea about CNN's enthused with animal cortex institute. In late 1961 Hubble proposed a theory named receptive fields, where they invent composite provision of cells those have animal illustration cortex in charge of light exposure and miniature sections of sub-fields. They observed how neurons in animals take action when facing images, visualize in precise on a monitor in front of the animal, neurons early visual system counter to extremely definite outlines of light, like as specifically oriented bars, nevertheless reacts barely at all further corresponding outlines. Their work assists to exemplify many portions of brain function. Neurons in premature visual system react most powerfully to extraordinarily definite outlines/patterns of light like in particular oriented bars although react hardly all other patterns. CNN provides more average weight to most recently happened or calculated values. Convolution can use in more than one axis means it can perform commutative property. The commutative possessions of convolution occur since we can flip kernel comparative to input, in the sense as m increase, the index into input enlarge, but an index into kernel decreases. The lone motive to flip kernel is to commutative possessions (Goodfellow et al., 2018; Simonyan et al., 2015).

Convolution neural networks have three motivational functions that can improve machine learning performances those are namely sparse interaction, parameter sharing, and equivariant representations. Basically in traditional neural network matrix multiplication performed in each layer means matrix of parameters by means of the separate parameter relating interface among each input-unit with each output unit. In this operation, each output-unit interacts by each input unit which increases computational complexity as well as a storage volume. However in sparse interactions kernel smaller than the input. Here kernels with meaningful features occupy only a small number of parameters that will reduce memory requirement of the model and increase the efficiency of the algorithm. Additionally, images as raw inputs straightly imported to the system, thus avoid feature extraction process in regular learning algorithms. In parameter sharing rather than learning all parameters at every location, try to earn one parameter set and rotate all over received data set. In a conventional neural net, each element of the weight matrix is utilized just once while computing output of a layer. The equivariant representation which is very important in any kind of operation in machine learning or any other, which shows variations if input changes slightly output also change.

Convolution neural network includes two layers those are convolution layer, as well as a sub-sampling layer, the interconnection between these two layers, forms a new middle part of the network. Figure 2: Architectural Structure Convolution Neural Networks Input image convolved by way of the trainable filter at every potential filter and fabricate with features maps in the first convolution layer and correlation weights are integrated into every filter. Additional feature map is produced in a sub-sampling layer by passing through a sigmoid function. This operation carries on all available convolution and sub-sampling layers obtain feature maps. At last, the values of these pixels showed in one particular vector as the output of the network. Convolution films habitually apply to extract features when the input of neuron connected with the receptive field of the preceding layer. After collect all extracted attribute or feature relationship among them can be estimated. Sub-sampling layer works as a feature map which split weights and shapes a plane. Furthermore, a sigmoid function applied as activation function Figure 3: Various forms of nonlinear activation functions suitable to its minor influence on function kernel. Filters in CNN utilized to hook-up a succession of overlap receptive fields, renovate 2d image into distinct unit output. If dimensionality of input alike to output filter it will tricky to continue transformation invariance hence classifier may cause over-fitting. In 1988 pooling method initiate to trim down the general magnitude of the signal. Pooling task utilizes to replace the output of the system at a definite location. A max-pooling technique designed in LeNet for sub-sampling where we use summarization of nearby statistical outputs and obtain maximum output in a rectangular neighborhood. Pooling utilizes to acquire invariance in image/figure alteration. This progression will direct to improved heftiness against noise. It is pointed out presentation of mixture of pooling process depend on numerous factors, like declaration at which low-level features are extracted and association among model cardinalities (William et al., 2018; Mehdi et al., 2017; Szegedy et al., 2014; Thompson et al., 2014;).

Recent convolution networks involve containing above one million units, parallel computations implemented to provide for more power to above-mentioned networks. Other than selecting the appropriate convolution algorithm for a specific application is also speed up the network. Convolution is equivalent to convert input as well as the kernel to frequency field with the assist of Fourier transform where pointwise reproduction performed and convert back to the time domain with inverse Fourier transformation. A typical convolution layer contains three phases. In the first phase, numerous convolutions in corresponding to construct a set of linear activations. In the second phase, those above-mentioned linear activations run through a non-linear activation which is also named as detector stage. The third phase is named as pooling where the output of layer changes at a definite place with summary statistics of adjacent outputs. Figure 4: Various forms of pooling Operations, For instance, max pooling process, outputs maximum with a rectangular neighbor. L2 norm of the rectangular neighborhood, an average of the rectangular neighborhood, a weighted average based on distance from the central pixel. The main advantage of pooling operation is it invariant to small translation or changes of input. Means if we convert input by little quantity, most of the pooling values do not transform. Invariance to local translation very constructive property if we care more regarding whether very few features are present than precisely where it is which was most essential when we work convolution with images. The utilize of pooling viewed as the addition of considerably strong proceeding that the function layer learns must be invariant to miniature transformation. When this supposition is correct it can significantly advance the statistical efficiency of the network. Stride makes a decision that how much we shift our window if we have a stride of one we shift across and down a single pixel. Through superior stride values, we shift huge quantity of pixels at a time hence construct slighter output volume (William et al., 2018; Mehdi et al., 2017; Szegedy et al., 2014; Thompson et al., 2014; Bengio et al., 2009; Bengio et al., 2016).

Figure 2.

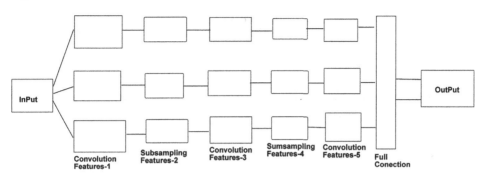

Training convolution neural networks is the same as traditional neural networks in the first stage; information or data set to transmit in feed-forward trend through dissimilar layers. Most important features acquire by the apply digital filter at every layer then values of output calculated. Throughout the second stage, error among anticipated and authentic values of output calculated. Backpropagating with minimizing this error, the weight matrix is more adjusted and system fine-tuned. Not like a further normal algorithm in image classification, the pre-processing is not frequently performed in CNN's. Instead of setting parameters, as traditional NNs, we just need to instruct filters in CNN's. Furthermore, in feature extraction, CNN's are self-governing of previous information and human intervention.

CNN's at this time apply roughly every mission in computer visualization area since it outperforms elder practices if there is a momentous quantity of data offered. A few applications are Object Detection (image, video), astronomy, Face recognition, X-ray diagnosis, Neural Art transfer, Satellite image analysis.

Figure 3.

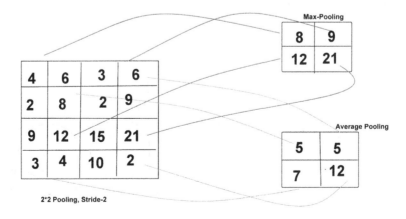

Figure 4.

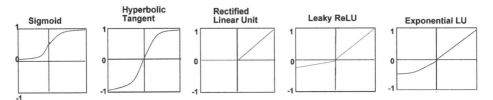

RECURRENT NEURAL NETWORK

Recurrent-neural-network or RNN is a group of deep networks that consider supervised or unsupervised with a sequential data processing whose length is as large as depth. In RNN data/information cycles through a loop. When it desires to make a decision, it takes concern about the current input and also what it has learned from inputs it established before. This is essential since the progression of data hold important information about what is coming next, which is why an RNN can do things other methods cannot. RNN can build in many ways, essentially any network consists recurrence named as a recurrent neural network. If recurrent neural network skilled to execute a mission, need to predict outlook from history. The output can read from RNN after a number of time steps which asymptotically linear in length of the input. There are many patterns in RNN some Recurrent neural networks that construct output at each node time stamp and contain recurrent relationship among hidden units, some Recurrent neural networks that construct output at each nodes time stamp and contain recurrent relationship with output of one time stamp to hidden units at next time stamp, some more Recurrent neural networks with recurrent relationship among hidden units as well as read complete sequence and then produce a single output. Computing gradient through a recurrent neural network is uncomplicated, simply apply the comprehensive back-propagation algorithm, No dedicated algorithms are essential. The use of back-propagation on the unrolled graph is called back-propagation via time (BPTT) algorithm. Gradients acquire by back-propagation may perhaps exploit with any general-purpose gradient-based procedure to teach an RNN (Chung et al., 2014).

Echo State Network

RNN is successfully applicable in model nonlinear time series like model finance data, electricity load forecast, sensor network event detection and prediction. Training RNN methods suffer troubles similar to sluggish convergence as well as vanishing gradients. Echo state network is a recent and efficient approach where the minor computational complication is the effect of using an unchanging, randomly associated reservoir of neural units in the recurrent layer, merely associations to output units are distorted throughout the preparation. Simply ESN networks have some detailed structural design and preparation process which aims to resolve the convergence rate of numerous RNN algorithms. ESN generally use with a distinct model means system dynamics are definite for disconnected time-steps t, they consist of inputs, a recurrently associated hidden layer and an output. The major dissimilarity among ESN to classical recurrent network advances is the setup of relationship weights and teaching process. To design an ESN, units in the input layer and hidden layer are accidentally associated. Correlation between the hidden layer and the output layer are only associations that are skilled. Most generally supervised learning approach employ for training, it follows as training data are utilized to teach and drive the network, each time stamp t, activations of all input units and all hidden units are saved to the new-fangled column as state matrix. At equivalent time preferred activations of output units are composed. Determine the weight output and squared error among training output and definite output, attempt to minimize error. To make an approach work productively, associations in the reservoir cannot completely accidental, but need to accomplish called echo state possessions. Reservoir computing recurrent system comparable to kernel machines where they plot an arbitrary length succession into a fixed-length vector where linear forecaster can be functional to solve the problem of attention (Chung et al., 2014; Goodfellow et al., 2018).

Bidirectional RNNs

All recurrent neural networks consider casual structure like a state at the time only capture information from past and present input. But in same application output depend entirely upon complete input succession. For illustration speech and character identification, the accurate explanation depends upon existing sound or character could depend on next phonemes or characters since co-articulations and potentially depend on next few words for the reason that linguistic among adjacent words or characters. Bidirectional RNN invented for these needs and has been an extensively successful character, image and voice recognition. In bidirectional RNN, input in hidden layer shift forward through time start of input succession at the same time there is another hidden layer where input shifts backward through time beginning from the end of succession. Clearly, input data transform from two hidden layers where one hidden layer transform data forward another hidden layer transform data backward. Finally, the output of two-hidden layers connects with the output layer. This idea boosts 2-dimensional input like images where RNNs can move four directions up, down, left and right. If RNN performs this operation compared to convolution network they can typically more expensive but one drawback is interaction among feature in the same feature map (Mehdi et al., 2017; Szegedy et al., 2014; Thompson et al., 2014; Goodfellow et al., 2018).

Long-Short-Term-Memory

Classical RNN is worked well when we deal with short term dependencies. RNN does not remember or register what was said before this happening, what it means. If we doing some work mean we learn about that work previously, we remember those things and applied. Here we are not going to learn every time from scratch. Long short-term memory expansion for the recurrent neural network. Basically, RNN expands its memory and introducing self-loops to produce path, therefore, it is very useful to learn from past important experience. LSTM has found extremely helpful in many appliances such as handwriting generation, image captioning, handwriting recognition and machine translation and many more (Goodfellow et al., 2018).

Compared to classical RNN, LSTM hidden units are replaced by memory blocks. Information can be stored in memory blocks called cell variable as shown in figure 5. LSTM's facilitate RNN's to memorize their inputs over a lengthy period of time. Since LSTM's enclose their information in a memory, which is much like computer memory since LSTM can understand, write and remove information from its memory. This memory is seen as gated cell, where gated means that cell makes a decision whether to store or delete information (e.g if it opens the gates or not), based on magnitude it assigns to information. The assigning of magnitude happens through weights, which also learned via an algorithm. Simply it learns over time which information is significant as well as which is not. Each memory block consists of a memory cell along with three gates namely input gate, output gate and forgets gate. Figure 5: LSTM-RNN Gate formation these gates determine whether or not to let new input in (input gate), delete the information since it is not vital (forget gate) or to allow it impact to output at existing time step (output gate). Entire memory block maintained by these three gates. The forget reorganize cell variable that guides to forget stored input Ct, whereas input as well as output gates answerable for reading input from Xt and writing output to ht correspondingly. Here variables it, ft are outputs of input, output and forget gates. Here be is bias term, W is weight matrix. Every memory block can regard as detach, self-determining unit. The activation vectors it, ft', Ct is the same size as ht. additionally; weight matrices from cells to gates are diagonal, which means that each gate is only dependent on a cell inside a similar memory block.

Figure 5.

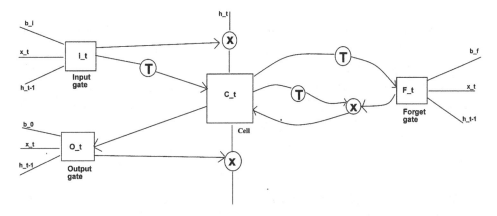

DEEP LEARNING MODELS: SHORT NOTE

From late 1900s deep learning models have been developed and many more on the construction stage. Every model has dissimilar network architecture with notable variations in layer shapes, layer numbers, and layer types moreover connection among layers. It is very important to understand these variations because of incorporating the right flexibility in any efficient Deep learning model (Vivienniesze et al., 2018; Lecun et al., 1998; Russakousky et al., 2015).

Alexnet

Alexnet contains five convolution layers, three fully connected layers which were first CNN to win Image-net 2012 challenge. Among these five convo layers, each of one contains 96 to 384 filters with filter dimension volumes starting 3×3 to 11×11 by 3 to 256 channels apiece. A ReLU non-linearity utilize in each layer. Max-Pooling of 3×3 employed to output layers 1, 2 and 5. The stride of 4 is applied to reduce at first layer of the network. Here notable difference identified between AlexNet and LeNet, number of weights much larger and natures differ from layer to layer. To decrease the number of weights as well as calculation on the second layer Conv layer, 96 output channels of the first layer are divided into two groups of 48 input channels for the second layer means the second layer have only 48 channels. Correspondingly, weights of fourth, fifth layers also divide into two clusters. In totality, AlexNet entails 61 million weights and 724 million MACs to process one 227×227 input image (Vivienniesze et al., 2018; Krizheusky et al., 2012).

Google Net

It is deeper with 22 layers with different sized filters 1×1, 3×3 and 5×5 moreover 3×3 pooling employ in favor of every parallel correlation and their outputs for component productivity. To improve the training speed of Google Net weights and activation functions stored in backpropagation during training. The 22 layers enclose three Conv layers, follow by nine inceptions layers and one fully connected layer (Vivienniesze et al., 2018; Lin et al., 2014; Szegedg et al., 2015).

LeNet

One of the first CNN approaches introduces in 1989. It was intended for assignment of digit taxonomy on grayscale images with size 28×28. The renowned version LeNet-5, include two CONV layers along with two fully connected layers. Every Conv layer exploits filters of range 5*5 with six filters inside first layers as well as 16 filters inside the second layer. Standard pooling of 2*2 exercises behind each conv along with a sigmoid utilizes for non-linearity (Vivienniesze et al., 2018).

Res-Net

ResNet, in addition, acknowledged as Residual Net, use residual associations to go deeper with 34 layers or more. ResNet was primary advance DNN in ImageNet confront that surpass human-level precision by top-5 error rate underneath 5% but here challenge with disappearance gradient throughout preparation as error back propagates throughout the network gradient minimize which distress capacity to modernize the weights in previous layers in support of extremely deep networks (He et al., 2015; Vivienniesze et al., 2018).

VGG-16

VGG-16 model deeper with 16 layers consist of 13 CONV along with 3 fully connected layers. For making balance while going deeper big filters (5×5) fabricate from multiple less important filters (3×3) those have fewer weights, however, accomplish similar effectual receptive fields (Vivienniesze et al., 2018; Simonyan et al., 2015).

Over Feat

Similar structural design as AlexNet contains 5 CONV along with 3 fully-connected layers. The most important dissimilarity is amount filter enlarged for layers 2, 3

(384 to 512), 4 (384 to 1024), and 5 (256 to 1024) but here layer 2 not divide to two groups. Moreover, the first FC layer has only 3072 channels quite than 4096 and the input size is 231×231 rather than 227×227 (Sermanet et al., 2014).

APPLICATIONS

From the last decade significant state of art applications concerning deep learning has been developed progressively and particularly in fields of natural language processing, handwritten character recognition, image, audio, videos and many more multimedia in addition to these improvements in big-data, cloud-computing has made feasible for machine learning prosperous, enable to essential data compilation and proliferation, increase computational complexity of deep learning models. Deep learning will likely to play a key role in healthcare, robotics fields as well as forecasting weather conditions, event detection, infrastructure, and finance fraud detections.

Natural Language Processing and Text Analysis

Developments in mobile devices make possible uninterrupted demands and compute challenges commencing anywhere, anytime. Inter-communication of social appliances creates massive continuous data that can be analyzed for sentimental and social understand levels. Both texts, as well as natural language processing, affords potential language understanding, transformation and conversation of human-computer systems via natural speech (Woodhouse et al., 2016; Long et al., 2015; Simonyan et al., 2014)

Image Audio Classification

The video contains a large amount of data, it takes first place at big data. Nowadays mostly it covers over 65% of internet traffic. A huge amount of data is collecting worldwide daily which nears to 800 million hours of data. Most part of DL appliances image and video conversions, investigation, identification, as well as the discovery, has seen a massive enlargement in modern years. Convolution neural networks play a great role in image and video processing where we convolve multiple channels and extracts most important features with help of pooling was dipping size of image, frame, fields and finally link fully connected layers before producing results (Woodhouse et al., 2016; Hinto et al., 2012; Van et al., 2016).

Medical Diagnostics

Medical diagnostics developed significantly from massive improvement in deep learning. Deep learning work towards in medical images shows considerable improvements in the detection of tumors, abnormal conditions and abnormal conditions in MRI scan images along with many more scan pictures. Internet of things in favor of medical application affords self-governing monitoring on patient moreover extracts functional information/data. Recent advance in deep learning increase precision of remote sensor metrics (Xian et al., 2015; Wang et al., 2016; Termyn et al., 2016; Alipanahi et al., 2015; Zhou et al 2015).

Finance Economics Market Analysis

Deep learning has capability learned from stochastic data and recognizes trends; predict stock trading and investment. In addition verification as well as validation of money transactions and can be used to detect anomalies behavior.

Autonomous Systems and Robotics

Deep learning methods widely produce significant improvements towards training to assists inside working autonomous machines in manufacturing, commercial appliances. Robotics manipulations with deep learning provide momentous towards rapid instruction of robotics arms in support of repeating manufacture tasks (Levine et al., 2016; Pfeiffer et al., 2017; Gupta et al., 2017; Zhang et al., 2016; Shalev et al., 2016).

Computational Biology

Same as medical diagnostics we apply deep learning for biological science which is most important for various innovations such as chemical, molecular interactions, micro and micro-organisms that can move toward a fine-grain understanding of uninterrupted mechanisms with the purpose of produce a result.

Cybersecurity

As the result of significant developments and utilization of various internet connected devices where most important information transform through communication technologies. However, it is now users attempt, subverting credentials, bypass security systems, attacks with network traffic. Make use of DL technology for cyber security analysis, event and intrusion detection be extremely appropriate.

REFERENCES

Alain, G., & Bengio, Y. (2013). What regularized auto-encoders learn from the data generating distribution. In *ICLR'2013*, arXiv:1211.4246.

Alipanahi, B., Delong, A., Weirauch, M. T., & Frey, B. J. (2015). Predicting the sequence specificities of DNA-and RNA-binding proteins by deep learning. *Nature Biotechnology*, *33*(8), 831–838. doi:10.1038/nbt.3300 PMID:26213851

Arel, I., Rose, D. C., & Karnowski, T. P. (2010). Deep machine learning-a new frontier in artificial intelligence research. *IEEE Computational Intelligence Magazine*, *5*(4), 13–18. doi:10.1109/MCI.2010.938364

Arnold, L., Rebecchi, S., Chevallier, S., & Paugam Moisy, H. (2011). An introduction to deep learning. In Proceedings ESANN, pp. 477–488.

Arsa, D. M. S., Jati, G., Mantau, A. J., & Wasito, I. (2016). Dimensionality reduction using deep belief network in big data case study: Hyperspectral image classification. In *2016 International Workshop on Big Data and Information Security (IWBIS)*, pp. 71–76. 10.1109/IWBIS.2016.7872892

Arulkumaran, K., Deisenroth, M. P., Brundage, M., & Bharath, A. A. (2017). Deep reinforcement learning: A brief survey. *IEEE Signal Processing Magazine*, *34*(6), 26–38. doi:10.1109/MSP.2017.2743240

Barabasi, A.-L. (2016). Network science. *Cambridge University Press*, 2016.

Goodfellow, I., Bengio, Y., & Courville, A. (2016). *Deep learning*. Book in preparation for MIT Press Online.

Bengio, Y., Courville, A., & Vincent, P. (2013). Representation learning: A review and new perspectives. *IEEE Pattern Analysis and Machine Intelligence*, *35*(8), 1798–1828. doi:10.1109/TPAMI.2013.50 PMID:23787338

Bengio, Y., Yao, L., Alain, G., & Vincent, P. (2013c). Generalized denoising autoencoders as generative models. In NIPS'2013.

Bengio, Y. (2009). Learning deep architectures for AI, *Foundations and trendsR in Machine Learning*, 2, 1, pp. 1–127.

Bonarini, A., Lazaric, A., Montrone, F., & Restelli, M. (2009). Reinforcement distribution in fuzzy Q-learning. Fuzzy Sets and Systems. *Special Issue: Fuzzy Sets in Interdisciplinary Perception and Intelligence*, *160*(10), 1420–1443.

Bottou, L. (2015). *Multilayer neural networks*. Deep Learning Summer School.

Caffe2. (2017). A new lightweight, modular, and scalable deep learning framework. Retrieved from *https://caffe2.ai/*

Chung, J., Gulcehre, C., Cho, K., & Bengio, Y. (2014). Empirical evaluation of gated recurrent neural networks on sequence modeling. *NIPS'2014 Deep Learning workshop*, arXiv 1412.3555.

Complete Visual Networking Index (VNI). (2016). Forecast, Cisco, San Jose, CA, June.

Deep learning. (2017). For data scientists who need to deliver. Retrieved from *https://skymind.ai/*

Deep learning for java. (2017). Open-source, distributed, deep learning library for the JVM.

Deng, L. (2013). Recent advances in deep learning for speech research at Microsoft. In *Proceedings of ICASSP, 2013*, pp. 8604–8608.

Doya, K. (1993). Bifurcations of recurrent neural networks in gradient descent learning. *IEEE Transactions on Neural Networks, 1*, 75–80.

Fadlullah, Z. M., Tang, F., Mao, B., Kato, N., Akashi, O., Inoue, T., & Mizutani, K. (2017). State-of-the-art deep learning: Evolving machine intelligence toward tomorrow's intelligent network traffic control systems. *IEEE Communications Surveys and Tutorials, 19*(4), 2432–2455. doi:10.1109/COMST.2017.2707140

Faust, O., Hagiwara, Y., Hong, T. J., Lih, O. S., & Acharya, U. R. (2018). Deep learning for healthcare applications based on physiological signals: A review. *Computer Methods and Programs in Biomedicine, 161*, 1–13. doi:10.1016/j.cmpb.2018.04.005 PMID:29852952

Ge, L. L., Wu, Y. H., Hua, B., Chen, Z. M., & Chen, L. (2017). Image registration based on SOFM neural network clustering. In *Proceedings 2017 36ᵗʰ Chinese Control Conference (CCC)*, pp. 6016–6020, July.

Gheisari, M., Wang, G., & Md, Z. A. B. (2017). A survey on deep learning in big data. *IEEE Computer Society. 2017 IEEE International Conference on Computational Science and Engineering (CSE) and IEEE International Conference on Embedded and Ubiquitous Computing (EUC)*. doi:10.1109/CSE-EUC.2017.215

Goodfellow, I., Bengio, Y., & Courville, A. (2018). *Deep learning*. MIT Press.

Gupta, S., Davidson, J., Levine, S., Sukthankar, R., & Malik, J. (2017). Cognitive mapping and planning for visual navigation. In *Proc. CVPR*, 2017, pp. 1252-1264.

Hatcher, W. G., Booz, J., McGiff, J., Lu, C., & Yu, W. (2017). Edge computing-based machine learning mobile malware detection. In National Cyber Summit.

Hatcher, W. G., & Yu, W. (2018). A survey of deep learning: Platforms, applications and emerging research trends. *IEEE transactions.* pp. 2169-3536.

He, K., Zhang, X., Ren, S. & Sun, J. (2016). Deep residual learning for image recognition. In *Proceedings of CVPR, 2016*, pp. 770–778.

Hinton, G., Deng, L., Yu, D., Dahl, G., Mohamed, A., Jaitly, N., ... Kingsbury, B. (2012). Deep neural networks for acoustic modeling in speech recognition: The shared views of four research groups [Nov]. *IEEE Signal Processing Magazine*, *29*(6), 82–97. doi:10.1109/MSP.2012.2205597

Jermyn, M., Desroches, J., Mercier, J., Tremblay, M.-A., St-Arnaud, K., Guiot, M.-C., ... Leblond, F. (2016). Neural networks improve brain cancer detection with Raman spectroscopy in the presence of operating room light artifacts. *Journal of Biomedical Optics*, *21*(9). doi:10.1117/1.JBO.21.9.094002 PMID:27604560

Jia, Y., Shelhamer, E., Donahue, J., Karayev, S., Long, J., Girshick, R., . . . Darrell, T. (2014). Caffe: Convolutional architecture for fast feature embedding. *arXiv preprint arXiv:1408.5093*.

Keras. (2017). The python deep learning library. Retrieved from https://keras.io/

Krizhevsky, A., Sutskever, I., & Hinton, G. E. (2012). ImageNet classification with deep convolutional neural networks. In Proceedings Advances in neural information processing systems (pp. 1097-1105). NIPS.

LeCun, Y., Bengio, Y., & Hinton, G. (2015). Deep learning. *Nature*, *521*(7553), 436–444. doi:10.1038/nature14539 PMID:26017442

Levine, S., Finn, C., Darrell, T., & Abbeel, P. (2016). End-to-end training of deep visuomotorpolicies. *Journal of Machine Learning Research*, *17*(39), 1–40.

Lin, M., Chen, Q., & Yan, S. (2014). Network in network. In *Proceedings of ICLR*.

Liu, W., Wang, Z., Liu, X., Zeng, N., & Liu, Y. (2016). A survey of deep neural network architectures and their applications. *Neurocomputing*, (December). doi:10.1016/j.neucom.2016.12.038

Long, J., Shelhamer, E., & Darrell, T. (2015). Fully convolution networks for semantic segmentation. In *Proceedings of CVPR-2015*, pp. 3431–3440.

Luo, T., & Nagarajan, S. G. (2018). Distributed anomaly detection using autoencoder neural networks in WSN for IoT. IEEE.

Marquardt, D., & Doclo, S. (2017). Noise power spectral density estimation for binaural noise reduction exploiting direction of arrival estimates. In *2017 IEEE Workshop on Applications of Signal Processing to Audio and Acoustics (WASPAA)*, pp. 234–238, October. 10.1109/WASPAA.2017.8170030

Nguyen, N. D., Nguyen, T., & Nahavandi, S. (2017). System design perspective for human-level agents using deep reinforcement learning: A survey. *IEEE Access: Practical Innovations, Open Solutions*, 5, 27091–27102. doi:10.1109/ ACCESS.2017.2777827

Pfeiffer, M., Schaeuble, M., Nieto, J., Siegwart, R., & Cadena, C. (2017). From perception to decision: A data-driven approach to end-to-end motion planning for autonomous ground robots. In *Proc. ICRA*, 2017, pp. 1527–1533.

Russakovsky, O., Deng, J., Su, H., Krause, J., Satheesh, S., Ma, S., ... Fei-Fei, L. (2015). ImageNet large scale visual recognition challenge. *International Journal of Computer Vision*, *115*(3), 211–252. doi:10.100711263-015-0816-y

Russakovsky, O., Deng, J., Su, H., Krause, J., Satheesh, S., Ma, S., ... Fei-Fei, L. (2015). ImageNet large scale visual recognition challenge. *International Journal of Computer Vision*, *115*(3), 211–252. doi:10.100711263-015-0816-y

Sermanet, P., Eigen, D., Zhang, X., Mathieu, M., Fergus, R., & LeCun, Y. (2014). OverFeat: Integrated recognition, localization and detection using convolutional networks. In *Proceeding ICLR*.

Shalev-Shwartz, S., Shammah, S., & Shashua, A. (2016). Safe, multi-agent, reinforcement learning for autonomous driving. In *Proc. NIPS Workshop Learn. Inference Control Multi-Agent Syst., 2016.* pp. 563-575.

Shi, S., Wang, Q., Xu, P., & Chu, X. (2016). Benchmarking state-of-the-art deep learning software tools. *ArXiv e-prints, Aug. 2016.*

Silver, D., Huang, A., Maddison, C. J., Guez, A., Sifre, L., van den Driessche, G., ... Hassabis, D. (2016). Mastering the game of Go with deep neural networks and tree search. [EP −, Jan]. *Nature*, *529*(7587), 484–489. doi:10.1038/nature16961 PMID:26819042

Simonyan, K., & Zisserman, A. (2014).Two-stream convolution networks for action recognition in videos. In *Proceedings of NIPS-2014*, pp. 568–576.

Simonyan, K., & Zisserman, A. (2015). Very deep convolutional networks for large-scale image recognition. In *Proceedings of ICLR*.

Simonyan, K., & Zisserman, A. (2015). Very deep convolutional networks for large-scale image recognition. In ICLR.

Sze, V., Chen, Y. H., Yang, T. J., & Emer, J. S. (2017). Efficient processing of deep neural networks: A tutorial and survey. *Proceedings of the IEEE, 105*(12), 2295-2329.

Szegedy, C. (2015). Going deeper with convolutions, *in Proceedings of CVPR*, 2015, pp. 1–9.

Szegedy, C., Liu, W., Jia, Y., Sermanet, P., Reed, S., Anguelov, D., . . . Rabinovich, A. (2014a). Going deeper with convolutions. Technical report, arXiv:1409.4842

The Microsoft cognitive toolkit. (2017). Retrieved from https://docs.microsoft.com/en-us/cognitive-toolkit/

Theano. (2017). Retrieved from http://deeplearning.net/software/theano/

Thompson, J., Jain, A., LeCun, Y., & Bregler, C. (2014). Joint training of a convolutional network and a graphical model for human pose estimation. In NIPS'2014.

Torch. (2017). A scientific computing framework for Luajit. Retrieved from http://torch.ch/

van den Oord, A. (2016). WaveNet: A generative model for raw audio. [Online]. Available: Bengio, Yoshua, Courville, Aaron, Vincent, Pascal. (2013). Representation learning: A review and new perspectives. *IEEE Transactions on Pattern Analysis and Machine Intelligence*, *35*(8), 1798–1828.

Wang, D., Khosla, A., Gargeya, R., Irshad, H., & Beck, A. H. (2016). Deep learning for identifying metastatic breast cancer. arXiv preprint arXiv:1606.05718.

Woodhouse, J. (2016, January). Big, big, big data: Higher and higher resolution video surveillance. [Online]. Available at http://technology.ihs.com

Xiong, H. Y., Alipanahi, B., Lee, L. J., Bretschneider, H., Merico, D., Yuen, R. K. C., ... Frey, B. J. (2015). The human splicing code reveals new insights into the genetic determinants of disease. *Science*, *347*(6218), 1254806. doi:10.1126cience.1254806 PMID:25525159

Yeshwanth, C., Sooraj, P. S. A., Sudhakaran, V., & Raveendran, V. (2017). Estimation of intersection traffic density on decentralized architectures with deep networks. In *2017 International Smart Cities Conference (ISC2)*, pp. 1–6, Sept.

Zeng, H., Edwards, M. D., Liu, G., & Gifford, D. K. (2016). Convolutional neural network architectures for predicting DNA–protein binding. *Bioinformatics (Oxford, England)*, *32*(12), i121–i127. doi:10.1093/bioinformatics/btw255 PMID:27307608

Zhang, T., Kahn, G., Levine, S., & Abbeel, P. (2016). Learning deep control policies for autonomous aerial vehicles with MPC-guided policy search. In *Proc. ICRA, 2016*, pp. 528–535.

Zhang, X., Pan, X., & Wang, S. (2017). Fuzzy DBN with rule-based knowledge representation and high interpretability. In *2017 12th International Conference on Intelligent Systems and Knowledge Engineering (ISKE)*, pp. 1–7.

Zhang, Z., Cui, P., & Zhu, W. (2018). Deep learning on graphs: A survey. *arXiv:1812.04202v1 [cs.LG] 11 Dec 2018.*

Zhou, J., & Troyanskaya, O. G. (2015). Predicting effects of noncoding variants with deep learning-based sequence model. *Nature Methods, 12*(10), 931–934. doi:10.1038/nmeth.3547 PMID:26301843

Chapter 2
A Journey From Neural Networks to Deep Networks:
Comprehensive Understanding for Deep Learning

Priyanka P. Patel

ⓘD https://orcid.org/0000-0002-2618-072X

Chandubhai S. Patel Institute of Technology, CHARUSAT University, India

Amit R. Thakkar

Chandubhai S. Patel Institute of Technology, CHARUSAT University, India

ABSTRACT

The chapter is about deep learning fundaments and its recent trends. The chapter mentions many advanced applications and deep learning models and networks to easily solve those applications in a very smart way. Discussion of some techniques for computer vision problem and how to solve with deep learning approach are included. After taking fundamental knowledge of the background theory, one can create or solve applications. The current state-of-the-art of deep learning for education, healthcare, agriculture, industrial, organizations, and research and development applications are very fast growing. The chapter is about types of learning in a deep learning approach, what kind of data set one can be required, and what kind of hardware facility is required for the particular complex problem. For unsupervised learning problems, Deep learning algorithms have been designed, but in the same way Deep learning is also solving the supervised learning problems for a wide variety of tasks.

DOI: 10.4018/978-1-7998-1159-6.ch002

INTRODUCTION

DL is a subclass of ML and ML is a sub-branch of AI. Capabilities of deep learning diverge in many key respects from ancient machine learning. Deep learning acquiesces to computers to resolve a number of complex, advanced and novel issues that have been not somewhat be tackled by Ancient machine learning approaches (Arel, I. et al, 2010; LeCun et al, 2015; Schmidhuber, J., 2015). These issues are that swathes of issues in the real world are not a good fit for such simple models means some advanced and high configuration models, techniques, and approach is required. A handwritten number recognizing is one of the examples of these complex real-world problem. To resolve such problem one needs to gather a huge dataset related to handwritten numbers also the computer system should handle such data. Every digit between 0 and 9 can be written in numerous ways also the size and exact shape of each handwritten digit can be very different depending on whose writing and in what circumstance. So to manage the diversity of these multiple feature set and to further communication between them is where deep learning and deep neural networks become very beneficial as compare to Ancient learning. Neural networks are mathematical models whose construction of the network is broadly inspired by the human brain. Each neuron of the network is a mathematical function which receives data through an input layer and, transforms that input data into a more responsible form, and then it will spit it out through an output layer. You can think of neurons in a neural network as being arranged in layers, as shown below (Adamczak et al, 2004; Buduma et al, 2017; Goodfellow et al,2016; LeCun et al, 2015). The terms like Deep Belief Nets, Convolutional Nets, Backpropagation, non-linearity, Image recognition, and so on or maybe across the big Deep Learning researchers like Geoff Hinton, Andrew Ng, Yann LeCun, Andrej Karpathy, Yoshua Bengio. If we follow and see the news of technology we may have even heard about Deep Learning in big companies NVidia and its GPUs, Apple and its self-driving Car, Google buying DeepMind for 400 million dollars, and Toyota's billion dollars AI research investment(Arel et al, 2010).

Deep Learning is About Neural Networks

The neural system's structures and any other simple network's structures are the same structure. Nodes of webs are interconnected with each other. Nodes are called neurons and we called edges to those joints which are used to join node to node. The main function of neural networks is to collect or receive a set of inputs, do some complex and progressively calculate some process and end up with some useful information called the output of the problem (Adamczak et al, 2004; Buduma et al, 2017; LeCun et al, 2015Schmidhuber et al, 2015).

Figure 1. Neural Network

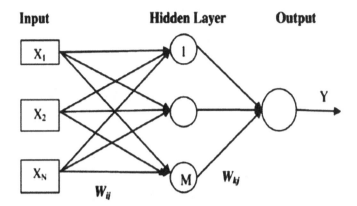

The current state-of-the-art in deep learning is to recognition pattern through deep learning which is worth noting. In ancient learning, attempting to training a network with a backpropagation method, we fall into a basic error called the vanishing gradient, sometimes it is called as the exploding gradient. Once the vanishing gradient the error encounters, the training task takes an extremely long time and consequently, the accuracy of the network will suffer extremely (Arel et al, 2010; LeCun et al, 2015; Patterson et al, 2017).

When we are training a neural network, we are constantly computing a cost-value. Generally, the cost-value is the excellence between the net's predicted output and the actual output from a group of labeled training data. The cost value is then dropped by making slight changes or adjusts to the weights and biases over and over throughout the training method until the lower possible value are obtained. Here is

Figure 2. Deep Neural Network

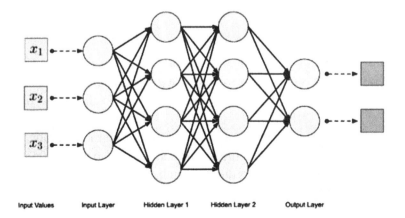

Figure 3. Cheat sheet on Neural Networks and deep networks topologies (Fjodor van Veen)

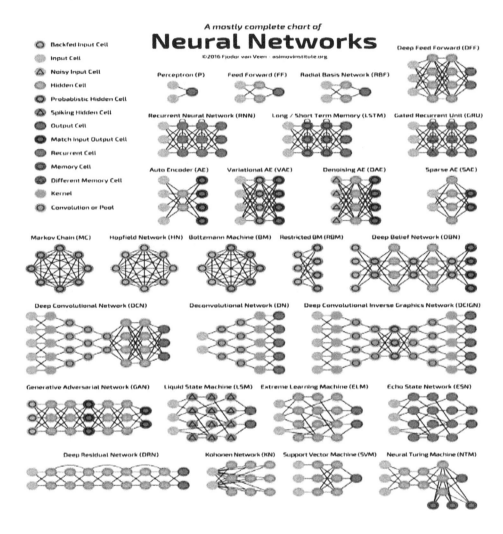

that forward propagation again; and here are the instance weights and biases. The training process utilizes one factor spoken as a gradient, which measures the rate at that the cost will change with respect to a change in weight or bias (Brownlee, J., 2016; LeCun et al, 2015).

For complex machine learning problems such as facial recognition, the deep architectures are the best and sometimes only choice. But up until 2006, there was no way to accurately train deep nets due to a fundamental problem with the training process and the problem of the vanishing gradient. For example, think that Gradient

Figure 4. AI, ML, and DL (Copeland, B. M., 2016)

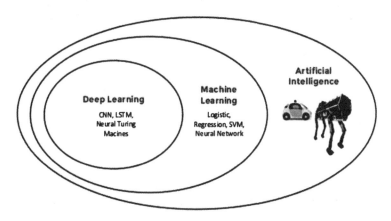

is like a slope and the training process like a rock rolling down that slope. A rock will roll quickly down a steep slope but will barely move at all on a flat surface. The same is true with the gradient of a deep net. When the gradient is larger, the network will train speedily. When the gradient is smaller, the net will train slowly. Here's that deep net again. And here is how the gradient could potentially vanish or decay back through the net. As we can see, the gradients are much smaller in the earlier layers. As a result, the early layers of the network are the slowest to train. But this is a fundamental problem! The early layers are responsible for detecting the simple patterns and the building blocks – when it came to facial recognition, the early layers detected the edges which were combined to form facial features later in the network. And if the early layers get it wrong, the result built up by the net will be wrong as well. It could mean that instead of a face like this, our net looks for this. The method used for training a neural net is called back- propagation or back-prop. We saw before that forward prop starts with the inputs and works forward; back-prop does the reverse, calculating the gradient from right to left. For example, here are 5 gradients, 4 weight, and 1 bias. It starts with the left and works back through the layers, like so. Each time it computes a gradient, it usages all the previous gradients up to thereto purpose (Brownlee, 2016; Copeland, B. M., 2016; LeCun et al, 2015).

LEARNING TYPES

Two types of learning terminology are described here: supervised and unsupervised learning. In unsupervised learning – it extracts patterns from a set of unlabelled data – then it will utilize either a Restricted Boltzmann Machine or an auto-encoder (Adamczak et al, 2004; Goodfellow et al, 2016; LeCun et al, 2015; Zhang, G. P.,

2000). In Supervised Learning: Labelled data for supervised learning and it will build a classifier, there are several different options depending on our application. For text processing tasks like sentiment analysis, parsing, and named entity recognition – use a Recurrent Net or a Recursive Neural Tensor Network, which we'll refer to as an RNTN (Adamczak et al, 2004; Goodfellow et al, 2016; LeCun et al, 2015).

CLASSIFICATION

Neural systems are utilized for heaps of various distinctive applications here they have examined about classification problem (Kotsiantis et al, 2007). Classification is the way toward sorting or categorizing a group of objects while just utilizing some fundamental information or feature of that objects includes that portray them with the help of those highlighted features (Adamczak et al, 2004; Kotsiantis et al, 2007). There are lots of classifiers available today like Logistic Regression, Naive Bayes, Support Vector Machines, Neural networks (Goodfellow et al, 2016; Zhang, G. P., 2000).

The Activation or output of a classifier is generally known as the score. For example, to predict that the patient is sick or healthy? The data required for prediction are the patient's height, weight, and body temperature. The classifier would receive these patient data and, process the data with complex calculations, and finally, it will catch out a confidence-score. The patient is sick if the confidence score is high, and a low score would indicate that the patient is fit. For the classification task, neural nets are used where an object can dive into one of at least two different categories of classification Not at all like different networks sort of a social network and the NN is extremely organized, structured plus NN comes in the layer by layers. The input layer is the first year of the network also called primary layer. The last layer is the output Layer or classification layer and all the layers in between input and the output layers are declared as hidden layers (Brownlee, J., 2016; Yu, F. R., & He, Y.). As a result of every node within the hidden and output layers have its own classifier, the neural internet is viewed because of the results of spinning classifiers along in an exceedingly layered net (Brownlee, J., 2016; Buduma et al, 2017; Deng, L., 2014; Nielsen et al, 2015; Zhang, G. P., 2000).

Take that node for example - it gets its inputs from the input layer, and activates. Its score is then passed on as input to the next hidden layer for further activation. The principal neural nets were conceived out of the need to address the error of an early classifier, the perception. It was demonstrated that by utilizing a layered web of perceptron's predictions accuracy could be made progress. Subsequently, this new type of neural nets was known as a Multi- Layer Perceptron or MLP. Since then, the nodes within neural nets have replaced perceptron's with a lot of powerful classifiers, however, the name MLP has stuck. Take that node for instance — it gets its inputs from the input layer, and activates. Its score is then passed on as input to succeeding hidden layer for advanced activation.

The principal neural nets were planned out of the necessity to handle the error of associate early classifier, the perception. It absolutely was incontestable that by utilizing a superimposed net of perceptron's predictions accuracy may well be created progress. Afterward, this new style of neural nets was called a Multi-Layer Perceptron or MLP. Since then, the nodes within neural nets have replaced perceptron's with additional powerful classifiers, however, the name MLP has stuck (LeCun et al, 2015).

Forward propagation: every node has a similar classifier, associated none of them fire randomly; if we repeat an input, we get a similar output. Thus, if each node within the hidden layer received a similar input, why didn't all of them fireplace out a similar value? The explanation is that every set of inputs is changed and modified by distinctive weights and biases. As an example, for that node, the primary input is changed by a weight of 10 the second by 5, the third by 6 then a bias of 9 is added on top. Every edge incorporates a distinctive weight, and every node incorporates a distinctive bias. This implies that the combination used for every activation is also distinctive that explains why the nodes fire otherwise (LeCun et al, 2015).

NEURAL NETWORK ACCURACY IS PREDICTED BASED ON WEIGHTS AND BIASES.

What we want from the neural net is the net to predict a value that is as close to the actual output as possible every single time. In other words, we want that accuracy to

Figure 5. Bias and Weights

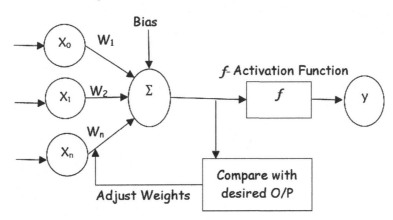

Figure 6. Deep Learning Techniques

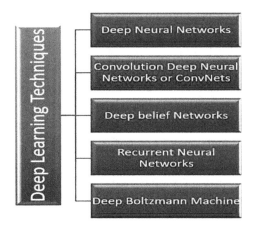

be high. The process of improving accuracy of a neural networks is called training, much the same as with other machine learning techniques. Here's that forward propagation again - to prepare the network, the yield from forward propagation is contrasted with the yield that is known to be right and the cost is the distinction of the two. The purpose of training is to make that cost as little as would be prudent, crosswise over a huge number of training cases. To do this, the net changes the weights and biases step by step in well-ordered until the point when the prediction intently coordinates the right yield. Once prepared well, a neural net can possibly set aside a few minutes. This is a neural net more or less (Adamczak et al, 2004; Bengio, Y., 2009; Géron, A., 2018; Schmidhuber et al, 2015). Figure-1 Shows the Deep learning techniques.

- Deep Belief Network or a Convolutional Net, and Recurrent Net are used for image recognition.
- Convolutional Net or an RNTN uses for object recognition
- Recurrent Net use for speech recognition

In general, Deep Belief Networks and Multilayer Perceptron's with rectified linear units – also known as RELU – are both good choices for classification. For time series analysis it's best to use a Recurrent Net (Adamczak et al, 2004; Goodfellow et al, 2016; LeCun et al, 2015).

DEEP LEARNING DRAWBACKS

One of the biggest disadvantages of deep learning training phase required huge data. Before some time ago Facebook announced that they had used one billion images for their image-recognition system to accomplish record-breaking compliance. So, in deep learning always large datasets are required to train systems and it can take vast amounts of time, it also required distributed computing power or GPU to access it.

Another drawback is the training cost of the network. Because of the large datasets and a huge number of training cycles it requires high computing -powered GPU and GPU array (Copeland, B. M., 2016. To train Deep network is also challenging, because of the vanishing gradient problem, but there are solutions in deep learning to solve it. When more layers are added to the network the vanishing gradient error will occur and it will result in the unfeasible mode and also compromise the accuracy. The problem doesn't trouble every network, but it will affect those which use gradient-based learning methods. so, these kinds of problems can be addressed by choosing a suitable activation function means instead of using sigmoid function use ReLu function or Leaky ReLu function or there are many other variations of ReLu Functions are also available (Arel et al, 2010; Shi, S. et al, 2016).

Deep learning does not have a strong theoretical foundation. It is like a black box because when the network generates features no one can figure out how it will be calculated. There's no fundamental mathematics for that. This leads to the next disadvantage. To decide the topology and hyper-parameters for deep learning is a black art with no theory to guide you.

HARDWARE REQUIRED FOR LEARNING

Hardware requirement for deep learning network to the training process is GPU, for that two options are here:

- Build own deep learning ring
- Hire the Hardware from GPU clouds from a cloud provider like Amazon, NVIDIA, IBM, Google, and Azure. The advantage of using Cloud is they offer machine driven systems that streamline the training process another advantage is the learning Model also offers drag- and-drop tools to setting parameters (Copeland, B. M., 2016; Shi, S. et al, 2016).

Figure 7. Training and validating a Network

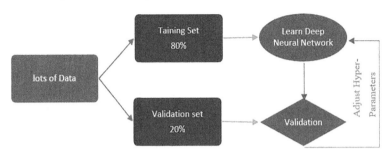

TRAINING OF DEEP NEURAL NETWORKS

As covers about deep neural networks. Due to large numbers of layers and the link between each neuron to the neuron in the middle layer deep neural networks are difficult to train. During the training time, the calculation and the adjustment of the parameter are too difficult for the very wide network. Also refer Drawback of Deep learning section. Figure-3 process shows the distribution of large dataset for training and validation set. It quite changes is the distribution of data as compared to ancient learning. During training time fine tune the hyper parameters to achieve desired accuracy from the network.

RESENT RESEARCH GOING ON DEEP LEARNING

Some leading organizations are work on it. Names are NVIDIA researchers making super- slow motion videos using deep learning, Google's making electronic health records, LG to NVIDIA and ARM doing IoT projects using deep learning (Copeland, B. M., 2016).

DEEP LEARNING MODELS

1. Restricted Boltzmann Machine

- The first researchers to devise a breakthrough idea for training deep nets and it was by Geoff Hinton at the University of Toronto. The researcher's approach directed to the creation of the Restricted Boltzmann Machine, also known as the RBM. Because of his pioneering work he declared to as one of the father of deep learning. A RBM is thin and one layered network. Mainly two layers:

- ○ The first layer- Visible layer
- ○ Second layer- Hidden layer
- That is why it also known as a shallow network. Visible layer's every node is connected with each node of the hidden layer.
- A RBM is well-thought-out "restricted" since in a same layer there is a no connection between two nodes.
- A mathematical analogy of a two-way translation of the RBM is mentioned below,
  - ○ **Way -1:** The forward propagation, an RBM will take the inputs and translates them into an encrypted set of numbers.
  - ○ **Way-2:** The backward-propagation- it will take above encrypted set of numbers and translates them back to re-establish inputs.
- A well-trained net will be able to execute the backward translation with a high degree of accuracy.
- In each steps, the weights and biases have a really vital role. They permit the RBM to decode, the interrelationships among the input features plus they additionally facilitate the RBM to decide that input features are the foremost vital once when detecting patterns.
- Through many forward and backward passes, associate RBM is trained to recreate the input data.
- Mention steps are repeated over and over through the training process:
  - ○ **Step-1:** With a forward propagation, each input information is pooled with one general bias and different weights, and subsequently, the outcome is passed to the activated or not activate the hidden layer.
  - ○ **Step-2:** Next in a backward propagation, every activation is pooled with a specific weight and a total bias, and subsequently, the outcome will be transferred to the input layer for rebuilding.
  - ○ **Step-3:** At input layer, the rebuilding is compared against the original input which decided the quality of the outcome.
- For step 1, 2 and 3, RBM is using KL Divergence measure. Until the input and the re- construction are as close as possible the weights and biases are changing repetitive.
- A motivating aspect of an RBM is that the data does not need to be labelled. This turns out to be very important for real-world data sets like photos, videos, voices, and sensor data – all of which tend to be unlabeled.
- Rather than having people manually label the data and introduce errors, an RBM automatically sorts through the data, and by properly regulating the weights and biases, an RBM is able to extract the important features and reconstruct the input.

- An imperative and necessary annotation is that an RBM is essentially generated conclusions of which input features are significant and how those input features should be combined to form patterns.
- In other words, an RBM belongs to feature extractor neural network family, which are altogether intended to identify natural patterns in dataset. These nets are likewise known as"Auto-encoders" in light of the fact that, they need to encode their own structure (Deng et al, 2013).

2. Deep Belief Nets (DBN)

- RBM can extract features and reconstruct inputs plus help to out of the vanishing gradient problem? By combining RBMs together and introducing an adroit training method, it obtain a powerful new model that finally solves the vanishing gradient problem. Now take a look at a Deep Belief Network. Just like the RBM, DBN were also conceived by Geoff Hinton as an alternative to backpropagation. Because of his accomplishments, he was hired for image recognition work at Google, where a large- scale DBN project is currently believed to be in development. In terms of network structure, a DBN is identical to an MLP (multi-layer perceptron). But when it comes to training, they are entirely different. In fact, the key factor is the difference in training methods which enables DBNs to outpace their shallow equivalents. DBN, the hidden layer of one RBM is the visible layer of the one "above" it. It can be viewed as a stack of RBMs.
- Training of DBN is as follows:
  a. Earliest RBMs were trained to re-build input as correctly as it promising.
  b. Earliest RBM- The hidden layer is salted as the visible layer for the second and also the second RBM is trained using the outputs from the first RBM (Glauner et al, 2015)
  c. The whole above process is repeated until each layer within the network is trained. An important note about a DBN is that every RBM layer learns the whole input (Glauner et al, 2015).
- In other kinds of models – alike convolutional networks, primary layers detect simple edges patterns and later layers recombine them to follow abstract feature from the layers to layers. For example in facial recognition application, the early layers would detect edges from the entire face image, next layers would detect more abstract feature and later layers would use these results to form facial features. On the other hand, A Deep Belief Networks generally, the model slowly improves, when fine-tune the complete input in progression– it's like a camera lens slowly focusing a picture. The reason that a DBN is highly technical and it works so well. A stack of RBMs will outperform a

single unit – just like a Multilayer perceptron was able to outperform a single perceptron working alone. After this primary training, the RAM creates a model that can detect natural patterns in the data, but we still don't know exactly what the patterns are called. Now, labels the all patterns and fine-tune the network with supervised learning to finish training, to complete training, one need tiny set of labelled dataset so that the features and patterns can be associated with a name. The biases and weights are adjusted slightly, due to this small change the net's perception of the patterns are also change, and sometime the over-all accuracy also increase slightly. Fortunately, the set of labelled data can be slight relative to the original data set, which as we've discussed, is extremely helpful in real-world applications. So, Deep Belief Nets is provided the solution of problem vanishing gradient (Glauner et al, 2015; Hinton et al, 2009).

3. Convolution Neural Network

- Convolution Neural Network also referred to as CNN or ConvNets. CNNs have wide range of applications in all the space some of them are Image Detection and Image Recognition, Detection in Video data, Recommender Systems, Video Recognition, and Natural Language Processing (Dehghan et al, 2017; Lan, S. et al, 2018). ConvNets are very similar to regular Neural Net's. Convolutional Neural networks enable computers to see and visualize, means CNN are used to recognize images by transmuting the original image through layers by layers to a class scores. The network was inspired by the visual cortex on every occasion that can see something by our eyes, a series of layers of neurons gets activated, and every layer will detect a group of features such as lines, edges. The initial layers of network will detect more complex features in order to recognize what layers are detects edges and finally the last layer of the network will decide the result or outcome of the problem based on score value. So, the process is like, the networks are made up of neurons and each neurons have weights and biases. Each weight and biases are learnable. So every neuron receives inputs, accomplishes with a dot product and optionally follows it with a nonlinearity (Lan, S. et al, 2018). So, how are Convolutional Neural Networks different than Neural Networks? Figure 8 shows the architecture of a regular 3-layer Neural Network (Kumar et al, 2017).
- A CNN gathers neurons in over-all three dimensions which are the depth, height, and width, as visualized in one of the layers. Each layer of a CNN's transforms the 3D input volume to a 3D output volume of neuron activations. In figure 9 example of architecture, the input holds the image red bar, so its

Figure 8. A regular 3-layer Neural Network (Johnson et al, 2015)

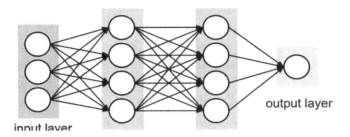

dimensions are width and height of the image, and also the depth would be 3 channels Red, Green, Blue.

- A CNNs is a sequence of layers, every layer of a ConvNet transforms one volume of activations to different through a differentiable function. ConvNet has two parts:
  - Feature learning and
  - Classification.
- Convolution, Relu, Poolings are the used to generate and craft the feature of the Image and to classify the Image fully connected layer and the softmax are used.

For an instance we can make a flow like;

- There are three main kinds of layers to make Convolution Neural network architectures: Convolutional Layer, we'll stack these layers to create a full ConvNet design.
  - Conv Layer,
  - Pool Layer,
  - Fully-Connected Layer
- Typical architecture of CNN is shown below.

Step-1 The Training of Input Data

- The input volume or input layer is an image that has the sequel dimensions: It is a matrix of pixel values.

Example: In input, here The depth, represents R, G, B channels.

Figure 9. A ConvNet with 3channeks (Johnson et al, 2015)

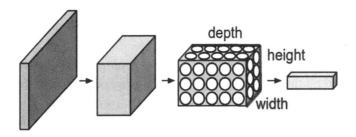

Figure 10. Example of CNN architecture (Johnson et al, 2015)

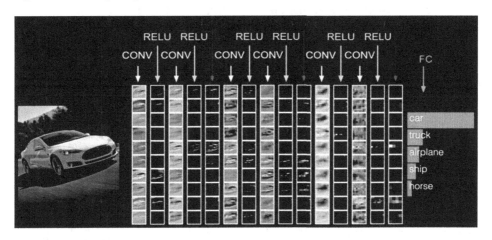

Figure 11.

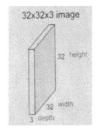

[32 x 32 x3]=> (Height=32, Width=32, Depth=3)

Step-2 CONV Layer

- A convolution is an operation that changes a function into something else. Means to get more information out of it.
- The whole input image is associated with progressive Conv layer in this manner, if all the pixels of the input layer is associated with the Conv layer, it will be exceptionally expensive in terms computation. So to apply dot products between a receptive field and a filter on all the dimensions. The final product of this task operation is a single integer of the output volume which is also referred as a feature map. Then after the filter over the successive receptive field of the same input image by a Stride and compute again the dot products between the new receptive field and the same filter. Repeat this process until go through the entire input image. The next layer input would be the output of the previous layer.

Figure 12. Conv layer with K = 2 filters, with a spatial extent F = 3, stride S = 2, and input padding P = 1 (Johnson et al, 2015)

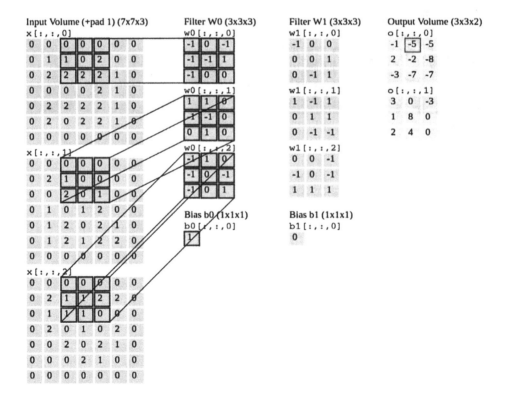

- The whole input image is associated with progressive Conv layer in this manner, if all the pixels of the input layer is associated with the Conv layer, it will be exceptionally expensive in terms computation. So to apply dot products between a receptive field and a filter on all the dimensions. The final product of this task operation is a single integer of the output volume which is also referred as a feature map. Then after the filter over the successive receptive field of the same input image by a Stride and compute again the dot products between the new receptive field and the same filter. Repeat this process until go through the entire input image. The next layer input would be the output of the previous layer.

Need to Know

- **What is Feature detector or the Filter or the Kernel:** Convolutions aren't a new notion. They have been used in image and signal processing for quite a while. Be that as it may, convolutions in machine learning are unique in relation to those in picture handling. Numerous filters are available like sobel, horizontal, vertical filter. It is an odd number small matrix used for features detection. A typical filter on the primary layer of a ConvNet might have a size [5x5x3]. The filter is also known as convolutional matrix.
- **Feature Map:**
  - It is the output volume formed by sliding the filter over the image and computing the dot product.
  - It is also referred as Convolved Feature, conv feature, Activation Map.
- **Receptive field:** It is a local region of the input volume that has the equivalent size as the filter.
- **Depth column:** It is the set of neurons that are all pointing to the same receptive field.
- **Depth:** the amount of filters.

Figure 13. Input Image matrix, Filter matrix, result convoluted feature matrix

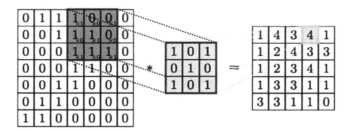

Figure 14. Convolution matrix or, filter computation with layer (Johnson et al, 2015)

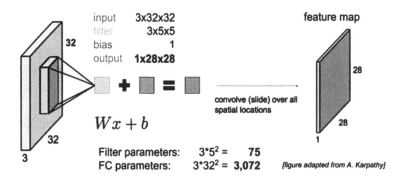

- **Stride:** it has the objective of building smaller output volumes spatially. For instance, if the image is larger than the size of the filter, the filter shifting one unit at time to the various parts of the image and perform the convolution task. Each time it will generate a new pixel in the output image. The amount of filter shifting unit to unite on whole input image k with kernel is known as the stride.
- **Zero-padding:** it includes zeros around the outside of the input volume so that the convolutions end up with the same number of outputs as inputs. . In the event that we don't utilize padding the information at the borders will be lost after each Conv layer, which will reduce the size of the volumes as well as the performance.

$$ZeroPadding = \frac{K-1}{2}, . \text{ Where K Filter size,}$$

The formula for calculating the output size for any given conv layer is,

$$Output = \frac{(W - K + 2P)}{S} + 1$$

→ So, [W2xH2xD2] compute the Output value:

$$W2 = \left[\frac{w1 - F + 2P}{S}\right] + 1, \ H2 = \left[\frac{H1 - F + 2P}{S}\right] + 1, \ D2 = K1, \text{ where:}$$

[W1xH1xD1]: input volume size

F: receptive field size

S: stride

P: amount of zero padding used on the border.

K: depth

○ The first Convolutional Layer output volume with given input size is: [227x227x3], W=227, F=11, S=4, P=0, and K=96.

$$W2 = \left[\frac{227 - 11 + 2(0)}{4} \right] + 1 = \left[\frac{227 - 11}{4} \right] + 1 = \frac{216}{4} + 1 = 55$$

$$H2 = \left[\frac{227 - 11 + 2(0)}{4} \right] + 1 = \left[\frac{227 - 11}{4} \right] + 1 = \frac{216}{4} + 1 = 55$$

D2= 96, So, [55x55x96] is the Conv layer output volume.

- **Parameter Sharing:** it is also known as weight sharing. If a feature is beneficial it will also be beneficial to look for it everywhere in the image. . Be that as it may,, occasionally, it is odd to share the same weights in some cases. For instance, in a training data that contains faces centered, we don't have to look for eyes in the bottom or the top of the image.
- **Dilation:** It is a new hyper-parameter introduced to the Conv layer. Dilation is filters with spaces between its cells. for instance, we have one dimension filter W of size 3 and an input X:

Dilation of 0: w[0]*x[0] + w[1]*x[1] + w[2]*x[2].

Dilation of 1: w[0]*x[0] + w[1]*x[2] + w[2]*x[4].

- ***ReLU layer:*** *ReLU Layer applies an elementwise initiation function max(0,x), which turns negative values to zeros means thresholding at zero. This layer does not change the size of the volume and there are no hyperparameters.*
- **POOL layer:** Pool Layer completes a function to reduce the spatial dimensions of the input, and the computational complexity of our model. And it also controls overfitting. It operates independently on every depth slice of the input. There are different functions such as Max pooling, average pooling, or L2-norm pooling. However, Max pooling is the most used type of pooling which only takes the most important part (the value of the brightest pixel) of

the input volume. Example of a Max pooling with 2x2 filter and stride = 2. So, for each of the windows, max pooling takes the max value of the 4 pixels.

- Pool layer doesn't have parameters, and no zero padding, but it has two hyperparameters: Filter (F) and Stride (S).All the more generally, having the input W1×H1×D1, the pooling layer produces a volume of size W2×H2×D2 where:

  ○ W2= {(W1−F)/S}+1

  ○ H2={(H1−F)/S}+1

  ○ D2=D1

- A typical type of a Max pooling is filters of size 2x2 applied with a stride of 2. The Pooling sizes with larger filters are too destructive and they usually lead to worse performance.

- Numerous individuals do not likes using a pooling layer since it throws away information and they replace it with a Conv layer with increased stride once in a while.

Step-3 Fully Connected Layer (FC)

- Fully connected layers connect each neuron in one layer to each neuron in another layer. The last fully-connected layer usages a softmax activation function for classifying the generated features of the input image into numerous classes on the training dataset. Example, Classification Of a ConvNet architecture:

- [INPUT—CONV—RELU—POOL—FC]

4. Recurrent Nets

- Recurrent neural networks is also a deep learning model and it also has a simple structure with a fundamental feedback loop, permitting it to perform as a predicting machine.

Figure 15. Max pooling with 2x2 filter and stride = 2

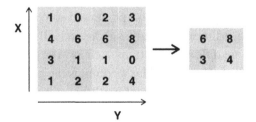

Figure 16. Operation upon the pixel space

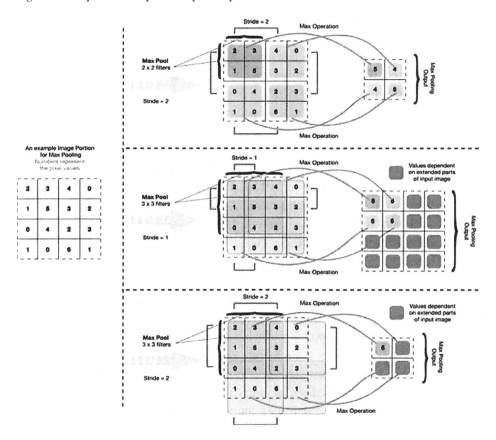

- Recurrent nets, or rnns, have a long history, but their recent popularity is mostly due to the works of Juergen Schmidhuber, Sepp Hochreiter, and Alex Graves. Their applications are extremely versatile – ranging from speech recognition to driverless cars.
- All the nets we've seen up to the present purpose are feedforward neural networks. During a feedforward neural network, the flow of signals is in one single direction from the input layer to the output layer solely and one layer at a time. During a recurrent network, succeeding input is that the output of a previous layer and it'll other and fed back to a similar layer, that is usually the sole layer within the whole network.
- For illustration, we can think of this progression as a passage through time – shown here are 4 such time steps.
  - At t = 1, the network takings the output of time t = 0 and sends it back into the network along with the next input.

- ○ The network repeats this for t = 2, t = 3, and so on.
- Unlike feedforward networks, a recurrent networks input is a sequence of, and it may turn out a sequence of values as output.
- The ability to work with sequences exposes these nets to a large type of applications. Here square measure some examples. Once the input is odd and also the output may be a sequence, a possible application is image captioning. A sequence of inputs with one output is often used for document classification. Once each the input and output square measure sequences, these nets will classify videos frame by frame. If a time delay is introduced, the cyber web will statistically forecast the demand in provide chain designing.
- Classically, an RNN is a particularly challenging network to train. Subsequently these networks use back propagation, we have a tendency to yet again run into the matter of the vanishing gradient. Unfortunately, for RNN the vanishing gradient is exponentially worse The reason for this is that every time step is that the equivalent of a complete layer during a feed-forward network. Thus training an RNN for a hundred time steps are like training a 100-layer feed forward net — these end up in exponentially small gradients and a decay of information through time. There are numerous methods to address this kind of problem - the most popular of which is Gating.
- The method that helps the network to make a decision once to forget the current input, and once to recollect it for future time steps is called Gating. The foremost well-liked gating sorts these days square measure GRU and LSTM. Besides gating, there are a couple of different techniques like gradient clipping, steeper gates, and better optimizers.
- When it involves training a recurrent network, GPUs are a unit an understandable alternative over a normal processor like CPU. The investigation team of Indico has validated this. Which usages these networks on text process tasks like sentiment analysis and effectiveness extraction. The team initiate that GPUs we have a tendency tore ready to train the nets 250 times faster than the CPUs! That's the distinction between in some unspecified time or one day time of training and over eight months! Thus beneath what circumstances would we use a recurrent net over a feedforward net? We all know that an output of feedforward networks is one value, that in several cases it was a category or a prediction.
  - ○ When it includes preparing a repetitive system, GPUs region unit a reasonable option over an ordinary processor like CPU. This was approved by an examination group at Indico, which utilizes these nets on content process assignments like feeling investigation and supportiveness extraction.

- A recurrent network is appropriate for statistic knowledge, time series data, wherever the output is following value during a sequence or following next several values. Thus the answer depends on whether or not the application calls for classification, regression, or forecasting.

5. Autoencoders

- There are times when it's extremely useful to figure out the underlying structure of a data set. Having access to the most important data features gives us a lot of flexibility when we start applying labels. Autoencoders are an important family of neural networks that are well-suited for this task.
- In a previous model we looked at the Restricted Boltzmann Machine, which is a very popular example of an autoencoder. But there are other types of Autoencoders like DE noising and contractive, just to name a few. Just like an RBM, an autoencoder is a neural net that takings a set of typically unlabeled inputs, and after encoding them, tries to reconstruct them as accurately as possible. Subsequently, as an outcome of this, the net must choose which of the data features are the most vital, essentially acting as a feature extraction engine.
- Autoencoders are typically very shallow, and are usually encompassed of an input layer, a hidden layer and the output layer. An RBM is an example of an autoencoder with only two layers. Here is a forward pass that ends with a reconstruction of the input. There are two steps - the encoding and the decoding. Typically, the same weights that are used to encode a feature in the hidden layer are used to reconstruct an image in the output layer.
- Autoencoders are trained with backpropagation, using a metric called "loss". As opposed to "cost", loss measures the amount of information that was lost when the net tried to reconstruct the input. A net with a small loss value will produce reconstructions that look very similar to the originals.
- Not all of these nets are shallow. In fact, deep Autoencoders are extremely useful tools for dimensionality reduction. Consider an image containing a 28x28 grid of pixels.
- A neural net would need to process over 750 input values just for one image – doing this across millions of images would waste significant amounts of memory and processing time.
- A deep autoencoder could encode this image into an impressive 30 numbers, and still maintain information about the key image features. When decoding the output, the net acts like a two-way translator. In this example, a well-trained net could translate these 30 encoded numbers back into a reconstruction that looks similar to the original image. Certain types of nets also introduce

random noise to the encoding-decoding process, which has been shown to improve the robustness of the resulting patterns.

- Deep Autoencoders perform better at dimensionality reduction than their predecessor, principal component analysis, or PCA. Below is a comparison of two letter codes for news stories of different topics – generated by both a deep autoencoder and a PCA. Labels were added to the picture for illustrative purposes.

6. Deep learning Platforms

- A platform may be a set of tools that others will devolve on from top to bottom of. As an example, consider the applications which will be designed off of the tools provided by Windows, Android, iOS, MacOS, and IBM Websphere, and even Oracle BEA. Thus a Deep Learning platform provides a collection of tools associated an interface for building custom.

- Deep Learning platform provides a collection of tools asssociated an interface for building custom deep networks. Typically, they provide a user with a spread of deep nets to determine on from DBN/MLP, RBM, Convo Net, Autoencoder, RNN, and RNTN. Beside the ability of knowledge-mining to integrate data from extremely different sources, manipulate information, and manage models through a UI. Some platforms collectively facilitate with performance if a net should be trained with huge data set.

- There are some benefits and downsides of employing a platform vs. employing a software code library. A platform is associate out-of-the-box application that enables us to put together a deep net's hyper-parameters through associate intuitive UI; with a platform, we don't have to be compelled to grasp something concerning about coding so as to use the tools. The drawback is that we constrained by the platform's selection of deep nets and also the configuration choices. Except for anyone trying to quickly deploy a deep web, a platform is that the best approach to go.

- A software library is a set of functions and modules that we can call through our own code in order to perform certain tasks. Deep net libraries give us a lot of extra flexibility with net selection and hyper-parameter configuration. For example, there aren't many platforms that let we build a Recursive Neural Tensor Net, but we can code our own with the right deep net library! The obvious downside to libraries is the coding experience required to use them, but if we need the flexibility, they really are a great resource.

- Ersatz Labs - a dedicated Deep Learning platform that handles all the technical issues like code, deployments, and performance – and allows the user to go straight to modelling. Two machine learning software system

Figure 17. Platform and set of tools

Figure 18. Deep learning tools and Techniques

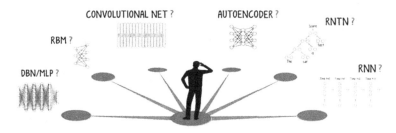

Figure 19. Platform

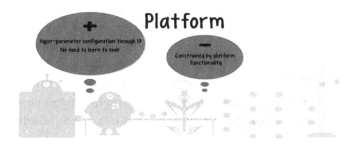

Figure 20. Libraries

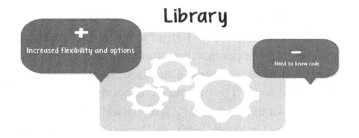

platforms referred to as H2O, and GraphLab produce, each of which supply Deep Learning tools.

- Set of functions and modules that we can call through our own programs. Libraries are typically created by highly-qualified software teams, and popular libraries are regularly maintained. Many libraries are open-source, and are surrounded by big communities that provide support and contribute to the codebase.
- Deep Learning has plenty of great libraries available like,
  - deeplearning4j
  - Torch
  - Caffe
  - Theano
  - Deepmat
- Google's TensorFlow library may be a great alternative for building commercial-grade deep learning applications with Python. There is a lot of popularity and hype encompassing TensorFlow.
- TensorFlow grew out of Associate in earlier Google library referred to as "DistBelief", that may be a proprietary deep web library developed as a part of the Google Brain project.
- Much like the Theano library, Tensor Flow is predicated on the conception of a computational graph.
- In a computational graph, nodes represent either persistent data or a math operation and edges represent the flow of data between nodes. The data that flows through these edges is a multi-dimensional array known as a tensor, hence the library's name, "TensorFlow".
- The output from one operation or set of operations is then fed as an input into the next. Even though TensorFlow was designed to support neural networks, it can support any domain where computation can be modelled as a data flow graph. TensorFlow also adopts several useful features from Theano such as auto differentiation, shared and symbolic variables, and common sub-expression elimination. And for an open source library, it has comprehensive and informative.
- TensorFlow users have to work with an additional library called Keras if this flexibility is required. Right now TensorFlow has a "no-nonsense" interface for C++, and the team hopes that the community will develop more language interfaces through SWIG, an open-source tool for connecting programs and libraries. Recently, Jason Toy of Somatic announced the release of a SWIG interface to Ruby for the summer of 2016. TensorFlow performed reasonably well in the ImageNet category, with no Theano-based libraries listed in the analysis. Another improvement over Theano comes in the form of parallelism.

- Even though most Deep Learning Libraries support CUDA, very few support OpenCL, a fast-rising standard for GPU computing.

GPU ACCELERATE DEEP LEARNING

- To train a complex model with a large dataset.
- Deep learning networks need a lot of computational power for building a model. In deep learning pipeline, the training phase of the modelling is the most intensive task, and the most time consuming one.
- Deep learning is an iterative process. When we train a deep learning model, two main operations are performed:
  - Forward Pass and
  - Backward Pass.
- In the forward pass, after processing the input which is passed through the neural network, the output is generated (Shaikh, F., 2017).
- In the backward pass, first, on the basis of the error(s) which received from forward pass, update the weights of the neural network. Second, deep learning involves heavy computations.
- For Example: in below Convolutional Neural Network figure 16 has each pixel within a single image becomes a feature point after being multiplied by the colour channel. We can consider the first array as the input to the neural network, and the second array can be considered as weights or a filter of the network. The size of these matrices are usually very big, that is, the data is high-dimensional here. So, considering that training is an iterative process, and Neural Networks have usually many weights, which should get updated with each iteration, it involves expensive computations that are mostly matrix multiplication. Therefore, Deep Learning requires much computing power (Shaikh, F., 2017).

Figure 21. Deep learning Need for Acceleration

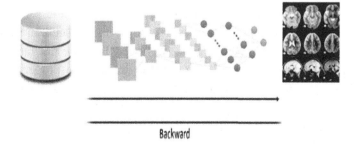

Backward

Figure 22. Deep learning Need for Acceleration

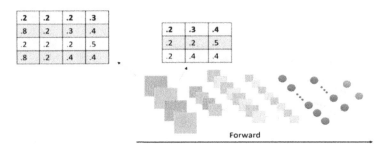

Figure 23. Matrix Multiplication in CNN

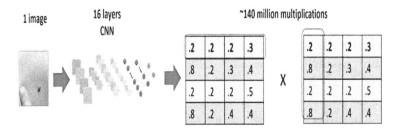

- Multiplication done as we seen in CNN, but the thing is where the data is going to instruct and process and store. We know that The CPU is responsible for executing a sequence of stored instructions, which in our case are multiplications. We need to fetch data and instructions from main memory to be run by the CPU. CPU is good at fetching small amounts of memory quickly, but not very well for big chunks of data, like big matrices, which are needed for deep learning. CPUs run tasks sequentially, rather than in parallel, even though they have 2 or 4 cores.
- Some companies used to build multiple clusters of CPUs to have a powerful system to do their processing in parallel, for example, built for training huge nets.These systems are usually very expensive and as such, most businesses can't afford them. So, we can conclude that CPUs are not fast enough for operations on big chunks of data and they're not the proper use for high parallelism, as they are very slow for these kinds of tasks (Shaikh, F., 2017).

Figure 24. Multiplication on CPU

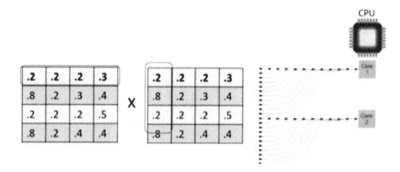

Figure 25. Multiplication on GPU

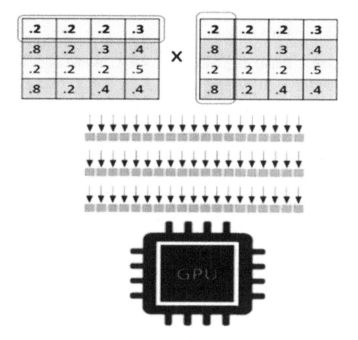

DISTRIBUTED DEEP LEARNING

- Distributed Deep Learning is a bunch of software systems, packages and algorithms that automatize and optimize the parallelization of huge and complex computing task across hundreds of GPU accelerators attached to dozens of servers. Most popular deep learning frameworks configure with a single server along with multiple GPUs, but, not configured with multiple servers along with GPUs. To reduce training times for large models with large datasets here distributed Deep Learning is introduced. It solves major-challenge scaling issue by distributing deep learning training across large numbers of servers and GPUs.

REFERENCES

Adamczak, R., Porollo, A., & Meller, J. (2004). Accurate prediction of solvent accessibility using neural networks–based regression. *Proteins*, *56*(4), 753–767. doi:10.1002/prot.20176 PMID:15281128

Arel, I., Rose, D. C., & Karnowski, T. P. (2010). Deep machine learning-a new frontier in artificial intelligence research. *IEEE Computational Intelligence Magazine*, *5*(4), 13–18. doi:10.1109/MCI.2010.938364

Bengio, Y. (2009). Learning deep architectures for AI. Foundations and trends® in Machine Learning, 2(1), 1-127.

Brownlee, J. (2016). *Master machine learning algorithms: Discover how they work and implement them from scratch*. Jason Brownlee.

Buduma, N., & Locascio, N. (2017). *Fundamentals of deep learning: Designing next-generation machine intelligence algorithms*. O'Reilly Media.

Copeland, B. M. (2016). The difference between AI, machine learning, and deep learning?. The Official NVIDIA Blog. Np, 29.

Dehghan, A., Masood, S. Z., Shu, G., & Ortiz, E. (2017). View independent vehicle make, model and color recognition using convolutional neural network. arXiv preprint arXiv:1702.01721.

Deng, L. (2014). A tutorial survey of architectures, algorithms, and applications for deep learning. APSIPA Transactions on Signal and Information Processing, 3.

Deng, L., Hinton, G., & Kingsbury, B. (2013, May). New types of deep neural network learning for speech recognition and related applications: An overview. In *Proceedings 2013 IEEE International Conference on Acoustics, Speech, and Signal Processing (ICASSP)*, (pp. 8599-8603). IEEE.

Fjodor van Veen from Asimov Institute compiled a wonderful cheatsheet on NN topologies.

Géron, A. (2018). Neural networks and deep learning.

Glauner, P. O. (2015). Comparison of training methods for deep neural networks. arXiv preprint arXiv:1504.06825.

Goodfellow, I., Bengio, Y., Courville, A., & Bengio, Y. (2016). *Deep learning* (Vol. 1). Cambridge, MA: MIT Press.

Hinton, G. E. (2009). Deep belief networks. *Scholarpedia*, *4*(5), 5947. doi:10.4249cholarpedia.5947

Johnson, J., & Karpathy, A. (2015). *Convolutional neural networks for visual recognition. Convolutional neural networks for visual recognition* (p. 94305). Stanford, CA: Stanford University.

Kotsiantis, S. B., Zaharakis, I., & Pintelas, P. (2007). Supervised machine learning: A review of classification techniques. Emerging artificial intelligence applications in computer engineering, 160, 3-24.

Kumar, V., & Garg, M. L. (2017, November). Deep learning in predictive analytics: A survey. In *Proceedings International Conference on Emerging Trends in Computing and Communication Technologies (ICETCCT)*, (pp. 1-6). IEEE. 10.1109/ICETCCT.2017.8280331

Lan, S., He, Z., Chen, W., & Chen, L. (2018, July). Hand gesture recognition using convolutional neural networks. In *2018 USNC-URSI Radio Science Meeting (Joint with AP-S Symposium)* (pp. 147-148). IEEE. 10.1109/USNC-URSI.2018.8602809

LeCun, Y., Bengio, Y., & Hinton, G. (2015). Deep learning. *Nature, 521*(7553), 436.

Nielsen, M. A. (2015). *Neural networks and deep learning* (Vol. 25). USA: Determination Press.

Patterson, J., & Gibson, A. (2017). *Deep learning: A practitioner's approach.* O'Reilly Media.

Schmidhuber, J. (2015). Deep learning in neural networks: An overview. *Neural Networks*, *61*, 85–117. doi:10.1016/j.neunet.2014.09.003 PMID:25462637

Shaikh, F. (2017). *Why are GPUs necessary for training deep learning models?* Analytics Vidhya.

Shi, S., Wang, Q., Xu, P., & Chu, X. (2016, November). Benchmarking state-of-the-art deep learning software tools. In *2016 7th International Conference on Cloud Computing and Big Data (CCBD),* (pp. 99-104). IEEE. 10.1109/CCBD.2016.029

Yu, F. R., & He, Y. (n.d.). Deep reinforcement learning for wireless networks.

Zhang, G. P. (2000). Neural networks for classification: A survey. *IEEE Transactions on Systems, Man and Cybernetics. Part C, Applications and Reviews, 30*(4), 451–462. doi:10.1109/5326.897072

Chapter 3
Current Trends in Deep Learning Frameworks With Opportunities and Future Prospectus

Chitra A. Dhawale
P. R. Pote College of Engineering and Management, India

Krtika Dhawale
Indian Institute of Information Technology, Nagpur, India

ABSTRACT

Artificial Intelligence (AI) is going through its golden era by playing an important role in various real-time applications. Most AI applications are using Machine learning and it represents the most promising path to strong AI. On the other hand, Deep Learning (DL), which is itself a kind of Machine Learning (ML), is becoming more and more popular and successful at different use cases, and is at the peak of developments. Hence, DL is becoming a leader in this domain. To foster the growth of the DL community to a greater extent, many open source frameworks are available which implemented DL algorithms. Each framework is based on an algorithm with specific applications. This chapter provides a brief qualitative review of the most popular and comprehensive DL frameworks, and informs end users of trends in DL Frameworks. This helps them make an informed decision to choose the best DL framework that suits their needs, resources, and applications so they choose a proper career.

DOI: 10.4018/978-1-7998-1159-6.ch003

INTRODUCTION

Artificial intelligence (AI) is everywhere, possibility is that we are using it one way or the other and sometimes even we do not know about it. In recent years, most of the researchers are getting attracted towards AI domain due to its major applications including multimedia (text, image, speech, video) recognition, social network analysis, data mining, natural language processing, driverless car and so forth are using machine learning which leads this sub domain to the top of popularity amongst researchers and industrialist. Most AI applications are indeed using Machine learning and it currently represents the most promising path to strong AI. On the other hand, Deep Learning (DL), which is itself a kind of Machine Learning (ML) is becoming more and more popular and successful at different use cases and is at the peak of developments hence DL is becoming a leader in this domain.

One can implement simple deep learning algorithms from scratch using python or any other programming language, But it becomes difficult and time consuming task for individual programmer to implement the complex models or algorithms such as Convolutional Neural Network (CNN) (Hinton, G. E., 2009), (LeCunn, Bengio, & Hinton, 2015), (Al-Ayyoub, et. al, 2018) Recurring Neural Network (RNN) [Cho et al.,, 2014; Hinton, G. (2015)., Al-Ayyoub, et. al, 2018, or Deep Generative Networks (DGN) (Hinton, G. E., 2009), (LeCunn, Bengio, & Hinton, 2015), (Al-Ayyoub, et. al, 2018)which are frequently needed as a part of these applications. Deep learning frameworks offer building blocks for designing, training and validating deep neural networks, through a high level programming interface. Frameworks make the development and deployment of applications easy and fast. Almost all frameworks are open source and can easily downloaded and used in programming part.

Few papers are published related to the comparative analysis related to hardware performance, applications and other features of various Deep learning frameworks. But no one has covered the details about the current state of art for various frameworks. This type of study and analysis are very useful in order to enable people who are interested in applying Deep Learning in their applications and or/research work so that they can choose proper framework suitable for their work.

Bahrampour et al. (2015) published the comparative studies between DL frameworks. The authors compared five DL frameworks: Caffe, Neon, TensorFlow, Theano, and Torch, in terms of speed (gradient computation time and forward time), hardware utilization and extensibility (ability to support different types of DL architectures) after applying various convolutional algorithms on the aforementioned frameworks (Maas et al., 2011).

Shi et al. (2016) presented a comparative study between several DL frameworks including Caffe, MXNet, CNTK, TensorFlow, and Torch based on running time and convergence rate.

Goldsborough (2016) showed the timeline of machine learning software libraries for DL. He focused on TensorFlow's results and its basic properties including computational paradigms, its distributed model and programing interface.

Chintala (2017) applied different ImageNet benchmarks for a variety convolutional network types including AlexNet, GoogleNet, Overfeat, and OxfordNet using different opensource DL frameworks such as Caffe, Theano, Torch, TensorFlow, Chainer, etc.

Kovalev et al. (2016) presented a comparative study between different DL frameworks namely Theano, Torch, Caffe, TensorFlow, and DeepLearning4J in terms of training and prediction speed and classification accuracy. They used MNIST dataset of handwritten digits for testing five FCN frameworks (Yu et al., 2014).

This chapter presents the unique review of various DL frameworks based on the current state of art and their applications.

DEEP LEARNING FRAMEWORKS

Deep learning frameworks offer building blocks for designing, training and validating deep neural networks, through a high-level programming interface. Each framework is built in a different manner for different purposes.Widely used deep learning frameworks such as Tensorflow, CNTK, Theano, Keras, Torch, Caffe and others rely on GPU-accelerated libraries such as cuDNN, NCCL and DALI to deliver high-performance multi-GPU accelerated training. There are many more frameworks available, out of which we will take a review of most demanding and popular ones with their features and applications along with their comparative analysis and current state of art.

Tensorflow

Tensorflow is an open-source machine learning library developed by Google Brain Team at Google. TensorFlow offers APIs for beginners and experts to develop applications for desktop, mobile, web, and cloud. It is an interactive multiplatform programming interface which is scalable and much as compared to other deep learning libraries (G. team, 2018). Tensorflow specially designed for processing of mathematical expressions involving multi-dimensional arrays, provides high scalability of computation across machines and huge data sets, These features made TensorFlow, the perfect framework for machine intelligence at a production scale. TensorFlow uses data flow graphs for evaluation of computation. Each node of the graph represents an instance of a mathematical operation (like addition, division, or multiplication) and each edge is a multi-dimensional data set (tensor) on which the operations are performed Edges in TensorFlow can be grouped in two categories:

Normal edges transfer data structure (tensors) where it is possible that the output of one operation becomes the input for another operation and special edges, which are used to control dependency between two nodes to set the order of operation where one node waits for another to finish .

Few notable companies using tensorflow are: The **Airbnb** engineering and data science team applies machine learning using TensorFlow to classify images and detect objects at scale, helping to improve the guest experience. **Airbus** is using tensorflow to extract information from satellite images and delivering valuable ouput to their clients. **China Mobile** has created a deep learning system using TensorFlow that can automatically predict cutover time window, verify operation logs, and detect network anomalies. Tensorflow enabled **Coca Cola** Company to achieve long slot frictionless proof of purchase capability. **GE Healhcare** using Tensorflow enabled deep learning's automated workflow tool AIRx is tool for MRI brain scanning that automatically "prescribes" slices to help reduce redundant, manual steps. It uses deep learning algorithms built right into the MRI technologist's workflow to automatically identify anatomical structures to prescribe the slice locations, and the angle of those slices, for neurological exams, delivering consistent and quantifiable results. **Google** using tensorflow enabled tools in gmail, serach, translate, even to forge changes in humanitarian and environmental changes. **LAIX Inc.** ("LAIX" or the "Company") is an artificial intelligence (AI) company in China that creates and delivers products and services to popularize English learning. Its proprietary AI teacher utilizes cutting-edge deep learning and adaptive learning technologies, big data, well-established education pedagogies and the mobile internet. Liulishuo using it for learning new language. **NAVER Shopping** is a shopping portal service provided by NAVER. NAVER Shopping matches products to categories in order to organize products systematically and allow easier searching for users. Of course, the task of matching over 20 million newly registered products a day to around 5,000 categories is impossible to do manually. **Paypal** is using tensorflow to stay at the cutting edge of fraud detection. **Sinnovation Ventures**: detecting diseseas with retinal image, **Swisscomm** improved business operation by classifying text, Twitter using tensorflow for ranked timelines, which makes user not to miss important tweet among thousands of users, **WPS-Office** encorporated Tensorflow for its intelligent office .

CNTK

Microsoft Cognitive Toolkit (CNTK) is an Open source DL framework developed by Microsoft Research. Microsoft Research used a specific high-level script language, BrainScript, for CNTK implementation. It supports different DL architectures like Feedforward, Convolutional, Recurrent, LSTM, and Sequence-to-Sequence NN. A Computational Network learns any function by converting it to a directed graph where each leaf node consists of an input value or learning parameter, and other nodes represent a matrix operations upon their children (Yu et al., 2014). In this case, CNTK has an advantage as it can automatically find the derive gradients for all the computation which are required to learn the parameters. In CNTK, users specify their networks using a configuration file that contains information about the network type, where to find input data, and the way to optimize parameters (Yu, Yao & Zhang, 2015). CNTK interface supports different APIs of several languages such as Python, C++ and C# across both GPU (CUDA) or CPU execution. According to its developers [Microsoft,2018], CNTK was written in C++ in an efficient way, where it removes duplicated computations in forward and backward passes, uses minimal memory needed and reduces memory reallocation by reusing them. Few notable companies using CNTK are: Amazon, Boeing, Johns Hopkins University, General Electric, Thermofisher Scientific, First American Title Insurance Company (Al-Bdour, G. (2017)

Theano

Theano is an open source Python library developed at MILA lab at University of Montreal in 2007. Its main objective is to optimize and evaluate mathematical expressions using a NumPy library which is Python library that supports a large and multi-dimensional arrays. Theano first evaluates the computations automatically, optimize it and translates them into other machine learning languages such as C++ or CUDA (for GPU) and then compiles them into Python modules in an efficient way on CPUs or GPUs. Several software packages have been developed to build on top of Theano, with a higher-level user interface which aims to make Theano easier to express and train different architectures of deep learning models, such as Pylearn2, Lasagne, and Keras (Al-Rfou, et al., 2016). Few companies using Theano are: Vuclip, Doctrine,Zetaops, cyanapse,visual.ai

Keras

Keras, a open source DL library developed in python by Google engineer Chollet (2015) in 2015 as a part of research project ONEIROS (Open-ended Neuro-Electronic Intelligent Robot Operating System). It runs on top of CNTK, Theano or TensorFlow frameworks. It allows fast expression with deep neural networks, easy and fast prototyping with modularity and extensibility . Companies using keras are: Capital one, JPMorgan Chase, Apple,Citi,Cisco (Collobert, Kavukcuoglu, & Farabet, 2011)..

Torch

Torch was first released in 2002 and its extended version with its deep learning feature released in 2011 combined with Facebook's deep learning CUDA library (fbcunn), data-level parallel computation. Recently, Torch released its Python interface, PyTorch, and the usage of this framework has greatly increased due to its flexibility. Although it is released after Tensorflow but has grown rapidly in popularity. It allows customization that TensorFlow does not. It has the backing of Facebook (Kovalev, et al., 2016). It supports a powerful N-dimensional array, lots of routines for indexing, slicing, transposing, amazing interface to C, via LuaJIT, linear algebra routines, neural network, and energy-based models, numeric optimization routines, Fast and efficient GPU support, Embeddable, with ports to iOS and Android backends

Main objectives of Torch is to have maximum flexibility, speed and in building scientific algorithms while making the process extremely simple. It is used in machine learning, computer vision, signal processing, parallel processing, image, video, audio and networking among others, and builds on top of the Lua community.

At the heart of Torch are the popular neural network and optimization libraries which are simple to use, while having maximum flexibility in implementing complex neural network topologies. You can build arbitrary graphs of neural networks, and parallelize them over CPUs and GPUs in an efficient manner (Jia, et al., 2014)..

Caffe

A deep learning framework made with expression, speed, and modularity in mind. It is developed by Berkeley AI Research (BAIR) and by community contributors. Yangqing Jia created the project during his PhD at UC Berkeley. Caffe is released under the BSD 2-Clause license. Its Expressive architecture encourages application and innovation. Models and optimization are defined by configuration without hard-coding. Switch between CPU and GPU by setting a single flag to train on a GPU machine then deploy to commodity clusters or mobile devices, Extensible code fosters active development. In Caffe's first year, it has been forked by over 1,000 developers and had many significant changes contributed back. Its Speed makes Caffe perfect for research experiments and industry deployment. Caffe can process over 60M images per day with a single NVIDIA K40 GPU*. That's 1 ms/image for inference and 4 ms/image for learning and more recent library versions and hardware are faster still. Caffe is among the fastest convnet implementations available. Caffe already powers academic research projects, startup prototypes, and even large-scale industrial applications in vision, speech, and multimedia.

MXNET

This framework is incubated by Apache and used by Amazon. It supports several interfaces, including C++, Python, R, Scala, Perl, MATLAB, Javascript, Go, and Julia MXNet has the most comprehensive functionality, but the performance is not optimized as much as other state-of-theart frameworks. In its core is a dynamic dependency scheduler that automatically parallelizes both symbolic and imperative operations on the fly. A graph optimization layer on top of that makes symbolic execution fast and memory efficient. The library is portable and lightweight, and it scales to multiple GPUs and multiple machines.

Apache MXNet is an open-source deep learning software framework, used to train, and deploy deep neural networks. It is scalable, allowing for fast model training, and supports a flexible programming model and multiple programming languages (including C++, Python, Julia, Matlab, JavaScript, Go, R, Scala, Perl, and Wolfram Language.).

The following table gives the comparative analysis of the above frameworks:

EVALUATION OF DL FRAMEWORKS

For the current state of art of frameworks, We chose the following categories to provide a well-rounded view of popularity and interest in deep learning frameworks.

Online Job Listings

What deep learning libraries are in demand in today's job market? We searched job listings on LinkedIn, Indeed, Simply Hired, Monster, and Angel List.

TensorFlow is the clear winner when it comes to frameworks mentioned in job listings. We searched using the term machine learning followed by the library name. So TensorFlow was evaluated with machine learning TensorFlow and tested several search methods and this one gave the most relevant results.

Usage

KDnuggets, a popular data science website, polled data scientists around the world on the software that they used. They collect the data using question-answering method like: What Analytics, Big Data, Data Science, Machine Learning software you used in the past 12 months for a real project? Here are the results for the frameworks in this category.

Table 1. Comparative Analysis of DL Frameworks

Framework	Founder	Language	Description	BackPropogation	Parameters	Update Formulae	Graph	Licence
TensorFlow	Google Brain Team	Python	Computation using data flow graphs for scalable machine learning	Extended Graph	Separate Nodes	Part of graph	Static	Apache
CNTK	Microsoft Research Laboratory	C++, Python	supports different DL architectures like Feedforward, Convolutional, Recurrent, LSTM, and Sequence-to-Sequence NN.	Directed graph	Nodes	Part of graph	Static	MIT
Theano	MLA Laboratory, University of Montreal	Python	Theano is a Python library that allows you to define, optimize, and evaluate mathematical expressions involving multi-dimensional arrays efficiently.	Extended Graph	Separate node	Part of the graph	Static	BSD
Keras	Google Research Project - ONEIROS (Open-ended Neuro-Electronic Intelligent Robot Operating System)	Python	Deep Learning library for Python. Runs on TensorFlow, Theano, or CNTK	Sequential model, a linear stack of layers, arbitrary graphs of layers.	Nodes	Part of the graph	dynamic	MIT
Torch	Facebook	Lua	Torch is a scientific computing framework with wide support for machine learning algorithms that puts GPUs first	Through Graph	Hidden in operators	Outside of graph	Static	BSD
PyTorch	Facebook's AI Research Team	Python	Tensors and Dynamic neural networks in Python with strong GPU acceleration	Through graph	Separate nodes	Outside graph	Dynamic	BSD
Caffe	UC Berkely	C++	Fastest Convolution Network	Through Graph	Hidden in Operators	Outside graph	Static	BSD
MXNet	DMLC team, University of Washington	Python/ C++	Lightweight, Portable, Flexible Distributed/ Mobile Deep Learning with Dynamic, Mutation-aware Dataflow Dep Scheduler; for Python, R, Julia, Scala, Go, Javascript and more	Extended Graph	Separate nodes	Outside graph	Static	Apache

Figure 1. Online Job Listing

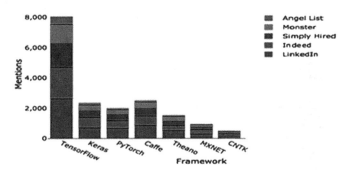

Keras showed a surprising amount of use—nearly as much as TensorFlow. It's interesting that US employers are overwhelmingly looking for TensorFlow skills, when—at least internationally—Keras is used almost as frequently. This category is the only one that includes international data because it would have been cumbersome to include international data for the other categories. KDnuggets reported several years of data. While we used 2018 data only in this analysis, we should note that Caffe, Theano, MXNET, and CNTK saw usage fall since 2017.

Google Search Activity

Web searches on the largest search engine are a good gauge of popularity. Google doesn't provide absolute search numbers, but it does provide relative figures.

Keras was not far from TensorFlow. PyTorch was in third and other frameworks had relative search volume scores at or below four. These scores were used for the power score calculations.

Figure 2. KDnuggets Usage

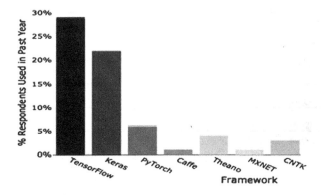

Figure 3. Google Search

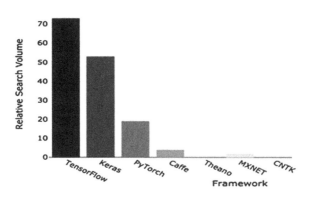

Publications

We included several publication types in the power score. Let's look at Medium articles first.

Finally, a new winner. In terms of mentions in Medium articles, Keras broke the tape ahead of TensorFlow. FastAI outperformed relative to its usual showing.

Figure 4. Medium Articles

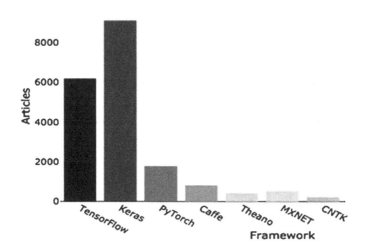

Figure 5. Amazon Books

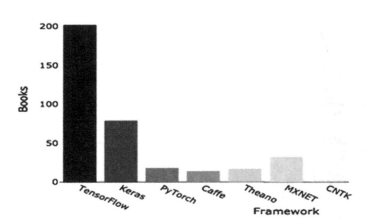

We hypothesize that these results might have occurred because Keras and FastAI are beginner friendly. They have quite a bit of interest from new deep learning practitioners, and Medium is often a forum for tutorials.

We used Google site search of Medium.com over the past 12 months with the framework name and "learning" as the keyword. This method was necessary to prevent incorrect results for the term "caffe". It had the smallest reduction in articles of several search options. Now let's see which frameworks have books about them available on Amazon.

Amazon Books

We searched for each deep learning framework on Amazon.com under Books->Computers & Technology.

TensorFlow for the win again. MXNET had more books than expected and Theano had fewer. PyTorch had relatively few books, but that may be because of the framework's youth. This measure is biased in favor of older libraries because of the time it takes to publish a book.

ArXiv Articles

ArXiv is the online repository where most scholarly machine learning articles are published. I searched for each framework on arXiv using Google site search results over the past 12 months.

Figure 6. ArXiv Articles

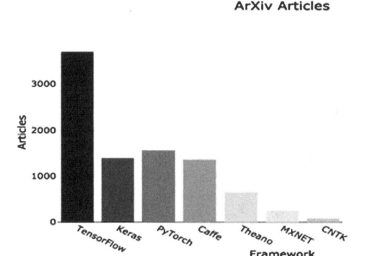

More of the same from TensorFlow for scholarly articles. Notice how much more popular Keras was on Medium and Amazon than in scholarly articles. Pytorch was second in this category, showing its flexility for implementing new ideas. Caffe also performed relatively well.

FUTURE DIRECTIONS AND SUGGESTIONS

From the overall discussion, it is cleared that as of now TensorFlow is firmly on top in case of number of client companies, jobs, publicatation, repository..etc. It seems likely to continue to dominate in the short term. Given how quickly things move in the deep learning world though, that may change. Time will tell if PyTorch surpasses TensorFlow as React surpassed Angular. Python based Torch i.e PyTorch is flexible frameworks backed by Facebook and often considered easier to use than their Google-backed competitors.

If you are considering learning one of these frameworks and have Python, numpy, pandas, sklearn, and matplotlib skills, you can start with Keras. It has a large user base, is in demand by employers, has lots of articles on Medium, and has an API that is easy to use. If you already know Keras, it might be tricky to decide on the next framework to learn. Reader can also either TensorFlow or PyTorch and learn it well.

CONCLUSION

We took a quick tour of most of the DL frameworks depending on various parameters. It is found that Tesorflow is on the top position in every terms. But the others frameworks are also in the race. No matter which frameworks to choose, we hope that reader have a better understanding of which deep learning frameworks are most in demand, most in use, and most written about and which will be in demand in future.

REFERENCES

Al-Ayyoub, M., Nuseir, A., Alsmearat, K., Jararweh, Y., & Gupta, B. (2018). Deep learning for Arabic NLP: A survey. *Journal of Computational Science*, *26*, 522–531. doi:10.1016/j.jocs.2017.11.011

Al-Bdour, G. (2017). Comparative study between deep learning frameworks using multiple benchmark datasets. (Doctoral dissertation, Master's thesis, Jordan University of Science and Technology).

Al-Rfou, R., Alain, G., Almahairi, A., Angermueller, C., Bahdanau, D., Ballas, N., & Bengio, Y. (2016). Theano: A Python framework for fast computation of mathematical expressions. arXiv preprint arXiv:1605.02688.

alexeyo26. (n.d.). News - Cognitive Toolkit - CNTK. Retrieved from https://docs.microsoft.com/en-us/cognitive-toolkit/news

Bahrampour, S., Ramakrishnan, N., Schott, L., & Shah, M. (2015). Comparative study of deep learning software frameworks. arXiv preprint arXiv:1511.06435.

Building deep neural networks in the Cloud with Azure GPU VMs, MXNet, and Microsoft R Server.

Case studies: TensorFlow. (n.d.). Retrieved from https://www.tensorflow.org/about/case-studies

Causevic, D. (2017, Nov. 29). Getting started with TensorFlow: A machine learning tutorial. Retrieved from https://www.toptal.com/machine-learning/tensorflow-machine-learning-tutorial

Chintala, S. (n.d.). Convnet benchmarks. Retrieved from https://github.com/soumith/convnetbenchmarks

Cho, K., Van Merriënboer, B., Gulcehre, C., Bahdanau, D., Bougares, F., Schwenk, H., & Bengio, Y. (2014). Learning phrase representations using RNN encoder-decoder for statistical machine translation. arXiv preprint arXiv:1406.1078.

Chollet, F. (2015). *Keras.* Retrieved from http://keras. io

Collobert, R., Kavukcuoglu, K., & Farabet, C. (2011). Torch7: A matlab-like environment for machine learning. In BigLearn, NIPS workshop (No. CONF).

G. team. Google. (n.d.). Retrieved from https://www.tensorflow.org/

Goldsborough, P. (2016). A tour of tensorflow. arXiv preprint arXiv:1610.01178.

Harris, D. (2014, June 2). A startup called Skymind launches, pushing open source deep learning. Retrieved from GigaOM.com.

Hinton, G. E. (2009). Deep belief networks. *Scholarpedia*, *4*(5), 5947. doi:10.4249cholarpedia.5947

Jia, Y., Shelhamer, E., Donahue, J., Karayev, S., Long, J., Girshick, R., & Darrell, T. (2014, November). Caffe: Convolutional architecture for fast feature embedding. In *Proceedings of the 22nd ACM international conference on Multimedia* (pp. 675-678). ACM. 10.1145/2647868.2654889

Kovalev, V., Kalinovsky, A., & Kovalev, S. (2016). Deep learning with theano, torch, caffe, tensorflow, and deeplearning4j: Which one is the best in speed and accuracy?

Kovalev, V., Kalinovsky, A., & Kovalev, S. (2016). Deep learning with theano, torch, caffe, tensorflow, and deeplearning4j: Which one is the best in speed and accuracy?

LeCun, Y., Bengio, Y., & Hinton, G. (2015). Deep learning. *Nature 521*.

Maas, A. L., Daly, R. E., Pham, P. T., Huang, D., Ng, A. Y., & Potts, C. (2011, June). Learning word vectors for sentiment analysis. In *Proceedings of the 49th Annual Meeting of the Association for Computational Linguistics: Human language technologies-Vol. 1* (pp. 142-150). Association for Computational Linguistics.

Microsoft. (n.d.). The Microsoft cognitive toolkit. Retrieved from https://docs. microsoft.com/en-us/cognitive-toolkit/cntk-evaluationoverview

Microsoft. (n.d.). The Microsoft cognitive toolkit. Retrieved from https://docs. microsoft.com/en-us/cognitive-toolkit/cntk-evaluationoverview

MXNet - Deep learning framework of choice at AWS - All things distributed. Retrieved from www.allthingsdistributed.com

Novet, J. (2014, June 2). Skymind launches with open-source, plug-and-play deep learning features for your app.

Shi, S., Wang, Q., Xu, P., & Chu, X. (2016, November). Benchmarking state-of-the-art deep learning software tools. In *2016 7th International Conference on Cloud Computing and Big Data (CCBD)* (pp. 99-104). IEEE. 10.1109/CCBD.2016.029

Skymind intelligence layer community edition. (n.d.). Retrieved from deeplearning4j. org.

Skymind's Deeplearning4j, the Eclipse Foundation, and scientific computing in the JVM. *Jaxenter.*

Towards data science. (n.d.). Retrieved from https://towardsdatascience.com/

Yu, D., Eversole, A., Seltzer, M., Yao, K., Huang, Z., Guenter, B., & Droppo, J. (2014). An introduction to computational networks and the computational network toolkit. Microsoft Technical Report MSR-TR-2014–112.

Yu, D., Yao, K., & Zhang, Y. (2015). The computational network toolkit [best of the web]. *IEEE Signal Processing Magazine, 32*(6), 123–126. doi:10.1109/MSP.2015.2462371

Chapter 4
Emotion Recognition From Speech Using Perceptual Filter and Neural Network

Revathi A.
SASTRA University, India

Sasikaladevi N.
SASTRA University, India

ABSTRACT

This chapter on multi speaker independent emotion recognition encompasses the use of perceptual features with filters spaced in Equivalent rectangular bandwidth (ERB) and BARK scale and vector quantization (VQ) classifier for classifying groups and artificial neural network with back propagation algorithm for emotion classification in a group. Performance can be improved by using the large amount of data in a pertinent emotion to adequately train the system. With the limited set of data, this proposed system has provided consistently better accuracy for the perceptual feature with critical band analysis done in ERB scale.

INTRODUCTION

Speech signal is considered as the acoustic signal obtained by exciting the vocal tract by quasi periodic pulses of air for voiced sounds and noise like excitation for unvoiced sounds. Speech utterances reveal the linguistic content, accent, slang and emotional state of a speaker. It is really cumbersome to recognize the emotions from speech with limited set of data. Emotion recognition from speech has found applications in

DOI: 10.4018/978-1-7998-1159-6.ch004

call centers and unmanned control of risky processes. This system would be useful for treating the mentally retarded patients and patients with depression and anxiety. Web related services, retrieval of information and synthesis of data would use this automated emotion recognition system. These systems will find place in operating robots for the speech commands given by the emotional operator. Modulation spectral feature is used as a new feature by Siging Wu et.al (Wu, 2011) for emotion recognition. Chi-Chun Lee et.al (Lee, 2011) have used hierarchical binary classifier and acoustic & statistical feature for emotion recognition. K. Sreenivasa Rao et.al (Rao, 2012) have used MFCC and GMM for recognizing emotions. Ankur Sapra et.al (Sapra, 2013) has used modified MFCC feature and NN classifier for emotion recognition. Shashidar G. Koolakudi et.al (Koolagudi, 2012) have used MFCC and GMM for speaker recognition in emotional environment. In this chapter on speaker independent emotion recognition, SVM is used to create templates for all emotions and system is evaluated with the speeches of a speaker not considered for training. Training speeches are converted into set of features and SVM models are developed as representative of emotions. During testing, group classification is done using minimum distance classifier and subsequently individual emotion classification is done in a group containing pertinent emotion models using linear binary classifier. Perceptual linear predictive cepstrum with critical band analysis done in BARK and ERB scale are used as features in this work and they provide complimentary evidence in assessing the performance of the system based on ANN modeling technique. ANN modeling technique is based on the selection of hidden layers and number of neurons in hidden layer. Weights between the layers are optimized using iterative procedure and output layer with two neurons to choose one of the two emotions in a group. This chapter also deals with the comparative analysis between the features and analysis is done comprehensively to assess the performance of the speaker independent and dependent emotion recognition system.

Affective computing has played a pivotal role in acting as an interface between humans and machines. Speech based emotion recognition system is difficult to be implemented because of the dataset which is containing limited set of speech utterances spoken limited set of speakers. Emotion recognition from speech is performed by using various databases. This chapter on multi speaker independent emotion recognition encompasses the use of perceptual features with filters spaced in Equivalent rectangular bandwidth (ERB) and BARK scale and vector quantization (VQ) classifier for classifying groups and artificial neural network with back propagation algorithm for emotion classification in a group. Performance can be improved by using the large amount of data in a pertinent emotion to adequately train the system. With the limited set of data, this proposed system has provided consistently better accuracy for the perceptual feature with critical band analysis done in ERB scale with overall accuracy as 76% and decision level fusion classification yielded 100% as accuracy for all emotions except FEAR and BOREDOM. Overall accuracy of the decision level fusion classifier is 78%. Speaker dependent emotion recognition system has provided 100% as accuracy for all the emotions for perceptual feature with critical band analysis done in ERB scale and perceptual linear predictive cepstrum has given 100% as accuracy for all emotions except anger and fear emotions.

MATERIALS AND METHODS

PLPC and ERBPLPC Extraction

The extraction of perceptual linear predictive cepstrum deals with computation of spectrum using FFT technique, wrap the spectrum along the BARK and ERB frequency scales, performing convolution between the warped spectrum and power spectrum of the simulated critical band masking curve, performing pre-emphasis by simulated loudness equalization, mapping between the intensity and the perceived loudness done by cube root compression, generation linear predictive (LP) coefficients and conversion into LP derived cepstrum. Probability is computed by counting the number of samples whose spectral energy is greater than the threshold by total number of samples in a frame of 16 msecs duration. Procedure (Revathi, 2018) used for Mel frequency perceptual feature extraction is detailed below.

1. Compute power spectrum on windowed speech.
2. Perform grouping to 21 critical bands in BARK scale and 35 critical bands in ERB scale for the sampling frequency of 16 kHz.
3. Perform loudness equalization and cube root compression to simulate the power law of hearing.
4. Perform IFFT
5. Perform LP analysis by Levinson -Durbin procedure.
6. Convert LP coefficients into PLP and ERBPLP Ccpstral coefficients.

The relationship between frequency in BARK and ERB with frequency in Hz is specified as in (1) &(2)

$$f\left(bark\right) = 6 * \sinh^{-1} f((Hz) / 600) \tag{1}$$

$$f(erb) = 21.4 * \log 10(4.37e^{-3} * Hz + 1) \tag{2}$$

Experimental Analysis Based on Clustering Technique

The way in which L training vectors can be clustered into a set of M code book vectors is by K-means clustering algorithm (Jeyalakshmi, 2016). Classification procedure for arbitrary spectral analysis vectors that chooses the codebook vector is by computing Euclidean distance between each of the test vectors and the M cluster centroids. The spectral distance measure for comparing test feature vector v_i and cluster centroid v_j is as in (3).

$$d\left(v_i, v_j\right) = d_{ij} = 0 \quad when \quad v_i = v_j \tag{3}$$

If codebook vectors of an M-vector codebook are taken as y_m, $1 \le m \le M$ and new spectral vector to be classified is denoted as v, then the index m^* of the best codebook entry is as in (4)

$$m^* = \arg\left(\min\left(d\left(v, y_m\right)\right)\right) \quad for \quad 1 \le m \le M \tag{4}$$

Clusters are formed in such a way that they capture the characteristics of the training data distribution. It is observed that Euclidean distance is small for the most frequently occurring vectors and large for the least frequently occurring ones.

Emotion Recognition Based on ANN Modeling Technique

Performance of the any recognition system mainly depends on the database used. EMO-DB Berlin database used in this work contains only ten speeches uttered by ten speakers in the age group 21 to 35 years in different emotions such as Anger, Boredom, Disgust, Fear, Happy, Neutral and Sad. Robustness of the system depends on the amount of data considered for training to create templates for emotions. This work on emotion recognition from speech contains two phases namely training and testing. During training phase, speech signal is generated by concatenating the utterances in pertinent emotion from nine speakers and speech vector is allowed to pass through the conventional pre-processing stages namely pre-emphasis, frame blocking and windowing. Then perceptual features and probability are extracted for each speech frame of 16 msecs duration. Neural network models are created for emotions in a group. ANN is one of the types of supervised learning neural network. In the back propagation neural network, the network weights are updated on the basis of the error between the target output and the actual output by means of the back-propagation of the errors (Scanzio, 2010). This network has input layer, hidden layer and output layer. The training of the back propagation neural network (Fausett, 1994) proceeds as follows:

- Initialize the network weights with small random values.
- The input pattern is assigned to input neurons x_i, $i = 1, 2 \ldots n$ and broadcast to the next layer. In hidden layer z_j, $j = 1, 2 \ldots p$, each node sums the weighted inputs and applies its sigmoid activation function to compute its output signal as in equation (5).

$$z_{in\,j} = a_{0j} + \sum_{i=1}^{n} x_i \, a_{ij}$$

$$z_j = Activation(z_{in\,j})$$

$$Activation(z_{in\,j}) = \frac{1}{1 + \exp^{(-z_{in\,j})}} \tag{5}$$

- The z_j is broadcast to the next layer. In output layer y_k, $k = 1, 2 \ldots m$, each node sums the weighted inputs and applies its sigmoid activation function to compute its output signal as in equation (6).

$$y_{in\,k} = b_{0k} + \sum_{j=1}^{p} z_j \, b_{jk}$$

$$y_k = Activation(y_{in\,k})$$

$$Activation(y_{in\,k}) = \frac{1}{1 + \exp^{(-y_{in\,k})}} \tag{6}$$

- The output layer computes the error between target output and actual output.

$$e_k = t_k - y_k$$

- Compute error information term and propagate back as in equation(7)

$$\delta_k = e_k \, F^{'}(y_{in\,k})$$

$$F^{'}(y_{in\,k}) = Activation(y_{in\,k})[1 - Activation(y_{in\,k})] \tag{7}$$

- Compute its weight correction term as in equation (8), which is used to update weights a_{ij} and b_{jk}

$$\Delta b_{0k} = \alpha\, \delta_k$$

$$\Delta b_{jk} = \alpha\, \delta_k\, z_j \tag{8}$$

α - Learning rate
- The hidden layer sums the weighted output data as in equation (9)

$$\delta_{in\,j} = \sum_{k=1}^{m} \delta_k b_{jk} \tag{9}$$

$\delta_{in\,j}$ is multiplied by the derivative of its sigmoid activation function to compute its error information term as in equation (10)

$$\delta_j = \delta_{in\,j}\, F^{'}(z_{in\,j}) \tag{10}$$

- Calculate its weights correction term as in equation (11)

$$\Delta a_{0j} = \alpha\, \delta_j$$

$$\Delta a_{ij} = \alpha\, \delta_j\, x_i \tag{11}$$

- The hidden layer updates its bias and weights as in equation (12)

$$a_{ij}(new) = a_{ij}(old) + \Delta a_{ij} \tag{12}$$

- The output layer updates its bias and weights as in equation (13)

$$b_{jk}(new) = b_{jk}(old) + \Delta b_{jk} \tag{13}$$

The flow diagram shown in Fig.1 indicates the process used for back propagation training algorithm using artificial neural network

Figure 1. Flow diagram – BPNN algorithm

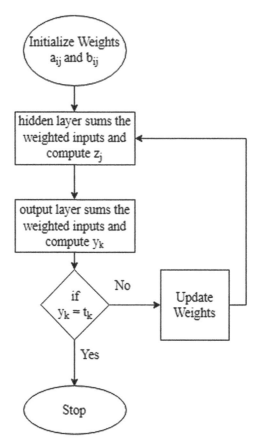

Test speech vector is pre-emphasized by using single order high pass filter so that flattening of speech spectrum is done. After getting speech vector passing through the pre-emphasis stage, speech vector is divided into overlapping frames of 16 msecs duration with 50% overlap between frames enabling no loss of information. Each speech frame is windowed by using Hamming window so that signal discontinuity at the beginning and end of the speech frame is eliminated. Speech frame after pre-processing would undergo FFT filtering, critical band analysis, Loudness equalization, cube root compression, LP coefficients extraction and deriving cepstrum from the LP coefficients. These extracted features are applied to the group specific models and group is identified correctly based on minimum distance classifier. Then, the features are given to the emotion specific models in a group and emotion recognition accuracy is computed by counting the number of speech segments correctly classified out of total number of segments considered for each emotion.

RESULTS AND DISCUSSION

This multi-speaker independent emotion recognition system from noisy test speeches is evaluated by using the implementation of the parallel group classifier and parallel specific emotional pattern classifier [7] to improve the accuracy of the system. Parallel group classifier and parallel emotion specific classifier is indicated in Figure 5.The concatenated test speech vector is applied to the pre-processing techniques namely pre-emphasis, frame blocking and windowing and the extracted feature vectors are applied to the vector quantization (VQ) templates for identifying a group and applied to the ANN templates and based on the minimum error criterion test speech is classified as association with pertinent emotion. Group classification is done based on minimum distance classifier and individual emotion in a group is classified based on ANN based minimum mean squared error classifier. After conventional pre-processing stages, extracted perceptual features are applied to the group models and group should be correctly classified based on minimum distance classifier. Then the features are applied to the emotion specific ANN models as shown in Figures (2 -4) and classification of the pertinent emotion is done by calculating the mean squared error for each feature vector with neural network models. This process is repeated for all feature vectors and indices are extracted. Finally, classification is done pertaining to the model which provides maximum of the index selection among the emotions in a group. For creating ANN templates by using back propagation algorithm, fourteen frames with 13 coefficients are concatenated and normalized. These features are applied to the neural network with one hidden layer containing half the number of neurons as compared to the input layer. Output layer contains the number of neurons corresponding to the number of classes. Weights between the layers are initialized with random values. Using iterative procedure, weights are optimized to march toward the target error. For testing using ANN, feature vectors extracted for the test speech utterances in pertinent emotion after group classification are applied to the ANN templates, and based on the minimum mean squared error criterion, emotions are classified.

Evaluation of the multi-speaker independent emotion recognition using ANN for ERBPLP is shown in Table 1.

Multi speaker independent emotion recognition from speech is evaluated using PLP as a feature and ANN as a modeling technique. Performance is depicted in Table2

Decision level fusion classifier is evaluated using both features and ANN as a modeling technique. Table 3 depicts the performance of the system using decision level fusion classifier.

Table 4 indicates the performance of the speaker dependent emotion recognition system for perceptual features with filters spaced in ERB scale.

Figure 2. BPNN structure – classification of Anger and Fear

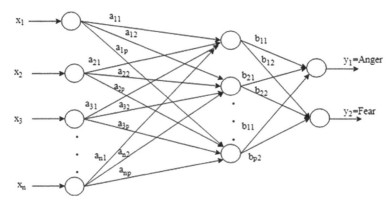

Figure 3. BPNN structure – classification of Boredom and Disgust

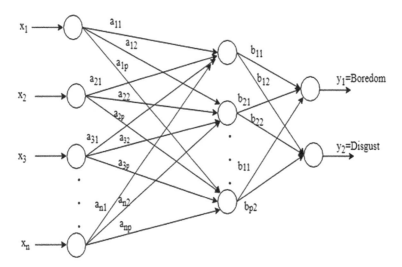

Multi speaker dependent emotion recognition from speech is evaluated using PLP as a feature and ANN as a modeling technique. Performance is depicted in Table 5

Decision level fusion classifier is evaluated using both features and ANN as a modeling technique. Table 6 depicts the performance of the speaker dependent system using decision level fusion classifier.

From the tables, it is understood that perceptual features with critical band analysis done in ERB scale performs better than that of the features with filters spaced in BARK scale for both speaker independent and dependent emotion recognition system.

Figure 4. BPNN structure – classification of Neutral and Sad

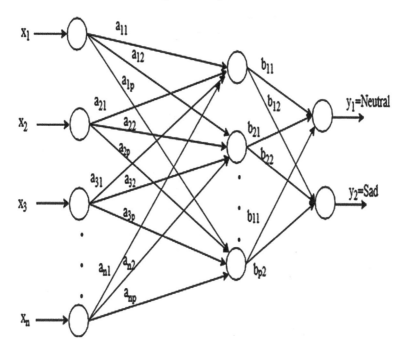

Table 1. Performance evaluation of speaker independent system – ERBPLP based ANN

Emotion	Anger	Fear	Emotion	Boredom	Disgust	Emotion	Neutral	Sad
Anger	25	0	Boredom	8	17	Neutral	8	0
Fear	5	0	*Disgust*	*0*	26	Sad	0	22

Table 2. Performance evaluation of speaker independent system – PLP based ANN

Emotion	Anger	Fear	Emotion	Boredom	Disgust	Emotion	Neutral	Sad
Anger	25	0	Boredom	5	20	Neutral	8	0
Fear	5	0	*Disgust*	*0*	26	Sad	0	22

Table 3. Performance evaluation of speaker independent system – Decision level fusion classifier

Emotion	Anger	Fear	Emotion	Boredom	Disgust	Emotion	Neutral	Sad
Anger	25	0	Boredom	11	14	Neutral	8	0
Fear	5	0	*Disgust*	*0*	26	Sad	0	22

Figure 5. Decision level fusion classifier using ANN

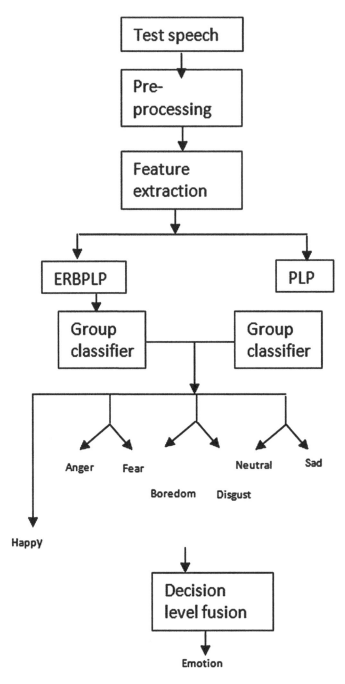

Table 4. Performance evaluation of speaker dependent system – ERBPLP based ANN

Emotion	Anger	Fear	Emotion	Boredom	Disgust	Emotion	Neutral	Sad
Anger	243	0	Boredom	149	0	Neutral	136	0
Fear	0	109	*Disgust*	*0*	*91*	Sad	0	172

Table 5. Performance evaluation of speaker dependent system – PLP based ANN

Emotion	Anger	Fear	Emotion	Boredom	Disgust	Emotion	Neutral	Sad
Anger	154	89	Boredom	149	0	Neutral	136	0
Fear	50	59	*Disgust*	*0*	*91*	Sad	0	172

Table 6. Performance evaluation of speaker dependent system – Decision level fusion classifier

Emotion	Anger	Fear	Emotion	Boredom	Disgust	Emotion	Neutral	Sad
Anger	243	0	Boredom	149	0	Neutral	136	0
Fear	0	109	*Disgust*	*0*	*91*	Sad	0	172

CONCLUSION

This chapter discusses the use of perceptual features with critical band analysis done in ERB and BARK scale and artificial neural network for creating templates as representative models for emotions. Features are extracted from the concatenated training speeches pertaining to the emotions. Extracted features pertaining to arousal and soft emotions are used to create set of clusters representing group models. Features extracted using pertinent emotional speech utterances are neural networks with initialization of random weights between the layers. Back propagation algorithm is used to optimize the weights between the layers by using minimization of mean squared error criterion. Iterative procedure is used to update the weights by fixing the target error and neural network models are created for each emotion. During testing, test speeches are concatenated to form a test vector and features are extracted after applying initial pre-processing stages namely pre-emphasis, frame blocking and windowing. Pre-emphasis stage is done to spectrally flatten the test speech signal. Frame blocking is used to convert the speech vector into frames of 16msecs duration with 8msecs overlapping in order to avoid the information loss. Windowing is done to remove the signal discontinuities at the beginning and end of speech frames. Features extracted from the pre-processed speech vector are applied to the group models to identify a group based on minimum distance classifier and further classification is done in a group containing pertinent emotion models based on minimum mean squared error criterion. Perceptual features with filters spaced in ERB scale has provided the better accuracy of 76% as compared to the perceptual features with filters spaced in BARK scale for which the accuracy is found to be 74%. Decision level fusion classifier has yielded the accuracy as 78%. Speaker dependent emotion recognition system is implemented by using same set of utterances for training and testing. Perceptual features with critical band analysis done in ERB scale has provided 100% as accuracy for all emotions and perceptual features with filters spaced in BARK has given 100% as individual accuracy for all emotions except Anger and Fear. Decision level fusion classifier using both the features and ANN as modeling technique has given the accuracy as 100% for all emotions. Emotion recognition from speech would find applications in business processing centers, web analysis, medical diagnosis of patients, and automated services based on the emotional state of a speaker.

REFERENCES

Fausett, L. (1994). *Fundamentals of neural networks: architectures, algorithms, and applications*. Prentice-Hall.

Jeyalakshmi, C., Revathi, A., & Yenkataramani, Y. (2016). Integrated models and features-based speaker independent emotion recognition. *International Journal of Telemedicine and Clinical Practices*, *1*(3), 277–291. doi:10.1504/IJTMCP.2016.077920

Koolagudi, S. G., Sharma, K., & Rao, K. S. (2012, August). Speaker recognition in emotional environment. In *International Conference on Eco-friendly Computing and Communication Systems* (pp. 117-124). Berlin, Germany: Springer.

Lee, C. C., Mower, E., Busso, C., Lee, S., & Narayanan, S. (2011). Emotion recognition using a hierarchical binary decision tree approach. *Speech communication*, *53*(9-10), 1162–1171. doi:10.1016/j.specom.2011.06.004

Rao, K. S., Kumar, T. P., Anusha, K., Leela, B., Bhavana, I., & Gowtham, S. V. S. K. (2012). Emotion recognition from speech. *International Journal of Computer Science and Information Technologies*, *3*(2), 3603–3607.

Revathi, A., & Jeyalakshmi, C. (2018). Emotions recognition: different sets of features and models. *International Journal of Speech Technology, 1-10*.

Sapra, A., Panwar, N., & Panwar, S. (2013). Emotion recognition from speech. *International Journal of Emerging Technology and Advanced Engineering*, *3*(2), 341–345.

Scanzio, S., Cumani, S., Gemello, R., Mana, F., & Laface, P. (2010). Parallel implementation of Artificial Neural Network training for speech recognition. *Pattern Recognition Letters*, *31*(11), 1302–1309. doi:10.1016/j.patrec.2010.02.003

Wu, S., Falk, T. H., & Chan, W. Y. (2011). Automatic speech emotion recognition using modulation spectral features. *Speech communication*, *53*(5), 768–785. doi:10.1016/j.specom.2010.08.013

Chapter 5
Ontology Creation

Anjali Daisy
🆔 https://orcid.org/0000-0003-1207-5002
SASTRA University, India

ABSTRACT

Neural networks are like the models of the brain and nervous system. It is highly parallel and processes information much more like the brain than a serial computer. It is very useful in learning information, using and executing very simple and complex behaviors, applications like powerful problem solvers and biological models. There are different types of neural networks like Biological, Feed Forward, Recurrent, and Elman. Biological Neural Networks require some biological data to predict information. In Feed Forward Networks, information flows in one way. In Recurrent Networks, information flows in multiple directions. Elman Networks feature Partial re-currency with a sense of time.

INTRODUCTION

Neural networks are like the models of the brain and nervous system. It is highly parallel and process information much more like the brain than a serial computer. It is very much useful in learning information, using and executing very simple and complex behaviours, applications like powerful problem solvers and biological models. There are different types of neural networks like Biological, Feed Forward, Recurrent and Elman neural networks. Biological Neural Networks: It requires some biological data to predict information. Feed Forward Networks: Information flows in one way. Recurrent Networks: Information flows in multidirectional. Elman Networks: Partial re-currency with sense of time.

DOI: 10.4018/978-1-7998-1159-6.ch005

Ontology Creation

Ontology

Ontology is closely connected to Natural Language Processing (NLP) - a field of artificial intelligence, computer science and linguistics. As such, NLP is related to the area of human–computer interaction. Because of that the production of software tools to support ontology and Semantic web has accelerated. In AI, ontology is defined as domain knowledge representation that facilitates common understanding of that domain. It is a logical combination of a domain concepts and their relationship. It is a good way to represent knowledge graphically.

Methods to Create Ontology

There are some methods to create ontology. They are as follows,

- Define concepts, i.e., classes.
- Organize them somehow in taxonomy.
- Define relations among the classes.
- Define the attributes and which values they can take.
- Define instances, i.e., "real" elements in our domain.
- Create axioms and functions.

Figure 1.

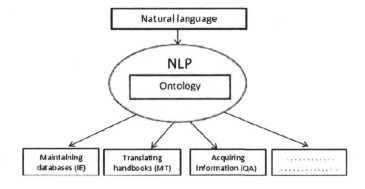

STEPS TO FOLLOW IN ONTOLOGY CREATION

Determine the Domain and the Scope or Purpose of Our Ontology

Basically, try to find an answer to questions such as:

- Which domain are we thinking of?
- What will we use the ontology for?
- Is it going to be just one, or will we need different sub ontologies to make it clearer?
- Who will use the ontology?

It is the hardest part to develop the ontology. It might be further clarified, but at least we need a good initial scope or purpose for our ontology. Formally, it is done using competency questions, which we think might prove useful once the ontology is started. Not the other way round. And remember, we can go through them as many times as needed. New questions will arise and former answers might change. Some other people prefer to make use scenarios of how/what for the ontology will be used.

Example: OASys (Ontology for Autonomous Systems) is ontology for the domain of autonomous systems, understanding as such systems capable of fulfilling a goal in an environment by adapting to changes to some extent (not to mention cognitive capabilities). We will try to use it to describe what such systems need to work as well as who and how they will be developed. Probably, we will need several sub ontologies(structure, behavior, agents), as the domain seems complex enough. The ontology is intended for autonomous systems developers and engineers.

Know Your Sources: (Documents, Experts and Existing Ontologies)

Either we are an expert on the domain or more common we have a partial knowledge of the domain. In the first case, we can be proud of ourselves and go ahead with the ontology. In the second case, we will need more knowledge that can come from:

- **Experts:** If available, ask everything we want to know. Remember, it is iterative, so we will have to do it several times. Grab their terminology, i.e., the words and terms they are familiar with when talking about the domain. Make notes.

- **Documents:** If we do not have people, we might have literatures, documents, technical information, etc. on the domain. Get a highlighter and start underlying nouns and verbs, which make sense both to us and the domain. Make as many notes.

- **Existing ontologies:** Our domain might have been modeled before with a different view point or purpose. There is a lot out there. Look for them, analyze the level of granularity (fancy word to describe if the existing ontology covers the same level of detail we want), select them and evaluate them. Usually, we are not the first one who has thought about the same domain.

Example: For OASys, We do not have the experts around but some miles away. Therefore, we had also searched and found ontologies that can be reused (ontologies for agent-based systems, taxonomies on autonomous systems).

Build the Ontology

An ontology development usually encompasses several tasks. Different methodologies order them differently, but in general we should.

a. Enumerate Important Terms

This is usually called among practitioners as Glossary of Terms, i.e., make a list or graphs of all the nouns and verbs we have considered. Use any tool we feel comfortable with handwriting lists, tables, graphs in any format. If we work within a group, agree on a common formalism and tool (remember the ontology is for sharing understanding, do not ruin by using different tools). For each term, try to write down at least a name, synonym, a natural language description, type, source, comments. Next, try to decide whether a noun in our list might be a concept, attribute or instance. Concepts tend to be nouns standing on their own, attributes look more like nouns that can describe type of things, and instances tend to be nouns about specific things. It will not come in one step, but a pre-classification can be useful. In case of doubt, leave it blank. Then, verbs will end up as relations we can make notes to remember between which concepts. Remember, it is not a closed list. The iterative process will uncover concepts and relations that did not show up initially.

b. Define Concept Taxonomies

The idea is to classify the concepts in a hierarchy (called among practitioners as taxonomy). Not all concepts will own a hierarchy, but as we were writing them down, some nouns seem to be related as types (subclasses) of other (super classes).

Traditionally, taxonomies/hierarchies are done following top-down (from general to specific), bottom-up (from specific to general) or combination processes. There are different types of taxonomic relations, i.e., how the subclasses are related to the super classes.

- **Subclass:** A concept C1 is subclass of concept C2, iff (if and only if) every instance of C1 is also instance of C2.
- **Disjoint Decomposition of C:** Set of subclasses of C that do not have common instances and do not cover C.
- **Exhaustive Decomposition of C:** Set of subclasses of C that may have common instances and subclasses and do cover C.
- **Partition of C:** Set of subclasses that do not share common instances but cover C.

Probably defining concepts and taxonomies is the most difficult part of developing an ontology.

c. Define Relations

Between concepts, there will be relations that so far, could have been represented as hand-made diagrams. It is time to describe each diagram and the relations in detail by giving a name, source concept, target concept, cardinality (how many instances of a concept are related with how many of the others), inverse name (we can read from A to B, but also from B to A. Sometimes, the distinction is important). We can further define the relation depending on a type, as it happens on UML or use predefined types on our chosen formalism.

d. Define Attributes

At this stage, some of our nouns in the list could have been considered attributes, i.e., terms used to describe others. Ontologists distinguish between class attributes (terms to describe concepts which take their values in the class they are defined, and they are not inherited in the hierarchy) and instance attributes (terms to describe concepts that take their values in the instance, and may be different for each instance). There is not a unique way to do this, but some guidelines could be:

- This step and the definition of taxonomies are intertwined: some classes might end up being attributes to describe the different classes and instances.
- Try to attach the attribute to the most general class/concept that can have that property.

- If it can have a well-defined type (integer, string, float) it is an attribute, not a class. Try to define type attributes (integer, string, float).
- Try to define a range, value, precision, related classes. Gather all the information about each attribute: name, concept name related to it, value type, range, value.

e. Define Instances

An instance is an individual of a class, we can describe in detail relevant instances that may appear by giving them a name, concept to which they are related, attribute names and values.

Taxonomy Evaluation

Defining Classes and Hierarchies: At the end, our ontology should be precise, consistent, complete and concise. Evaluating somehow is important. It is compulsory to evaluate the concepts and the taxonomies, attributes and relations we may have made. Otherwise the ontology might be useless.

Class Definition:
- ◦ Remember a class is a concept: Ontologists and modelers interchange the two terms. Generally, they prefer to talk about concepts in the end, as classes seem to be too related to other domains. However, we use them as synonyms.
- ◦ Classes represent concepts in the domain and not the language/words to denote them: Our nouns represent concepts regardless of being in English, Spanish or even the noun we have chosen. We can have a class named Car, which could be later change as Automobile. Remember, they are the same underlying concept • Synonyms for the same concept do not represent different classes: When listing our nouns, look for and detect synonyms referring to the same concept. Choose one and write down the rest for documentation. • A class is not only "real" entities in the domain: A common mistake is to think only of concepts that exist as real objects or entities in our domain. Firstly, a class can model abstract/mental concepts if need. Secondly, a class can be also be used to introduce concepts for modeling reasons
- ◦ Keep a balance: It is as bad to have few classes as to have too many. The same rules for subclasses, if we have only one, there might be a problem. If you have too many subclasses, our ontology might be crying for some new intermediate classes to be introduced.

○ Class or attribute: When modeling, we need to decide whether a distinction is modeled as a class or an attribute value. The answer lies in the scope defined for the ontology. Think on how important the distinction is for we, and especially for the domain. If we think it is important, and different values make us to think of different types of entities (objects), create a new class. If not, it will be probably an attribute with different values.

○ Class or instance: Once again, this depends on how the ontology will be used. It has to do with the level of granularity, i.e., the level of detail we need/want to achieve. Generally speaking, instances are the most specific concepts represented in the knowledge base.

Class Hierarchy:

○ Avoid class cycles (circularity errors): If class A has a subclass B, which in turn, is super class of A, we have a cycle. It is more likely that they are equivalent.

○ Classifying classes where they do not belong (semantic inconsistency error): When classifying classes or instances, we can classify a concept as a subclass of other concept to which it does not really belong. Be careful.

○ Careful with our classification (partition error): If we stick to the four types described before, be aware of instances and classes being common when they should not.

○ Incompleteness of taxonomies: Although we should not model all possible things, we have to define the ones we need for our level of detail and scope.

○ Redundancy: It happens when we have classes or instances with the same formal definition. Look for them.

USE OF ONTOLOGY IN FIELD NLP

Driven Ontology

Ontologies and Natural Language Processing (NLP) can often be seen as two sides of the same coin. An Ontology Model is the classification of entities and modeling the relationships between those entities. The purpose of NLP is the identification of entities, understanding the relationship between those entities. NLP- Driven

Figure 2.

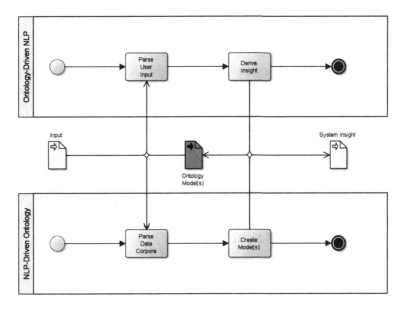

Ontology modeling means we're using natural language processing techniques to drive semantic models from unstructured data. Using Ontologies with NLP allows an enterprise to turn data into knowledge.

In this process diagram, we illustrate both Ontology-driven NLP (the use of the semantic layer to drive NLP parsing and insight at runtime) and the use of NLP-driven Ontology modeling (the use of NLP parsing to create and enhance Ontology models).

Ontology or Relational Database

Why would we use ontology over a relational database (RDB)? The use of a relational database is to make the following assertion – we can understand the data that exists in our domain completely, and that data is relatively static. That is not to say that changes may never happen, but the design of an ERD must remain relatively static for applications to effectively build on top of it. The use of an Ontology model (or models, there is no constraint toward using a single Ontology in an enterprise or industry) is to make the opposite assertion – we do not fully understand the data that exists in our domain we know that we'll never understand it completely, and far from being static, the data changes constantly.

The relational model has relations between entities established through explicit keys (primary, foreign) and, for many-to-many relationships, associative entities.

Changing relationships in this case is cumbersome, as it requires changes to the base model structure itself, which can be difficult for a populated database. Querying for this kind of data based on a relational model can also be cumbersome since it can result in very complicated where clauses or significant table joins.

Hierarchical models have similar limitations when it comes to real world updates and are not very flexible when it comes to trying to traverse the model "horizontally".

The graph model, which is how semantic models are implemented, makes it much easier to both query and maintain the model once deployed. For example, if a new relationship is needed to be represented that had not been anticipated during design. With a triple store representation that additional representation is easily maintained. A new triple is simply added to the data store. A critical point is the relations are part of the data, not part of the database structure.

Creating an Ontology Model

What exactly are semantic models and how are they helpful for this type of operations systems integration? When we talk about operational system integration based on information-oriented architecture, in this context, we are really referring to leveraging semantic models as the functional core of an application to provide a navigable model of data and associated relationships that represent knowledge in our target domain (Chortaras, Stamou, & Stafylopatis, 2005).

Semantic models allow users to ask questions about what is happening in a modeled system in a more natural way. As an example, an enterprise might consist of five geographic regions, with each region containing three to five drilling platforms, and each drilling platform monitored by several control systems, each having a different purpose. One of those control systems might monitor the temperature of extracted oil, while another might monitor vibration on a pump. A semantic model will allow a user to ask a question like, "What is the temperature of the oil being extracted on Platform 3?", without having to understand details such as, which specific control system monitors that information or which physical sensor is reporting the oil temperature on that platform.

Therefore, semantic models can be used to relate the physical world, as it is known to control systems engineers in this example, to the real world, as it is known to line-of-business leaders and decision makers. In the physical world, a control point such a valve or temperature sensor, is known by its identifier in a particular control system, possibly through a tag name like 14-WW13. This could be one of several thousand identifiers within any given control system, and there could be many similar control systems across an enterprise. To further complicate the problem of information referencing and aggregation, other data points of interest could be managed through databases, files, applications, or component services with each having its own interface method and naming conventions for data accessing (Ehrig & Sure, 2004).

A key value of the semantic model is to provide access of information in context of the real world in a consistent way. Within a semantic model implementation, this information is identified using "triples" of the form "subject-predicate-object";

For example:

- Tank1 *has Temperature* Sensor 7
- Tank 1 *is Part Of* Platform 4
- Platform 4 *is Part Of* Region 1

These triples, taken together, make up the ontology for Region 1 and can be stored in a model server, as is described in more detail later in this article. This information, then, can be easily traversed using the model query language to answer questions such as "What is the temperature of tank 1 on Platform 4", much more easily than was the case without a semantic model relating engineering information to the real world (Hariri, Abolhassani, & Sayyadi, 2006).

Likewise, you can traverse the model from many different perspectives to answer questions that you had not thought of at design time. In contrast, other types of database design might require structural changes to answer new questions that arise after initial implementation (Chicco, Sadowski, & Baldi, 2014).

Ontologies are fundamental for Natural Language Processing (NLP) and enhancing search through query expansion at runtime and search index creation on the back-end.

Semantic Search

Natural Language Processing (NLP) can be used to achieve advanced online question answering services. These services can provide effective access to information to everyone, computer-savvy or not, as interface barriers are eliminated. Answering any type of question is very challenging because it requires knowledge about the world, the user's task, inference capabilities, user modeling, linguistics knowledge, and knowledge about the pragmatics of discourse and dialog (Huhns & Singh, 1997).

Ontology-driven NLP parses natural language text and transposes it into a representation of its meaning, structured around events and their participants as mentioned in the text and known to the Ontology model. Queries can then be matched to this meaning representation in anticipation of any of the permutations which surface in the text. These permutations centrally include over specification (e.g. not listing all synonyms, which non-semantic search engines require their users to do) and more importantly, under specification. There is almost always an assume context in any statement or query (pulling [pipe] up, tripping [bit] out of hole, etc).

For the latter case, ambiguity can only be reduced by the process of query expansion, that is, giving the search engine what humans use for disambiguation, namely knowledge of the world as represented in an Ontology (Martinez-Gil & Aldana-Montes, 2011).

Query Expansion

Using Ontologies to drive the process of query expansion forms a cornerstone of "Semantic Search" (Pulido et al., 2006).

Ontology enabled query expansion can take the natural language query "does aspirin cure headaches" and automatically expand upon the query's meaning to produce a more thorough search. "Aspirin" would trigger a search not just for the word aspirin, but rather for all words linked to its ontology concept, and words linked to that concept's parent and child concepts – not only "aspirin" but "acetylsalicylic acid" and all of its known brand names, as well as generic words and brand names of conceptually similar drugs – other painkillers in the same family as aspirin. The same would be done for "cure", bringing up search results for other similar words such as "treat", "relieve" and "headache", etc. (Ritze, & Paulheim, 2011).

A non-Ontology enabled query would simply use a bag-of-words "keywords search" approach and would search for "aspirin headache" or "cure headache", and neither would produce all the desired results. Semantic search can attempt to optimize search results by expanding on the query. But in contrast to other applications, it can do so based on the meaning of the query.

CONCLUSION

Since ontologies define the terms used to describe and represent an area of knowledge, they are used in many applications to capture relationships and boost knowledge management. However, leaving ontology knowledge specifications completely for domain experts, who usually do not have description logic experience, may end-up in defining inconsistent domain knowledge specifications from real world knowledge, and hence this needs to be controlled.

REFERENCES

Chicco, D., Sadowski, P., & Baldi, P. (2014, September). Deep autoencoder neural networks for gene ontology annotation predictions. In *Proceedings of the 5th ACM conference on bioinformatics, computational biology, and health informatics* (pp. 533-540). ACM. 10.1145/2649387.2649442

Chortaras, A., Stamou, G., & Stafylopatis, A. (2005, September). Learning ontology alignments using recursive neural networks. In *Proceedings International Conference on Artificial Neural Networks* (pp. 811-816). Berlin, Germany: Springer.

Ehrig, M., & Sure, Y. (2004, May). Ontology mapping–an integrated approach. In *European semantic web symposium* (pp. 76-91). Berlin, Germany: Springer. 10.1007/978-3-540-25956-5_6

Hariri, B. B., Abolhassani, H., & Sayyadi, H. (2006). A neural-networks-based approach for ontology alignment. In Proceedings SCIS & ISIS 2006 (pp. 1248-1252). Japan Society for Fuzzy Theory and Intelligent Informatics.

Huhns, M. N., & Singh, M. P. (1997). Ontologies for agents. *IEEE Internet Computing*, *1*(6), 81–83. doi:10.1109/4236.643942

Martinez-Gil, J., & Aldana-Montes, J. F. (2011). Evaluation of two heuristic approaches to solve the ontology meta-matching problem. *Knowledge and Information Systems*, *26*(2), 225–247. doi:10.100710115-009-0277-0

Pulido, J. R. G., Ruiz, M. A. G., Herrera, R., Cabello, E., Legrand, S., & Elliman, D. (2006). Ontology languages for the semantic web: A never completely updated review. *Knowledge-based systems*, *19*(7), 489–497. doi:10.1016/j.knosys.2006.04.013

Ritze, D., & Paulheim, H. (2011, October). Towards an automatic parameterization of ontology matching tools based on example mappings. In *Proc. 6th ISWC ontology matching workshop (OM)*, Bonn, Germany. (pp. 37-48).

Chapter 6
Semantic Similarity Using Register Linear Question Classification (RLQC) for Question Classification

Shanthi Palaniappan

https://orcid.org/0000-0001-7721-8305
Sri Krishna College of Engineering and Technology, India

Sridevi U. K.
PSG College of Technology, India

Pathur Nisha S.
Nehru Institute of Technology, India

ABSTRACT

Question Classification(QC) mainly deals with syntactic parsing for finding the similarity. To improve the accuracy of classification, a semantic similarity approach of a question along with the question dataset is calculated. The semantic similarity of the question is initially achieved by syntactic parsing to extract the noun, verb, adverb, and adjective. However, adjectives and adverbs do give sentences an exact meaning that should also be considered for computing the semantic similarity. The proposed RLQC (Register Linear and Question Classification) model for semantic similarity of questions uses HSO (Hirst and St. Onge) measure with Gloss based measure to enhance the semantic similarity relatedness by considering the Noun, Verb, Adverb and Adjective. The semantic similarity of the question pairs for RLQC is 0.2% higher compared to HSO model. The highest semantic similarity of the proposed model achieves a better accuracy.

DOI: 10.4018/978-1-7998-1159-6.ch006

INTRODUCTION

Questions are usually 10-20 words long. Each question can be divided into different levels based on the taxonomy. The proposed work deals with level2 questions (Costa, 2001). QC provides the syntactic and semantic information that has the semantic similarity between concepts.

Earlier study on levels of questions including Costa taxonomy and Blooms taxonomy reveals the importance to focus on different categories of questions. To overcome these issues, a question classifier using Register Linear (RL) models for a specific domain is proposed by Shanthi (2015). The Register Linear (RL) Model classifies each input into one class for the complex questions in linear manner. The RL classification model is shown in the Figure 1. The Figure illustrates the RL model for Costa level questions.

The syntactic information of the question is more relevant in computing the semantic similarity. The meaning of a sentence does not depend only on the individual words; it also depends on the structural way the phrases are combined. The classification of questions by Shanthi (2015) takes only the noun and verb for semantic similarity using RL method. To improve the method, adjective and adverb are also considered to achieve the semantic relatedness of the concept. Semantic relatedness of the question is more suitable rather than the semantic similarity of questions to classify.

The evaluation process is carried out using the Stanford dataset used in the RL method to enhance the performance of the classification. As stated by Shanthi (2015), question classification is much essential for question answering. To improve the method further, the semantic similarity and the semantic relatedness is calculated. Register Linear Question Classification (RLQC) method is compared with the Syntax-based Measure for Semantic Similarity (SyMSS) to classify the questions efficiently. The semantic relatedness between the questions is done for a 100 pair of questions and compared with the existing approach. Corpus based methods use syntactical information that uses Latent Semantic Analysis (LSA). The disadvantage of LSA does not follow syntactic information. The antonyms and negations are not considered by LSA. For example, "Name the fruits that are red in color" and "Name the fruits that are not red in color" is not supported by LSA. The sentence "River passes though the lake" is different from "Lake passes through the river". There are some ongoing researches focusing on the improvement of LSA.

Earlier methods (Achananuparp, 2008; Li, 2006; Islam, 2008), use pseudo-syntactic information that justifies syntactic information is most essential to find the semantic similarity. Wiemer-Hastings (2004) and Li (2006), uses the semantic similarity between concepts. The different measures of semantic similarity were also compared in this model as given by Oliva et al., (2011). The syntactic information

Figure 1. Architecture diagram of RL classification model

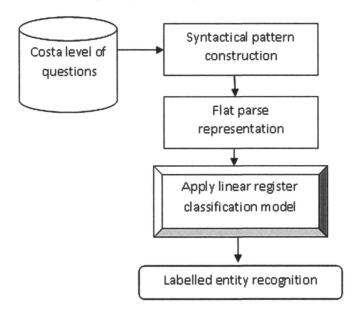

is more relevant for a sentence level for calculating the semantic similarity. In the proposed RL model, the syntactic information is extracted at the question level that considers noun, verb, adverb and adjective for the semantic relatedness process. Pelletier (1994) stated that the meaning of each word in the sentence depends not only on the hypothesis, it also depends on the structural way the words are combined. Sridevi (2018), proposed a comparison of information extraction in deep learning framework features of annotated framework. As stated by Pelletier (1994), the meaning of the question is also important for finding the similarity, which is considered in the proposed approach.

The proposed approach acquires semantic content from a lexical database such as WordNet that gives various kinds of measures to be applied to come across semantic similarity between questions. Syntactic details are obtained by parsing the phrases that structure the sentence and their syntactical information. The given question is analysed by semantic similarity approach and list out the similar questions that are presently available in the existing dataset along with the given question. If the given question is not in the existing data, it automatically updates in the existing dataset. Also the given question is placed in one of the classification question as specified in the previous work. If the classification doesn't exist earlier, then a new classification will be created and the question will be placed in the new classification.

RELATED WORK

Question Classification (QC) is a primary step in a Question Answering (QA) system that searches for the type of expected answer to retrieve the answer. The derivation of expected answer type is performed by a machine learning approach. The entire task depends on: (i) Taxonomy of answer types into which questions are to be classified. (ii) Corpus of questions prepared with the correct answer type classification. (iii) Algorithm that learns to make the actual predictions given in the corpus. The taxonomy needs to be designed perfectly and the corpus must be of appropriate size to get successful result.

A typical QA system involves steps like Question Classification (QC), identifying the answer for the type of the questions and answer retrieval. In a QA system, classifying the questions is the first step for finding the expected answer type using various approaches. In order to identify the expected answer for the given questions machine learning approaches are used. Previous researches in this area have produced some machine learning approaches, which have dealt with taxonomy to classify questions. Costa's taxonomy and Bloom's taxonomy are considered in this work for classifying questions based on the cognitive levels for enhancement of question and answering systems.

Semantic similarity plays an important role for a sentence/questions to classify that depends on the occurrence of the words. Even a single word in the phrases fails in achieving the exact similarity. There are three core types of methods used to compute semantic similarity namely corpus-based methods, word co-occurrence methods and hybrid methods.

Corpus-based methods use statistical information on words in a corpus. LSA is one such method that makes use of a phrase by using passage matrix to denote all the presence of words in the passages used. This matrix is decomposed by singular value decomposition. Its dimensionality is reduced by removing all small singular values. Finally, the sentences to be compared are represented on this lowered space as two vectors containing the meaning of their phrases. Semantic similarity between concepts is carried out to find the most suitable measure in the proposed method. There are various measures like Path Based Measure, Information Content Measure and Gloss Based Measure for finding the semantic similarity. Each of these categories uses several similarity measures for finding the exact semantic similarity. The proposed approach considers only on HSO, PATH from Path based measures, and LIN from Information content measure, since they provide better similarity ranking analysed in the recent work by Oliva et al., (2011).

Path Based Measure

Path based measures depends on the information from the shortest path. These measures are calculated by Least/Lowest Common Subsumer (LCS) or by finding the minimum path between the concepts. The length between the concepts is calculated by counting the number of nodes. Path measure and Hirst & St. Onge measure are some of the Path based measure considered for calculating the semantic similarity. The semantic similarity by Path based measure between the concepts can also be better achieved using the adjective structure of Wordnet with relations like "similar-to", "antonyms" and "see-also".

Path Measure - Semantic similarity is measured by the length between the concepts. This measure uses "is-a" relations between the nodes.

Hirst & St. Onge measure - This measure takes into account of "is-a" relations considering the antonyms and synonyms.

Information Content Measures

Information Content Measures (ICS) the specificity of a concept, which is higher for more specific concepts. Three different measures like Resnik measure, Jiang & Conrath measure and Lin measure are used in ICS.

Resnik Measure

Resnik measure is that two concepts are semantically similar that relies on the structure of the thesaurus. Resnik refine path bases approach using normalisations based on hierarchy depth. It represents the distance associated with each edge. So the measure is calculated as the information content of their lowest common subsumer (is the distance of the lowest nodes) in the hierarchy as given below:

$$Sim(c_1, c_2) = IC(lcs(c_1, c_2)) \tag{2.1}$$

Jiang and Conrath Measure

This measure calculates the distance between the concepts based on the Information Content (IC). Jiang measures the distance instead of the similarity. It transforms into the similarity by taking its reciprocal. The calculation is as follows:

$$Sim(c_1, c_2) = \frac{1}{IC(c_1) + IC(c_2) - 2 * IC(lcs(c_1, c_2))} \tag{2.2}$$

Lin Measure

This similarity between the two concepts C_1 and C_2 is measured by the ratio between the amount of information. Commonality of the concepts is identified by the information content of the common and the IC of the two concepts. The value of this similarity measure varies between 0 and 1. The information common between the two concepts is twice the information in the lowest common subsumer (LCS).

$$Sim(c_1, c_2) = \frac{2 * IC(lcs(c_1, c_2))}{IC(c_1) + IC(c_2)} \tag{2.3}$$

Gloss-Based Measure

Extended Gloss Overlap measure and Gloss Vectors measure are two types of Gloss based measures. Glosses measures the semantic relatedness of the concepts by their definition.

Extended Gloss Overlap Measure

This calculates the similarity of two concepts using Wordnet by comparing the glosses with multiple senses and the other words in the context. The sense of the target word whose common definitions matches with the neighbouring words are chosen as the best sense.

Gloss Vectors Measure

Wordnet glosses help to create the vector measures using the co-occurrence matrix. The average of all the context of the words found in the gloss is represented by a gloss vector. The semantic relatedness between the concepts is measured by finding the similarity between the pair of gloss vectors. It measures by forming the second order co-occurrence from the glosses. The pair-wise gloss vector measure is similar to the gloss vector measure except the adjacent glosses. Separate vector measures are created for the hyponyms, holonyms, meronyms, etc. that measures the individual cosine similarity of the corresponding gloss vectors. Gloss vector measure performs better than the Pair-wise gloss vector. Gloss based measure computes the similarity by considering the similarity between the adjectives and adverbs.

RLQc SIMILARITY

The semantic similarity between the concepts considers mainly on the syntactic structure. The similarities between the sentences are considered by calculating the sum of the similarities between the head of the sentence. It is also important to note that the gloss-based measures and HSO are the only measures that can be computed to find the similarity between the two words that are used in different Parts Of Speech(POS).

$$Sim(S_1, S_2) = \frac{1}{N} \sum_{i}^{n} sim(h_{1i}, h_{2i}) - lPF \qquad (3.1)$$

Let the sentence S1 is made of n phrases and their heads are $h_{11}, \ldots, h_{1n}$ and sentence S_2 is made of n phrases, and $h_{21}, \ldots, h_{2n}$ are their heads. The phrases of h_{1i} and h_{2i} probably have the same syntactic function. The syntactic role for one of the sentence is considered. A Penalisation Factor (PF) is introduced in case if one sentence phrase is not shared by the other sentence to reflect the fact that one of the sentences has extra information. If the heads are not present in WordNet like pronouns, they are ignored in the calculation unless the same word shares the same syntactic role in both the sentences. HSO method overcomes even in the absence of proper nouns in WordNet. In the proposed RLQC method, the penalisation factor is eliminated for calculating the semantic similarity between the questions. HSO uses the syntactic role of both the sentences, so that PF is not needed for calculating the similarity.

$$Sim(q_1, q_2) = \frac{1}{N} \sum_{i}^{n} sim(h_{1i}, h_{2i}) \qquad (3.2)$$

Let the question q_1 is made of n phrases and their heads are $h_{11}, \ldots, h_{1n}$ and question q_2 is made of n phrases, and $h_{21}, \ldots, h_{2n}$ are their heads; and moreover the phrases of h_{1i} and h_{2i} have the same syntactic function.

EXPERIMENTS AND RESULTS

In order to evaluate the question similarity measure with a larger dataset, the Stanford dataset of geographical questions are considered. This corpus consists of 5020 test pairs to find the semantic relatedness of the questions. The sample of word pairs are listed in the Table 1. The table also gives a comparative result of all the existing approach. The proposed approach on semantic similarity of questions used Hirst and St. Onge (HSO) measure to enhance the semantic similarity. In the proposed RLQC, the semantic similarity of questions of HSO is evaluated by considering the Noun, Verb, Adverb and Adjective. The semantic similarity of a set of sample questions given in the table below is considered for the experimental results with the existing and the proposed approach. The existing approach UMBC EBIQUITY-CORE: Semantic Textual Similarity Systems (UMBC) by Lushan Han (2013) uses refined standard corpus with relation similarity and concept similarity and Oliva et al., (2011) has proposed Syntax-based Measure for Semantic Similarity (SyMSS).

Table 1. Semantic Similarity of word pair

Sl.No	Word Pair	HSO	PATH	LIN
1	Identify, find	3	0.33	0.39
2	city, city	16	1.00	1.00
3	find, locate	4	0.50	0.88
4	determine, decide	16	1.00	1.00
5	clarify, determine	0	0.25	0.00
6	state, elevation	6	0.33	0.50
7	point, state	4	0.50	0.61
8	flow, run	16	1.00	1.00
9	cyclone, hurricane	4	0.50	0.98
10	little, small	16	0.11	0.00
11	lake, river	4	0.25	0.79
12	cock, rooster	16	1.00	1.00
13	city, capital	4	0.14	0.60
14	car, bus	5	0.50	0.60
15	highway, road	4	0.50	0.85
16	hill, mountain	5	0.33	0.86
17	autograph, signature	4	0.50	0.00
18	glass, tumbler	5	0.50	0.87
19	gem, jewel	16	1.00	1.00
20	geography, map	0	0.07	0.00
21	bottle, glass	5	0.33	0.75
22	automobile, car	16	1.00	1.00
23	train, automobile	5	0.20	0.71
24	state, city	5	0.33	0.79
25	population, people	5	0.50	0.78

The following table describes the similarity results of the existing approaches to show the different aspects of analysis by considering the similarity values for analysis. The results are analysed using the equation given below.

$$Sim(c_1, c_2) = \frac{1}{N} \sum_{1}^{n} sim(h_{1i}, h_{2i}) - IPF \tag{4.1}$$

$1/3(+1+1+0.0763) - 0.03 = (0.6921)-0.03 = 0.6621$

$$Sim(q_1, q_2) = \frac{1}{N} \sum_{1}^{n} sim(h_{1i}, h_{2i}) \tag{4.2}$$

$1/16(16+16+16+4) = 3.25 / 4 = 0.81$

Table 2. Comparison of similar questions

Sl.No	Similar Questions	Sim_{UMBC} Relation	Sim_{UMBC} Concept	Sim_{SyMSS}	Sim_{RLQC}
Q1	Identify the city named city of Newyork.	0.87	0.0	0.89	0.96
	Find the city name Newyork				
Q2	Categorise mountains in Alaska based on their height	0.76	0.51	0.87	0.95
	Classify mountains in Alaska based on their tallness				
Q3	Analyse the river of Delaware	0.67	0.0	0.98	0.99
	Explore the river of Delaware				
Q4	Identify the place that has lowest point of Alaska	0.61	0.0	0.96	0.98
	Find out the place that has smallest spot of Alaska				
Q5	Classify the river based on length which runs through Newmexico	0.94	0.0	0.97	1.00
	Categorise the rivers based on length which flows in Newmexico				
Q6	Categorise the rivers based on distance which flows via Newmexico	0.78	0.0	0.6621	0.81
	Classify the river based on length which passes through Newmexico				

Table 2 explains the pairs of questions and the comparison of these pairs of questions with the proposed approach are analysed. According to the results, the proposed approach gives a closer semantic similarity to achieve the accuracy of question classification.

The proposed approach used in RLQC, finds a semantic similarity of the given questions using HSO with semantic similarity relatedness to obtain the classification accuracy.

CONCLUSION

The proposed approach on semantic relatedness of question is compared with the existing approach that gives better result. The given question is analysed using semantic similarity approach and lists out the similar questions that are presently available in the existing data set along with the given question. If the given question is not already available in the existing data, the given question will be placed in one among the classification questions. If the classification doesn't exist earlier, then a new classification will be created and the question will be placed in the new classification. These classifications of questions help to reduce the retrieval time in answering the questions. As per the analysis, the efficiency of the system is achieved on closed domain answering rather than open domain.

REFERENCES

Achananuparp, P., Hu, X., Zhou, X., & Zhang, X. (2008). Utilizing sentence similarity and question type similarity to response to similar questions in knowledge-sharing community. In *Proceedings of QAWeb Workshop*. pp. 41-52.

Costa, A. L. (2001). *Developing minds: A resource book for teaching thinking* (3rd ed.). Alexandria, VA: Association for Supervision and Curriculum Development.

Han, L., Kashyap, A., Finin, T., Mayfield, J., & Weese, J. (2013). UMBC EBIQUITY-CORE: Semantic Textual Similarity Systems, Second Joint Conference on Lexical and Computational Semantics (*SEM), *Proceedings of the Main Conference and the Shared Task*, Atlanta, GA. Association for Computational Linguistic, vol. 1, pp. 44-52.

Islam, A., & Inkpen, D. (2008). Semantic text similarity using corpus-based word similarity and string similarity. *ACM Transactions on Knowledge Discovery from Data*, 178–190.

Li, Y., McLean, D., Bandar, Z., O'Shea, J., & Crockett, K. (2006). Sentence similarity based on semantic nets and corpus statistics. *IEEE Transactions on Knowledge and Data Engineering*, *18*(18), 1138–1149. doi:10.1109/TKDE.2006.130

Oliva, J., Serrano, J. I., Dolores del Castillo, M., & Iglesias, Á. (2011). SyMSS: A syntax-based measure for short-text semantic similarity. *Data & Knowledge Engineering*, *70*(4), 390–405. doi:10.1016/j.datak.2011.01.002

Palaniappan, S., & Krishnamurthi, I. (2015). Register linear based model for question classification using costa level questions, *WSEAS Transactions on Computers, 14*, pp. 369-381.

Pelletier, F. J. (1994). The principle of semantic compositionality. *Topoi*, *13*(1), 11–24. doi:10.1007/BF00763644

Sridevi, U. K., Shanthi, P., & Nagaveni, N. (2018). Deep model framework for ontology-based document clustering. In M. Habib (Ed.), *Handbook of research on investigations in artificial life research and development* (pp. 424–435). Hershey, PA: IGI Global. doi:10.4018/978-1-5225-5396-0.ch019

Wiemer-Hastings, P. (2004). All parts are not created equal: SIAM-LSA, *Proceedings of 26th Annual Conference of the Cognitive Science Society*, pp. 22-41.

Chapter 7
Knowledge Graph Generation

Anjali Daisy

(iD) https://orcid.org/0000-0003-1207-5002
SASTRA University, India

ABSTRACT

Nowadays, as computer systems are expected to be intelligent, techniques that help modern applications to understand human languages are in much demand. Amongst all the techniques, the latent semantic models are the most important. They exploit the latent semantics of lexicons and concepts of human languages and transform them into tractable and machine-understandable numerical representations. Without that, languages are nothing but combinations of meaningless symbols for the machine. To provide such learning representation, embedding models for knowledge graphs have attracted much attention in recent years since they intuitively transform important concepts and entities in human languages into vector representations, and realize relational inferences among them via simple vector calculation. Such novel techniques have effectively resolved a few tasks like knowledge graph completion and link prediction, and show the great potential to be incorporated into more natural language processing (NLP) applications.

INTRODUCTION

Nowadays, as computer systems are expected to be intelligent, techniques that help modern applications to understand human languages are in much demand. Amongst all the techniques, the latent semantic models are the most important, they exploit the latent semantics of lexicons and concepts of human languages and transform them into tractable and machine understandable numerical representations. Without which, languages are nothing but combinations of meaningless symbols for the machine.

DOI: 10.4018/978-1-7998-1159-6.ch007

To provide such learning representation, in recent years, embedding models for knowledge graphs have attracted much attention, since they intuitively transform important concepts and entities in human languages into vector representations, and realize relational inferences among them via simple vector calculation. Such novel techniques have effective resolved a few tasks like knowledge graph completion and link prediction, and show the great potential to be incorporated into more natural language processing (NLP) applications.

EMBEDDINGS

Embedding-based techniques project discrete concepts or words to a low-dimensional and continuous vector space where co-occurred concepts or words are located close to each other. Compared to conventional discrete representations (e.g., the one-hot encoding, embedding provides more strong representations, particularly for concepts that infrequently appear in corpora,(Narayanan et al., 2012) but are with significance of meaning. In this section, we state the background of embedding-based approaches that are frequently used in NLP tasks. We start with a brief introduction to word embeddings, then focus on addressing the past advance of knowledge graph embeddings (King,1983).

KNOWLEDGE GRAPH EMBEDDINGS

Lately, knowledge graph embedding methods are proposed to learn latent representation from structured corpora. Different from word embeddings, knowledge graph embeddings represent entities or concepts of the graphs as vectors, while the relations among them as different forms of vector calculation that is bound with specific relational semantics. There exist two families of knowledge graph embeddings, (Yeung et al., 2009) namely the translation-based and the non-translation-based. Recently, significant advancement has been made in using the translation-based method to train monolingual knowledge graph embeddings. To characterize a triple (h, r, t), models of this family follow a common assumption hr + r ≈ tr, where hr and tr are either the original vectors of h and t, or the transformed vectors under a certain transformation w.r.t. relation r. The forerunner TransE sets hr and tr as the original h and t and achieves promising results in handling 1-to-1 relations of entities. Later works improve TransE on multi-mapping relations by 1v(King, 1983) here means a embedding vector of a given word 10 introducing relation-specific transformations on entities to obtain different hr and tr, including projections on relation-specific hyperplanes in TransH, linear transformations to heterogeneous relation spaces in TransR(Yeung et al., 2009) dynamic matrices in TransD (Pick, 2015), and other forms. All these variants of TransEspecialize entity embeddings for different relations, therefore improving knowledge graph completion on multi-mapping relations at the cost of increased model complexity. Meanwhile translation-based models cooperate well with other models. For example, variants of TransE are combined with word embeddings to help relation extraction from text. In addition to these, there are non-translation-based methods.It applies a bilinear transformation between h and t, and (Narayanan et al., 2012) defines holographic mapping for relations. These models do not explicitly represent relation in forms of embeddings. SLM adopt neural networks to learn structured data, while (Umbrich et al., 2013) uses random walk on graphs to generate corpora for context-based training. These models are expressive and adaptable for both structured and text corpora, but they are too complex to be incorporated into an architecture supporting multilingual knowledge. Others including neural-based models and random-walk-based model which are expressive and adaptable for both structured and text corpora. These are too complex to be incorporated with other models, including the architecture supporting multilingual knowledge that is to be proposed in our research. To train a knowledge graph embedding model, a score function fr (h, t) is defined to measure the plausibility of any given triples according to the assumption of the model addressed as above. Then the training process minimizes the total loss, which is defined as the sum of scores, via convex optimization algorithms such as stochastic gradient descent and except for neural-based methods which are trained using neural or tensor networks. To accelerate in training process, negative sampling are sometimes used in training(Goldstein et al., 2000).

PROPERTIES PRESERVING KNOWLEDGE GRAPH EMBEDDINGS

Modelling

We hereby extend the formalization to reflect these special relations we are to handle. Now, we only consider any monolingual knowledge graph w.l.o.g. Thus, we omit any language mark L. However, now we extend the vocabulary of relations into R = Rtr∪Rs∪ Rh ∪ Ro 23 where Rtr is the set of transitive relations, Rs is the set of symmetric relations, Rh is the set of hierarchical relations, and Ro is the set of other simple relations. Thereof, Rtr and Rh are not required to be disjoint, while both of them are disjoint with Ro. For transitive relations for each r ∈Rtr, there exists three different entities e1, e2, e3 ∈ E such that (e1, r, e2), (e2, r, e3), (e1, r, e3) ∈ G. As for symmetric relations for each r ∈Rs, there exists two different entities e1, e2 ∈ E such that (e1, r, e2), (e2, r, e1) ∈ G. As for hierarchical relations, we further divide them into Rh = Rr∪Rc where Rr is the set of refinement relations, Rc is the set of coercion relations. The difference between relations in Rh and multi-mapping relations is that the former consider only the atomic relations (i.e. relations satisfying transitive reduction. (Samer, 2009).

ROLE-DEDICATED-MAPPING MODEL

The reason for which the previous translation-based mappings to fail to preserve relational properties of relations is that those relation-specific entity transformations place entities involved in transitive or symmetric relations into conflict positions.

JOINT EMBEDDINGS

A word and knowledge graph joint embedding model (or text-graph joint embeddings) is easily created by applying an alignment model between a word embedding model and a knowledge graph embedding model. The advantage of a joint model is that it accepts both signals from knowledge graph structures and plain text contexts, and has a large vocabulary like a word embedding model. Word embeddings are trained on the plain text document D that has a vocabulary V. A sliding window c reads the context of each word in the document D. The alignment model is trained on 27 the anchor file A that contains entity-word pairs (w, e) ∈ A such that w ∈ V and e ∈ E. Suppose the word embedding model is the Skip-gram model in Word2Vec [MCC13] which maximizes the log-linear energy function as below, Slog = X (w,c)∈D logp(c|w) = X (w,c)∈D (loge vc·vw − X c 0∈D loge vc 0·vw)

RESEARCH

Our future research focuses on two aspects, i.e. 1) continue developing the approaches for learning latent representation on multi-faceted relational knowledge, and learning joint with word contexts; 2) solve various natural language processing tasks based on the learnt latent representation. We propose the following research plan for the next 24 months. The schedule is tentative and content orders are subject to change.

- **Improving Property-Preserving Embeddings:** In Winter and Spring 2017 we will focus in implementing several variants of On2Vec obtained by adopting different role-dedicated mapping models and hierarchy models.

This stage of work also includes the release of a cleaned Yago-based data set, which being different from the two common data sets FB15k (Freebase-based) and WN18 (WordNet-based), contains a majority of triples with relational properties and hierarchical relations. The experiments of unsupervised relation extraction and link prediction will be extended on the Freebase-based and WordNet-based data sets to show the ability of On2Vec variants in encoding simple relations in ordinary knowledge graphs. The same study will also be conducted on the Yago-based data set to determine the performance on handling special graphs in Ontology graphs (Umbrich et al.,, 2013).

- **Joint Embeddings:** The text-graph joint embeddings will be implemented and tuned in Fall 2017 such that future work will be able to use it as the feature model for modeling sentences and documents. The best variant of On2Vec, TransR and TransE will be adopted as the 42 knowledge model component for training the joint embeddings, and Skip-gram or Glove will be adopted as the text model. For corpora, this model will be using on annotated Wikipedia dumpplus a Yago-based ontology graph that shares high coverage of the entity vocabularies with the annotated Wikipedia dump

- **Supervised Relation Extraction:** The research on supervised relation extraction from plain text will start from Summer 2017. A neural-based relation extractor will be implemented and experimentally evaluated on Google's knowledge graph project during the author's summer cooperation with Google Search Team. In detail, this version of model uses knowledge graph-augmented vector representation to model Wikipedia's entity short descriptions along with other (optional) signals including distant supervision and selective attention. Held-out evaluation will be conducted to reflect the effectiveness of the extractor, while the Search Team will also use our model to extract non-preexisting relational data. Starting from Winter 2018 to Spring 2018 the extractor will be further tested on extracting relations from Wikipedia articles when the text-graph joint embeddings are incorporated.

- **Sentiment Analysis:** Sentiment analysis experiments will be conducted in Summer 2017 to classify Wikipedia articles with missing domains, which is a part of the project assigned to the author by the Google Search Team. In Summer 2017 we will first use the same classifier structure (with modified layers) developed for supervised relation extraction. Since this task is going to be extended to different domain-specific learning resources as stated in Section 4.4, this work will be continued in Spring 2018 to Fall 2018, during which time we plan to implement the classifier using other neural-based models as well

- **Semantic Relatedness Analysis:** For monolingual semantic relatedness analysis, as stated we have developed the workflow for the analysis, which has already been used to evaluate the annotated Skip-gram-based approach. Therefore, during the time scale from Fall 2017 to Winter 2018, more results are expected as we incorporate newly-developed embedding models. We postpone the work on cross-lingual semantic relatedness analysis to 43 Winter 2019 since it is expected to follow the public release of MTransE and corresponding learning resources and requires cultivating rated multilingual documented sets for evaluating this task (Valduriez,2011).

- **Cross-Lingual Tasks:** We have completed the development of MTransE variants and evaluated their performance on knowledge alignment. Currently we are on our way in publishing this work and releasing the corresponding implementation and learning resources. We plan to improve MTransE by incorporating knowledge models with relation-specific entity transformations as well as alignment models with other characterization techniques after Winter 2019.

CONCLUSION

Thus, since neural networks for NLP is the developing field and it has great scope in future. we believe it to be easily portable to other knowledge graphs and suitable for KG's that change over time (such as DBpedia Live). However, we leave an evaluation of its portability for future work. In future work, the investigation of implicit or explicit segmentation modelling should improve subject prediction by better candidate pruning and reduce the noise for better learning of predicate patterns. Exploitation of external lexical resources could also prove advantageous as it should help to bridge the lexical gap.

REFERENCES

Goldstein, J., Mittal, V., Carbonell, J., & Kantrowitz, M. (2000). Multidocument summarization by sentence extraction. In *Proceedings of the 2000 NAACLANLP Workshop on Automatic summarization-Vol. 4*, pp. 40–48. ACL. 10.3115/1117575.1117580

Hassan, S. & Mihalcea, R. (2009). Cross-lingual semantic relatedness using encyclopedic knowledge. In Proceedings EMNLP, pp. 1192–1201.

Hu, M., & Liu, B. (2004). Mining and summarizing customer reviews. In Proceedings KDD, pp. 168–177. doi:10.1145/1014052.1014073

Huang, H.-H., & Kuo, Y.-H. (2010). Cross-lingual document representation and semantic similarity measure: A fuzzy set and rough set-based approach. *IEEE Transactions on Fuzzy Systems, 18*(6), 1098–1111. doi:10.1109/TFUZZ.2010.2065811

King, J. L. (1983). Centralized versus decentralized computing: Organizational considerations and management options. *ACM Computing Surveys, 15*(4), 319–349. doi:10.1145/289.290

Narayanan, A., Toubiana, V., Barocas, S., Nissenbaum, H., & Boneh, D. (2012). A critical look at decentralized personal data architectures. arXiv preprint arXiv:1202.4503.

Pick, R. A. (2015). Shepherd or servant: Centralization and decentralization in information technology governance. *International Journal of Management & Information Systems, 19*(2), 61–68.

Umbrich, J., Gutierrez, C., Hogan, A., Karnstedt, M., & Parreira, J. X. (2013, May). The ACE theorem for querying the web of data. In Proceedings *WWW* (pp. 133–134). Companion Volume.

Valduriez, P. (2011, August). Principles of distributed data management in 2020? In *Proceedings International Conference on Database and Expert Systems Applications* (pp. 1-11). Berlin, Germany: Springer. 10.1007/978-3-642-23088-2_1

Yeung, C. M. A., Liccardi, I., Lu, K., Seneviratne, O., & Berners-Lee, T. (2009, January). Decentralization: The future of online social networking. In *W3C Workshop on the Future of Social Networking Position Papers* (Vol. 2, pp. 2-7).

Chapter 8

Develop a Neural Model to Score Bigram of Words Using Bag-of-Words Model for Sentiment Analysis

Anumeera Balamurali
St.Joseph's College of Engineering, India

Balamurali Ananthanarayanan
Tamilnadu Agriculture Department, India

ABSTRACT

A Bag-of-Words model is widely used to extract the features from text, which is given as input to machine learning algorithm like MLP, neural network. The dataset considered is movie reviews with both positive and negative comments further converted to Bag-of-Words model. Then the Bag-of-Word model of the dataset is converted into vector representation which corresponds to a number of words in the vocabulary. Each word in the review documents is assigned with a score and the scores are later represented in vector representation which is later fed as input to neural model. In the Kera's deep learning library, the neural models will be simple feedforward network models with fully connected layers called 'Dense'. Bigram language models are developed to classify encoded documents as either positive or negative. At first, reviews are converted to lines of token and then encoded to bag-of-words model. Finally, a neural model is developed to score bigram of words with word scoring modes.

DOI: 10.4018/978-1-7998-1159-6.ch008

INTRODUCTION: KNOW THE BASIC TERMS?

Natural Language Processing or NLP is generally defined as the automatic understanding of natural language, like speech and text. The study of natural language processing has been popular around for more than fifty years and grew out of the field of linguistics with the evolutions of computers. Current end applications and research includes information extraction, machine translation, summarization, search and human computer interfaces. While complete semantic understanding remains a way still far from distant goal, researchers have studied a divide and conquer approach and identified several subtasks and methods needed for application development and analysis. These ranges varies from the syntactic methods, such as part-of-speech tagging, chunking and parsing, to the semantic method, such as word sense disambiguation, semantic-role labelling, named entity extraction and anaphora resolution. The field of Natural Language Processing (NLP) aims to convert human language into a formal representation which makes easy for computers to manipulate.

As Internet services for movies has increased in popularity, more and more languages are able to make their way online. In such a world, a need exist for the rapid organizing of ever expanding online reviews. A well-trained movie reviews can easily improves the quality of movies provided through online platform: there are so many different reviews other than movies like product review or feedbacks in so many different languages and most of them cannot be parsed immediately with a glance eye. Thus, an automatic language identification system is needed to analyse the reviews so the system is built to take this task. Because of the sheer volume of reviews in online to be handled, the categorization must be efficient, consuming as small storage and little processing time as possible.

N-gram models are the most widely used models for statistical language modelling and sentiment analysis, which is implemented by artificial neural networks (NN). NN is the powerful technique that is widely used in various fields of computer science. Most of the current NLP systems and techniques use words as atomic units which defines that there is no notion of similarity between words, as these are represented as indices in a vocabulary. The observation so far tells that the simple language models trained on huge amounts of data which outperform complex systems trained on less data. An example is the popular N-gram model used for statistical language modelling and text categorization in google, amazon etc...

Text categorization addresses the problem of splitting a given passage of text (or a document) to one or more predefined classes. This is an important area of sentiment analysis research that has been heavily investigated. The goal of text categorization is to classify the given reviews into a fixed number of pre-defined categories which is then listed as result to data analytics companies (Barry, 2016).

Deep learning architectures and algorithms have already created spectacular advances in fields like computer vision and pattern recognition (Brownlee, 2017).

Following this trend, the recent natural language processing is currently more and more specialized in the field of recent deep learning strategies. (Collobert et al., 2011) Deep learning algorithms is found to use the unknown structure for the input distribution to give good representations, usually at multiple levels, with higher-level learned features stated in terms of lower-level features. Deep learning strategies aim at learning feature hierarchies with features from higher levels of the hierarchy with which it is created by the composition of lower level features. Automatic learning features at multiple levels of abstraction permit a system to learn complex functions mapping the input to the output directly from data, while not relying fully on human-crafted features (Youngy et al.,, 2018).

Text Pre-Processing

Tokenization is a way of breaking a text into words or sentences. Tokenization is the method by which huge amount of text is splitted into smaller parts, referred as tokens. Natural language processing is employed for building applications like Text classification, intelligent chatbot, sentimental analysis, language translation, etc. It becomes important to grasp the pattern within the text to attain the above-stated purpose. These tokens are helpful for locating such patterns as well as taken a base step for stemming and lemmatization.

For example, consider the given input string –

Hi, how are you? ◊ the output ◊ ['Hi', 'how', 'are', 'you']

Removal of Stop Words is an initial step: Stop Words are the words that don't contain vital significance to be employed in Search Queries. Usually, these words are filtered out from search queries since the method huge quantity of unnecessary information. Each programming language offers its own list of stop words to use. Most of the stop words are used English language like 'as, the, be, are' etc.

Stemming is the method for removing suffixes from words in English. Removing suffixes is an operation that is very helpful in field of text classification. Stemming and Lemmatization is used in Text Normalization (or generally known as Word Normalization) techniques in the field of natural language processing that are found to prepare text, words, and documents for further process. Stemming and Lemmatization are studied, and algorithms are developed in computer science since the 1960's. Stemming and Lemmatization each generate the base format of the inflected words. The distinction is that stem won't be an actual word whereas; lemma is an actual language word. Stemming follows an algorithm with steps to perform on the words that makes it quicker. Whereas, in lemmatization, researchers used WordNet corpus and a corpus for stop words still provides lemma that makes it slower than stemming.

The architecture is divided into two parts: Training phase and Testing phase. In Training phase, the training data is given into pre-processing stages which includes tokenization. Tokenization is done by using two steps: at first stopwords are removed and then stemming or lemmatization is done. After which feature engineering methods are implemented in pre-processed data that includes: Bag-of-words, TF-IDF and word embedding. The model so far developed is trained and evaluated so that the test data is given as input to test the model. As the result the sentiment analysed predicted output is shown. Figure 1 shows the architecture of the project.

BACKGROUND: SIMILAR TO LITERATURE SURVEY

Comparing Neural Network Approach With NGram Approach For Text Categorization

Suresh Babu and Pavan Kumar(2010) compares Neural network Approach with N-gram approach, for text categorization. And also demonstrates that Neural Network approach is better than the N-gram approach but with less judging time. Both methods demonstrated in this project are aimed at language identification. Feature vectors are calculated from the presence of particular characters, words and the statistical information of word lengths. In an identification experiment the approach is compared with Asian languages where the neural network approach achieved 98% correct classification rate with 600 bytes, but it is six times faster than n-gram based approach.

Figure 1. Architecture for the language model
Source: Own

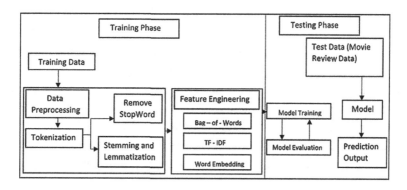

Figure 2. Schematic diagram of Neural network system
Source: *Comparing Neural Network Approach With NGram Approach For Text Categorization (A. Suresh Babu and P.N.V.S.Pavan Kumar (2010) International Journal on Computer Science and Engineering, Vol.2(1) pg: 80-83)*

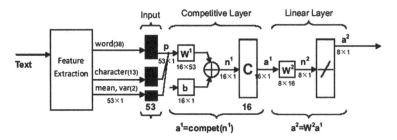

Above figure explains the step by step procedure of neural network approach which starts by text feature extraction to the final linear layer. In this project a method for identifying the 8 Roman alphabet language using Neural networks is proposed. Further the performance of other two N gram-based approaches has been compared to present the better approach. Now a days varies researches showed that the N-gram based approach gives an excellent performance on short strings. However, the information such as size of N-gram profiles and the speed of classification are not provided. The Neural network developed based on the proposed design of feature vectors are further distinguished by its high efficiency and accuracy of classification. The speed of classification are particularly useful when text of longer length has to be classified.

Understanding Bag-of-Words Model: A Statistical Framework

Yin Zhang, Rong Jin and Zhi-Hua Zhou (2012) proposed new bag-of-words model which is one of the most efficient representation methods for object categorization. The key idea of this project is to summarize each extracted key point into one of visual words, and then visualize each image by a histogram of the visual words. For this purpose, a clustering algorithm (e.g., K-means), is used to generate the visual words. Even though a number of studies have shown motivated results of the bag-of-words representation for object categorization. Theoretical studies about the properties of the bag-of-words model is almost unmarked, possibly due to the difficulties of using a heuristic clustering process. In this paper, a statistical framework is presented, which generalizes the bag-of-words representation. Where the visual words are provoked by a statistical process instead of using a clustering algorithm, while the factual performance is competitive to clustering-based method. A theoretical analysis based on statistical consistency is introduced for the proposed framework. Moreover, based on the framework two algorithms are developed which do not rely on clustering.

Statistical framework is presented for key point quantization that concludes the bag-of-words model by statistical expectation. Efficacy and the robustness of the proposed framework are verified by applying it to object recognition. In the future, proposed method can be improvised by introducing a plan to examine the dependence of the proposed algorithms on the threshold ρ [Chih-Fong Tsai. (2012)].

N-Gram Language Modeling Using Recurrent Neural Network Estimation

Ciprian Chelba, Mohammad Norouzi and Samy Bengio [Chelba et al.,, 2017] investigates the effective memory depth of Recurrent Neural Network models by using n-gram language model (LM) for smoothing purpose. LSTM is used in this work which means Long Short Term Memory which is a artificial recurrent neural network. Experiments done on a small corpus (UPenn Treebank, one million words of training data with 10k vocabulary) that have found the LSTM(Long Short Term Memory) cell with a dropout, which is a best model for encoding the n-gram state when compared with both feed-forward and vanilla RNN models. While allowing the dependencies across sentence boundaries, the LSTM with 13-gram language model has almost matched the perplexity of the unlimited history LSTM Language Model.

Developing a LSTM n-gram Language Models may be suitable for some practical situations they are: the state in a n-gram LM can be clearly represented with (n − 1)* 4 bytes which is stored in the identity of the words in the context and a set of n-gram contexts are processed in parallel. On the downside, this work concludes that the n-gram context encoding created by the LSTM is removed, that makes the model more expensive than a regular recurrent LSTM Language Model.

Recent Trends in Deep Learning Based Natural Language Processing

Tom Young et al has proposed deep learning methods that uses multiple processing layers to acquire a knowledge on hierarchical representations of data and then produces state-of-the-art results in different domains (Youngy et al., 2018). Now a days, a diversity of model designs and methods have been introduced in the context of natural language processing (NLP). In this work, significant deep learning related models and methods are employed for numerous NLP tasks which provides a overview of their evolution. Finally, various models are summarized, compared and contrast thus put forward a detailed understanding of the past, present and future of deep learning in Natural Language Processing.

To use Noam Chomsky's words, "researchers do not get discoveries in the sciences by just taking huge amounts of data, feeding data into a computer and doing a statistical analysis of data: that's not the way researchers understand things, there is a need of theoretical insights". Depending on machine learning in fact makes a good guess based on past experience, because some of the sub-symbolic methods creates correlation and the decision-making process is more probabilistic.

Figure 3. Schematic diagram of Convolutional Neural Network framework
Source: A unified architecture for natural language processing: Deep neural networks with multitask learning (Collobert and J. Weston in Proceedings of the 25th international conference on Machine learning. ACM, 2008, pp. 160–167)

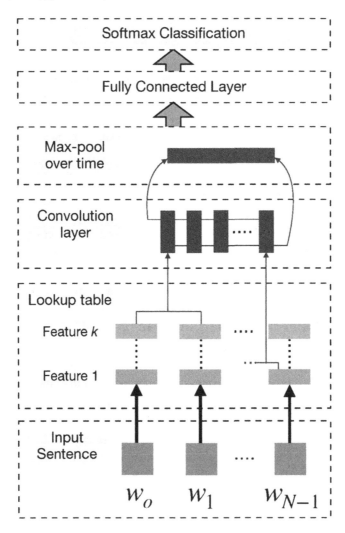

Neural Bag-of-Ngrams

Bofang Li et al introduced a Bag-of-ngrams (BoN) models that are commonly used to represent text (Bofang Li et al., 2017). One of the main disadvantages of traditional BoN models is the ignorance of n-gram's semantics. In this work, the concept of Neural Bag-of-ngrams (Neural-BoN) is proposed, which replaces one single n-gram representation in traditional BoN with different semantic n-gram representations by adding n-grams to word embeddings model. Two different representations are proposed to capture more semantics like topic or sentiment tendencies they are Text guided ngram representation and label guided n-gram representation . Neural-BoN with the former two n-gram representations achieves the results on 4 document level classification datasets and 6 semantic relatedness categories. Compared to traditional BoN models, proposed Neural-BoN is efficient, robust and easy to implement, so further expected it to be a strong baseline method and to be used in more real-world applications.

Neural-BoN model learns a text vector by calculating the belonging neural n-gram vectors along with weights (Bizzoni and Mehdi Ghanimifard, 2018). Compared to the unigram version, bigrams improve the performance of Neural-BoN on most of the datasets, while further trigrams needs larger dataset to improves the performance. As for future research three types of n-gram representations are introduced which shows effectiveness on text classification task and semantic relatedness task: Context Guided N-gram Representation (CGNR), Text Guided N-gram Representation (TGNR) and Label Guided N-gram Representation (LGNR).

THE INFLUENCE OF BIGRAM CONSTRAINTS ON WORD RECOGNITION BY HUMANS: IMPLICATIONS FOR COMPUTER SPEECH RECOGNITION

Ronald A. Cole et al has shown a way to bridge the gap between human and machine performance on speech recognition tasks. Recognition of words in telephone conversations is better than text representation (Cole, Yan and Bailey, 2001). Based on the experience this work summarize that human perception typically delivers much more accurate results than word recognition over the telephone.

One way to address the gap is to study the sources of linguistic information related to the speech signal which is important in word recognition, and then evaluate how well a machine utilize this information relative to humans. As an initial step in this direction, there is a need to measure word recognition performance of listeners presented with vocabulary words from the Switchboard corpus. Stimuli consisted of actual utterances of words that are taken from the Switchboard corpus, which includes high quality recordings of word utterances in Switchboard conversations. Also the recordings of word sequences with zero, medium and high bigram probabilities based on a language model computed from transcriptions of the same datasets. The results show that human listeners are good at understanding the words in the absence of word sequence constraints, but the statistical language models fails to capture much of the high level linguistic information needed to recognize words in a fluent speech.

MAIN FOCUS OF THE CHAPTER: WHATELSE NEEDED TO DO RESEARCH?

The existing Neural networks Language Models (NNLM) have evolved in recent years as an alternative to estimate and store n-gram Language Models. In NNLM, Words are generally represented using a method called embedding vectors. A simple NNLM architecture creates the Markov assumption and gets a input as the concatenated embedding vectors for the vocabulary words represented in the n-gram context to one or more layers each has an affine transform which is followed by a non-linearity function. The output of the last such layer is then given as input to the output layer consisting again an affine transform but this time it is followed by an exponential non-linearity function that is then normalized to get a guaranteed proper probability over the vocabulary words.

The NNLM with affine transform is commonly named as feed-forward architecture for an n-gram LM (FF-NNLM). But the proposed NNLM with recurrent properties uses sigmoid activation function which needs some basic knowledge to understand, so the following topics of main focus concentrates on fundamental terms of the NNLM.

Feature Engineering

The first fundamental term which is needed to be understood in feature engineering, that is usually done after text preprocessing. Nowadays text data offers a wide range of possibilities to generate different types of features. But sometimes, this process ends up with generating lots of different features, to an extent that processing of these features becomes a painful task. Hence there is a need to meticulously analyze the extracted features. Therefore, following methods explained below will help in reducing the dimension of the generated data set. Following subtopic is the list of popular feature engineering methods used now a days:

1. **N-grams:** N-gram is one of the popular feature engineering method which takes words as count from the dataset. In the dataset, one word is known as 1-gram, such as movie, tamil. Similarly, two word in the dataset is called as 2-gram, such as Thank You, Good Movie and then 3-gram etc. The objective behind the above all technique is to explore the chances of using one or two or more words in order to give more information to the neural model.

2. **Feature Hashing:** Feature Hashing method uses the hashing strategy that reduces the dimension of document by achieving lesser column. This method needs only lesser memory because it uses index to access data instead of wasting memory by accessing whole data.

3. **TF - IDF:** TF-IDF is abbreviated as Term Frequency - Inverse Document Frequency. This method proves that a learning algorithm gets more information from the rarely occurring words compared to frequently occurring words. By allocating weight for each terms in vocabulary this method declares importance of each word. While assinging weights for each term, frequently occuring terms are weighted lower and the rarely occurring terms get weighted higher. Term Frequency is calculated as a number of occurences of a term in a document divided by all the terms in the document. Inverse Document Frequency is calculated as a ratio of log for the total documents in the corpus divided by number of documents with the particular terms in the dataset. Finally, TF-IDF is calculated as TF multiplied by IDF.

4. **Jaccard Similarity:** This feature engineering method uses separate distance metric which is used in text analysis. Consider two vector representation created from word vocabulary thus a distance metric can be calculated as ratio of the terms which are found in both vectors divided by the terms which are available in either of the two vectors. In order to create features of the dataset using distance metrics, first create collection of similar documents and then assign a unique label to each document in a new column. So the formula used in this technique is: (A ∩ B)/(A U B).

5. **Cosine Similarity:** This technique is used to find the similar document from the corpus. Cosine similarity is one of the prevalently used method to calculate the distance metric which is used in text analysis. Distance metric is found by multiplying two vector representation created by using the words from vocabulary.

6. **Levenshtein Distance:** This method is used to create a new feature from the text which is based on the distance between two text. The distance metric is found by analysing long text from which shorter text is generated and then if another text is given, shorter text is found in both text. If both shorter text is found between the two text, then maximum value 1 is returned.

Bag of Word

BoW or Bag-of-Word model gives different methods to extract the features from the text of dataset, which is further used in modeling like machine learning algorithm, neural network etc.. A BoW approach is used to represent a text from vocabulary that defines the frequency of words within a document in dataset. This includes two important stages they are: First stage creates a vocabulary of a known words and the second stage calculates the frequency of a known words in dataset. A Bag-of-Word approach is a efficient and flexible method that proposes several different way to extract features from the document in dataset.

Bag-of-Word or BoW method is named so because this method ignore any information about the text that includes order or the structure of the text. This model is concerned about the fact that whether the known words are found in the document from the dataset or not in the dataset. In one of the famous natural language processing authors article, the BoW method is defined as a common feature extracting approach which includes both sentence and document from the dataset and also it includes a histogram of the text within the sentence. Thus, this method considers word count as a feature from the document.

Since the frequency of the word is counted from the document it is useful to find whether the documents from the dataset is similar or not. So the goal of Bag-of-word approach is to learn something about the meaning of the content. The complexity of this approach is increased based on the design of creating a vocabulary and also by calculating the presence of the known word from the document. In this work, the movie review document is analysed and the feature is extracted as word count, then finally given as input to the neural model developed.

Word Embedding

Next stage followed by the creation of the vocabulary with the known word is to create a vector representation for the filtered word from the document. By using word embedding method, individual words are considered to create vector representation. Important property for the word embedding method is to generate a similar representation for same words from the sentence or document in dataset. This step is considered as one of the key breakthroughs of deep learning challenge in natural language processing issues.

Each word in the document are represented as real-valued vectors in a predefined vector space [Chih-Fong Tsai, 2012]. Word Embedding is a technique in which individual words are mapped to one vector and that vector values are studied in order to represent those values in a neural network. Thus this technique is often collaborated with deep learning field to achieve good result. Vector representation of a words are displayed in two ways they are: sparse vector representation and dense vector representation. In dense vector representation, each words are mapped to one vector which has one or more dimensions. And in other hand, sparse vector representation uses thousands or millions of vector dimensions for each word that is often used in the hot encoding method.

The hot encoding method uses a individual hot encoded word that is mapped to a single word vector. The developed word vectors are summed up and fed as input into a supervised learning algorithms. But in case of recurrent neural network each word are given as individual input in sequence. Thus a method to learn a embedding layer in a neural network there is a need of lot of training data which makes the above process slow.

In order to learn word embedding process in neural network model, two different models are introduced they are: Continuous Bag-of-Words (CBOW model) and Continuous Skip-Gram model. The former learning model learns the word embedding process by predicting the current text based on the context. And the latter model learns the word embedding process by predicting the surrounding words based on the current word. In both model a configurable parameter is used which is a window of neighbouring words that gives context. This context is used in above both model to learn the word embedding process.

Bigram

Bigram is generated by using N-gram language model in which N=2. Bigram or Digram is a collection of two adjacent words from a string. Main application of bigram model is used for simple statistical analysis of text that is included in cryptography, speech recognition, computational linguistics and so on.

One of the variations from bigram is called as skipping bigram or gappy bigram in which gaps between the words are allowed. This kind of bigram allows some simulation of dependencies and also avoids connecting words. Gappy bigram with explicit dependency relationships are often found in head word bigrams. Bigram helps to calculate the conditional probability of a text given the preceding text.

Thus the conditional probability $P()$ of a word W_n given the preceding word W_{n-1} is equal to the probability of the particular word bigram, other method to find the probability by dividing the co-occurrence of the two words $P(W_{n-1}, W_n)$, by the probability of the preceding word. For example Thank you is a bigram, Indian Great Wall is a trigram and He is my neighbour is a 4-gram. The conditional probability of the bigram are categorized into three parts they are: zero bigram probability, medium bigram probability and high bigram probability.

Figure 4. Architecture diagram of Hybrid Model
Source: *Weakly Supervised Sentiment Analysis Using Joint Sentiment Topic Detection With Bigrams.*
Pavitra.R and PCD.Kalaivaani. (2015). IEEE Sponsored Second International Conference On
Electronics And Communication Systems.

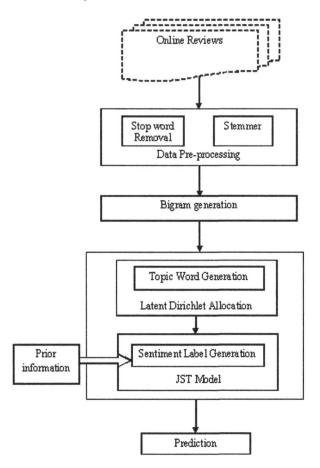

Text Classification In NLP

Text classification in nlp is similar to that of feature engineering that are more prevalently used in spam detection and sentiment analysis. The features are extracted from the text by using bag-of-word, TF-IDF, cosine similarity and other two different methods. In the text classification, first step is to pre-processing step in which punctuations are removed and all the text are converted into lowercase.

Second stage is to construct the vocabulary with a known word by using a different document from the dataset. After the construction of the vocabulary, vector representation is created for all the individual words in the vocabulary. Then a N-gram language model is constructed for the vector representation of each word that does sentiment analysis.

Most of the text classification methods are based on the document term matrix that are often referred as unigram or bag-of-words. In order to find the sentiment in a document each words from the document are analysed for example, consider a sentence "Good movie must watch it again" which has a sentiment of pleasure. In this sentence word "Good" indicates the happy feeling of the reviewer so a model can easily predict the sentiment of the sentence by analysing each individual words.

SOLUTIONS AND RECOMMENDATION

Movie reviews are categorized in this project by using RNN model which is developed by using keras library in python programming language. Different datasets of movie reviews are collected from online databases which is divided as training set and testing set with bigram words. Anaconda Navigator is used along with neuralnet keras library to implement inbuild RNN(Recurrent Neural Network) model. Most of the online reviews are categorized as very positive, regardless of content. In addition, most of the online movie reviews had almost equal amount likelihood of being in the very negative or very positive category with very positive being more likely most of the time.

Online movie reviews are either very positive or very negative so most of the content from the dataset will fall into one of these categories in the model. So, by adjusting the training data to have equal amounts of reviews for each category will yield better results. The Prediction API for a serious categorization task is implemented, with also a strong enough background in machine learning which tweaks the model before using the Prediction API to analyse and host it. In short, the Prediction API is used as cloud-based access to the existing model that already works with help of libraries. The backward nature of the Prediction API makes it difficult to diagnose and correct any data problems that exists.

The developed model is trained and tested by giving reviews which produced the following output. The reviews are analysed and the percentage of positivity or negativity is shown to the user inorder to differentiate between positive or negative reviews.

Review: [I would recommend it. Best Movie that I have seen ever!]
Sentiment: POSITIVE (59.25%)
Review: [Waste of time. Bad Movie]
Sentiment: NEGATIVE (70.51%)

Dataset

1.   Movie Review Data: http://www.cs.cornell.edu/people/pabo/movie-review-data/
2.   Corpora: Online Collection of text and speech which can be used as dataset
3.   Movie Review Polarity Dataset:http://www.cs.cornell.edu/people/pabo/movie-review-data/review_polarity.tar.Gz
4.   A Sentimental Education: Sentiment Analysis Using Subjectivity Summarization Based on Minimum Cuts, 2004. http://xxx.lanl.gov/abs/cs/0409058

Outputs and Discussions

The dataset is preprocessed by doing different operations like: splitting the tokens on white space, remove the punctuations from words, remove all the words which are not properly comprised of alphabetical characters, remove all the stop words and finally remove all the words that have less than or equal to one characters.

One of the important steps for bag-of-word model is to construct the vocabulary, which is predefined for the datasets. The frequent bigram words from all the datasets are created along with the count and stored in a class. Which is then parsed by a snippet to remove the low occurence bigram words from the vocabulary. Bag-of-word model has a most prevalent job to extract the features from the text which is then given as input to neural model, in this project it is a RNN(Recurrent Neural Network) model.

The vector representation is generated from the words in vocabulary which corresponds to the words in reviews. For example the vocabulary consist of bigram words like good movie, bad movie, not worth, pleasant time etc...Scoring methods are used in this step to provide the score of the words in the vector representation. So at the first stage, reviews are converted into lines of tokens and then reviews are encoded into the bag-of-word model representation. The bigram tokens are filtered from the dataset and lines of tokens are stored into new document. Labels are given to reviews as zero for negative reviews and one for positive reviews.

The encoded reviews are then given as input to the neural model in which the input layer is equal to the number of bigram words in vocabulary. The neural model developed in this project does the sentiment analysis work on the movie reviews. One of the advantages of the RNN model is that the previous output is given as input to the current neuron. The model has the hidden state which stores certain information. Nearly 50 neurons are assigned for hidden layer and the output layer works with stigmoid activation function to yield 0 for negative reviews or 1 for positive reviews.

Scoring methods which exists so far are: binary, count, tfidf and freq. Binary scoring method is used in this project which encounters positive(1) and negative(0) reviews. The aim of the probabilistic language modelling is to evaluate the probability of a sentence of sequence of bigram words:

$$P(w)=P(w_1,w_2,w_3,\ldots w_n)$$

and also used to find the probability of the next bigram word in the sequence:

$$P(w_5 | w_1,w_2,w_3,w_4)$$

A model that computes either of the operation is called a Language Model. There are different methods used for calculatiing probability and for markov assumption. They are:

Method for calculating probability

- Conditional probability
- Chain rule

Method using markov assumption

- Markov Property
- N-gram model

For the demonstration purpose, IMDB large movie review dataset is used that is made available in online by Stanford. The data in the above dataset contains the ratings given by the reviewer, the polarity and the full comment given by the online movie reviewer. First step is to convert the full comments into the individual sentences with bigram words, then introduce notation for both start and end of sentence and the text is cleaned by removing any punctuation and lowercase of all the bigram words. The unigram model which calculates the probability of words are developed and output is produced for input (has,been), shown in Figure 5.

Figure 5. Unigram probability predicted result
Source: Own

```
In [49]:   word1= 'has'
           word2='been'

           prob_word1 = w_list1[w_list['words'] == word1]['prob'].iloc[0]
           prob_word2 = w_list1[w_list['words'] == word2]['prob'].iloc[0]

           uni_prob = prob_word1*prob_word2

           print('The unigram probability of the word "been" occurring after the word "has" has the
           probability is: ', np.round(uni_prob,20))
```

The unigram probability of the word "been" occurring after the word "has" has the probability is: 0.00006895

Both unigram model and bigram model is developed for comparision purpose. The unigram model developed is not accurate, so the bigram estimation is introduced instead of later model. Applying the bigram model is more complex compared to unigram model, at first calculate the co-occurrences of each words into a word-word matrix fed into new document. The counts of the words are then normalised by the counts of the previous word as shown in the following equation:

$$P\,(w_i \mid w_{i-1}) \approx$$

Therefore, for example, if the calculation has to be improved for the P(been|has), at first count the occurrences of (has,been) and divide this by the count of occurrences of (t0). count (w$_{i-1}$). Thus the calculation is improved by using bigram language model which is shown in Figure 6.

As studied before, to effectively utilise the bigram language model their is the need to compute the word-word matrix for all bigram word pair occurrences. With this, there is a way to find the most likely word to follow the current word. Even though this also needs an exceptional amount of time if the dataset is large. The output in Figure 7 shows the word to word matrix of the vocabulary which is the first stage of bigram probability model.

Figure 6. Bigram probability predicted result
Source: Own

```
In [49]:   word1=' '+str ('has') +' '
           word2= str (' been ') +' '

           bigram_prob = len ( re.findall(word1 + word2, word2_list)) / len(re.findall(word2,word2_list))

           print('The bigram probability of the word " been " occurring after the word " has " has the
           probability is: ', np.round(bigram_prob,10))
```
The bigram probability of the word "been" occurring after the word "has" has the probability is: 0.0012500

Figure 7. Word Matrix generated by the model
Source: Own

words	\<s	best	movie	ever	seen	i	would	recommend	it
0	\<s	0.0	0.000569	0.000000	0.000000	0.000561	0.000000	0.002652	0.000000	0.000563
1	best	0.0	0.000000	0.000000	0.000000	0.000000	0.000000	0.000000	0.000000	0.000000
2	movie	0.0	0.000000	0.013256	0.368912	0.000000	0.000000	0.000000	0.000000	0.000000
3	ever	0.0	0.000452	0.000000	0.000000	0.000000	0.000000	0.000000	0.000000	0.365741
4	seen	0.0	0.000000	0.000000	0.134586	0.000000	0.555555	0.000000	0.000000	0.000000
5	i	0.0	0.000388	0.333333	0.000000	0.000000	0.000000	0.168952	0.265893	0.000000
6	would	0.0	0.000000	0.000000	0.000000	0.589423	0.000000	0.000000	0.000000	0.123689
7	recommend	0.0	0.000256	0.000000	0.000000	0.000000	0.000000	0.000000	0.000000	0.000000
8	it	0.0	0.000000	0.000000	0.000000	0.000000	0.000000	0.000000	0.589632	0.000000

As the final stage of sentiment analysis a graph is generated for most common word after a current word. This graph is used to predict the occurrence of next word which is used to predict the sentiment based on the reviews. This model is used in several other businesses like Amazon and Google to predict the users sentiment about particular product. With this, the graph shows some examples of the most likely word to follow the given word (Figure 8).

FUTURE RESEARCH AND DIRECTION

The neural network model developed in this work has a important shortcoming that error analysis is not done, this might lead to a interesting future contribution to this project. In future, a better improvement can also be done by implementing systematic analysis of the errors in the developed network model. Extension to this work can be done by elaborating the range of comparing different machine learning algorithms, so that each contribution of the input terms can be found. And the deep learning concept can be improved by included larger datasets with different set of features.

CONCLUSION

In this study, a neural network language model is developed in which bag-of-word approach is used to extract the word count feature for all the individual word from the vocabulary developed at preprocessing step. After extracting the features, bigram of words are maintained to get more accurate prediction as the result. Then the generated

Figure 8. Graph for Most Common word
Source: Own

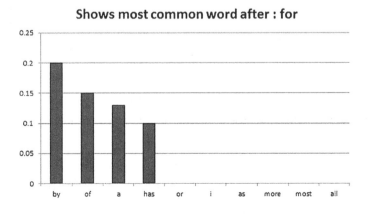

vector representation for each known words are given as input to network neural model. This model does the sentiment analysis of the movie reviews and produces the predicted result with the probability. The scoring method uses in binary count method which notes the occurrence of all known words.

REFERENCES

Barry, J. (2016). Sentiment analysis of online reviews using bag-of-words and LSTM approaches. Google Tech Report. A. Suresh Babu and P. N. V. S.

Bizzoni, Y., & Ghanimifard, M. (2018). Bigrams and BiLSTMs Two neural networks for sequential metaphor detection. In *Proceedings of the Workshop on Figurative Language Processing*, pp. 91–101. 10.18653/v1/W18-0911

Brownlee, J. (2017). Deep learning for natural language processing. Machine learning mastery. Edition: v1.1

Chelba, C., Norouzi, M., & Bengio, S. (2017, June 20). N-gram language modelling using recurrent neural network estimation. arXiv:1703.10724v2 [cs.CL]. Google Tech Report

Cole, R. A., Yan, Y., & Bailey, T. (2001). The influence of bigram constraints on word recognition by humans: Implications for computer speech recognition. ARPA HLT meeting.

Collobert, R., Weston, J., Bottou, L., Karlen, M., Kavukcuoglu, K., & Kuksa, P. (2011). Natural language processing (almost) from scratch. *Journal of Machine Learning Research*, 2493–2537.

Kumar, P. (2010). Comparing neural network approach with Ngram approach for text categorization. *International Journal on Computer Science and Engineering*, 2(1). pp. 80-83.

Li, B., Liu, T., & Zhao, Z., Wang, P., & Du, X. (2017). Neural bag-of-Ngrams. In *Proceedings of the Thirty-First AAAI Conference on Artificial Intelligence*. pp. 3067-3074.

Mikolov, T., Chen, K., Corrado, G., & Dean, J. (2013, Sept. 7). Efficient estimation of word representations in vector space. arXiv:1301.3781v3 [cs.CL]. Google Tech Report

Tsai, C.-F. (2012). Bag-of-words representation in image annotation: A review article. *ISRN Artificial Intelligence*, *2012*, 1–19. doi:10.5402/2012/376804

Youngy, T., Hazarikaz, D., Poria, S., & Cambria, E. (2018, November). Recent trends in deep learning based natural language processing. arXiv:1708.02709v8 [cs.CL]. Google Tech Report

Zhang, Y., Jin, R., & Zhou, Z.-H. (2012). Understanding bag-of-words model: A statistical framework. In *ECCV Workshop on Statistical Learning in Computer Vision*, Prague, Czech Republic

KEY TERMS AND DEFINITIONS

Bag of Words Model: The bag-of-words model is a method of representing text data while modeling text with machine learning algorithms.

Corpus: Corpus is a original repositories or online dataset which is used in most of the NLP projects.

Deep Learning: This method is also called as hierarchical learning or deep structured learning. It is one of the machine learning method that is based on learning methods like supervised, semi-supervised or unsupervised. The only difference between deep learning and other machine learning algorithm is that deep learning method uses big data as input.

Generalization: Generalization of markov assumption is done by calculating the probability of a word depending on the probability of the n previous words trigrams, 4-grams, etc.

Markov Assumption: Markov assumption calculates the probability of a word depends only on the probability of a limited history.

NLP: Natural Language Processing is prevalently used to analyse the text or speech inorder to make machine understand the words like human.

Sentence: Sentence is a unit of written words which forms a document in a dataset.

Tokens: Token is a total number of words in a sentence from the dataset.

APPENDIX: N-GRAM ANALYSIS

Natural Language Processing (NLP) is the method used to analyse the written dialect with the help of computer. The real time applications of NLP are sentiment analysis, relationship extraction, language modelling, question answering and much more. In order to understand the N-gram analysis considers a very simple sentence "Worst Experience would never watch this movie again".

First step is to split the sentence into consecutive set of words like (Worst, Experience), (Experience, would), (would, never), ... When splitting the words from sentence n-gram is implemented. Unigram, bigram and trigram are usually practiced in most of the nlp project.

While splitting the words it is important to remove the stop words for example "not a good" is predicted as positive and "good" is also predicted as positive. But the former word is negative, since the model only analyse each word in single manner by seeing "good" in "not a good" sentence it is wrongly predicted as positive. So the solution is to remove the stop word, thus "not a good" is changed into "not good". By considering two words a model can predict accurately the result. This is how the n-gram analysis is done in nlp projects.

Chapter 9

Deep Learning Approach for Extracting Catch Phrases from Legal Documents

Kayalvizhi S.
SSN College of Engineering, India

Thenmozhi D.
SSN College of Engineering, India

ABSTRACT

Catch phrases are the important phrases that precisely explain the document. They represent the context of the whole document. They can also be used to retrieve relevant prior cases by the judges and lawyers for assuring justice in the domain of law. Currently, catch phrases are extracted using statistical methods, machine learning techniques, and deep learning techniques. The authors propose a sequence to sequence (Seq2Seq) deep neural network to extract catch phrases from legal documents. They have employed several layers, namely embedding layer, encoder-decoder layer, projection layer, and loss layer to build the deep neural network. The methodology is evaluated on IRLeD@FIRE-2017 dataset and the method has obtained 0.787 and 0.607 as mean average precision and recall scores respectively. Results show that the proposed method outperforms the existing systems.

DOI: 10.4018/978-1-7998-1159-6.ch009

INTRODUCTION

In legal codes, tagging the documents with a set of keywords is essential. Keywords give out the meaning or motivation of the work in precise. The keywords extraction is a crucial task in many real time scenarios like summarizing the whole paragraph into a line, extracting the headlines in e-news, on-line correction of answer sheets, separating the e-mails as span or not, etc. In the legal domain, the keywords are referred to as catch phrases and so extracting them from the large legal documents becomes a very useful task in many aspects. For example, whenever lawyers prepare for their cases, they research extensively on prior cases which is a time consuming process. The legal practitioners can save a lot of time by quickly evaluating the relevance of the document. Thus, they play a crucial role in reducing the search time and also act as a tool for finding similarity between two documents. Legal texts are long and have complex structures. This makes their complete reading time-consuming and arduous. So, it is essential for advocates and judges to have a brief representation of the core legal issues described in the act of law. One way to list these issues is by using keywords or key phrases, which are known as catch phrases in the legal authority. Thus, an automated catchphrase extraction approach is needed toobtain context in legal documents. The catch phrase extraction is done by a deep learning approach which handles sequence to sequence problems.

Deep learning is the subset of machine learning which can process more data than the machine learning. The deep learning approach does not expect us to extract features as in machine learning which makes this approach much easier one. There are many deep learning approaches such as Convolution Neural Network, Recurrent Neural Network (RNN), Deep Belief Network, etc. Among these architectures, Long Short Term Memory (LSTM), a variant of RNN is made use since it processes the sequence to sequence related problem.

BACKGROUND

Natural Language Processing

Text processing refers to manipulation of text in an automated way. Manipulation of text can be anything like correcting errors, analyzing the mood, classifying the e-mails, tagging the important terms, summarizing the content, answering the questions, correcting the answers, translating the sentences, etc., Natural Language Processing (NLP) is concerned with making the computer to perform these text manipulation scenarios in natural language. The basic steps in NLP of text includes sentence segmentation, word tokenization, predicting Parts-of-Speech (POS), text lemmatization, cleaning the text, dependency parsing, named entity recognition. Segmentation refers to splitting up of sentences into words or meaningful phrases. Word tokenization is the process of making the sentences into tokens. Predicting the POS is the step where the parts of speech like nouns, adjectives, verbs, etc. are guessed. In lemmatization, the words of different forms like tenses, plurals are all made in into a single form of word. Cleaning the text refers to the removal of stop words and unwanted punctuation marks. In dependency parsing, a single parent will be selected for the depended words in the sentence. Named Entity Recognition is the process of labeling the noun phrases with named entities such as location, person, place, etc.

Considering a scenario of sentiment analysis of the text data, there are many approaches and classification methods. A typical machine learning approach is done by a steps which includes the above NLP phases of segmentation, tokenization, predicting POS, lemmatization, parsing and then vectorizing the text by any of the methods which includes Bag Of Words, word embeddings, glove, etc. and finally classifying by using classifiers.

Catch Phrase Extraction

In general, keywords can be extracted from a given a text by various approaches like scoring using deep neural networks (Tran et.al, 2018), RAKE (Bhat et.al, 2018), Kea (Nguyen et.al, 2007), ranking SVM (Xin Jiang et.al, 2007). These works are done with different approaches and are on different datasets. Different approaches such as statistical method, machine learning and deep learning methods are used to extract the catchphrases using the dataset IRLed@FIRE-2017. In probabilistic method (Kulkarni et.al, 2017) each of the training statements can be tokenized into a list and their Parts-of-Speech (POS) tags can be generated using Python NLTK library. B-LEGAL and I-LEGAL tags are then extracted for Begin and Intermediate of the catch phrases respectively and O for other tokens. CRF model can be generated which can then used to predict from test data. The CRF++ model could be used to predict custom NER tags that are served as catch phrases. Machine learning approaches (Koboyatshwene et.al, 2017) namely RAKE and MAUI are also used to extract catch phrases. RAKE is an unsupervised machine learning approach which does not require any training and works by first selecting candidates or key-words. MAUI is a supervised approach which was build based on four open-source software components: the Key phrase extraction algorithm (Kea) for phrase filtering and computing n-gram extractions, Weka for creating topic indexing models and applying them to new documents. Deep learning methodology (Bhargava et.al, 2017) involves a pipelined approach which is divided into four phase's namely pre-processing, candidate phrase generation, creating vector representations for the phrases, training a Long Short Term Memory (LSTM) network. Preprocessing includes removal of special characters, numbers and converting all characters to lower case. In candidate generation, n-grams with n in range one to four were created from the text. Then, the vectors are generated using Word2Vec model in creating vector representation phase. The training is done using LSTM. In statistical method (Das et.al, 2017) a set of potential meaningful phrases were created for each file and then are classified using deep neural network. Steps involved are preprocessing, phrase generation, feature selection, label the vectors, classification and training the model. In preprocessing, stop words, punctuation and non-ASCII characters and numbers are removed. In phrase generation, potential meaningful phrases based on common grammar of phrases were created. In feature selection, different features are extracted on these phrases. The features used here include grammar, TF-IDF, position in a document and are labeled as valid or invalid. Deep neural network was used for classification. During training gradient descent optimizer is used to optimize the result. Different machine learning techniques can be employed for the extraction of catch phrases. But, in our work, deep learning model is preferred since it is expected to give out better performance in short span of time.

Deep Learning Models

Deep learning is a subset of machine learning in which the machine learns the algorithm from input and output to perform a task instead of learning the procedure to perform the same. The major advantage in case of deep learning is that it does not expect us to extract the features as in machine learning. Considering a classification scenario of spam e-mails, the input is the email content and output is the class label of e-mail i.e. either spam or not-spam. For machine learning model the features must be extracted for the e-mail content and they should be given as input to the model whereas in deep learning model, the input can be the e-mails without any feature extraction. Considering the output, in machine learning model, the output will the probabilities of two classes while in deep learning, it will be the class labels. Deep learning models are built with the neural networks which accept input, processes it and expels the prediction. Deep learning architecture is a neural network with several layers in between the input layer and output layer. There are many deep learning architectures namely deep neural network, deep belief network, recurrent neural network and convolution neural network. Among these recurrent neural network processes sequence to sequence kind of problems such as video captioning, machine translation, sequence classification, value memorization, etc.

Deep Neural Network

Deep neural network is a neural network with more number of hidden layers. Thus, the level of complexity increases in deep neural networks than that of neural networks.

Deep Belief Network

Deep belief network is a deep neural network in which only the hidden layers are connected to each other but not the nodes. In this architecture, each layer is Restricted Boltzmann Machine for training phase and training is done by Contrastive Diversion algorithm. For fine tuning, feed forward network is used. These networks are used to extract features for text classification (Jiang et.al, 2018).

Convolutional Neural Network

Convolutional Neural Network (CNN) is a deep neural network with a layer that performs convolution. It is a simple mathematical operation which is the sum of multiples. CNN can have many different layers in addition to convolutional layer such as pooling layer, activation layer and dense layer. Each layer performs a different operation. CNN are also made use for a sentence classification (Jacovi et.al, 2018). In text classification, CNN considers the word embedding representation of the text. The raw text is converted into a word embedding representation which is given to a convolutional layer. This layer has 'm' filters which produces an m-dimensional vector. The m-dimensional vectors are all combined using a max-pooling layer. The final layer will be a ReLU activation whose result is passed to a linear classification layer.

Recurrent Neural Network

Recurrent Neural Network (RNN) is a deep neural network where the input of previous stage is given as input to next stage (i.e.) current stage. Thus, they are not independent of each other so it can perform sequence to sequence related problems. RNN converts the independent activations into dependent activations by providing weights and biases of all layers the same value, thus memorizing each previous outcome by giving it as input to the next hidden layer. There are two RNNs in which one is an encoder will be updating the hidden states which produces a "Context" vector. This vector is then fed to another RNN (decoder), which translates this context to a sequence of outputs.

Long-Short Term Memory

Long-Short Term Memory (LSTM) is a variant of RNN with additional gates and cell states. Gates are a way to optionally let information through. LSTM sorts the problem of long-term dependencies by remembering the content. The gates include input gate, forget gate and output gate. The input gate gets the input, forget gate decides the content which must be remembered and forgotten and the output gate gives us the output. The cell states remember values over arbitrary state of time intervals and the gates regulate the flow of information in the cell state. Among the deep learning architectures, LSTM is the one that processes the sequence to sequence problems.

Sequence to Sequence Model

Sequence to sequence model is the one that converts sequence of one domain into sequence of another domain. The sequence of one domain may be the sentence in one language and the sequence of another domain may be in another language. In trivial cases, the input and output sequences will be of same length. Sequence-to-Sequence model or the encoder-decoder model has an encoder and decoder. The encoder part will read the input sentence, understand its meaning, and then will create a learned representation. This representation will be forwarded to the decoder network which generates another sequence of representation. The sequence generated by the decoder part forms the output. As there is no explicit one-to-one relation between the input and output sequences, the lengths of input and output sequences need not be the same always.

Figure 1 explains an example of Sequence to Sequence model in which the next sentence is predicted. The input sequence is "How are you" and the output is expected to be an answer for that sequence. In this Seq2Seq model, the input is converted to a learned representation by the encoder which is transmitted to the decoder where it is decoded into the output "I am fine" with the help of previous learning of the machine.

Neural Machine Translation

Neural Machine Translation (NMT) is the Seq2Seq model made use in their work. An NMT system first reads the source sentence and builds a "thought" vector using an encoder. Thought vector is a sequence of numbers that represents the sentence meaning. The decoder processes the sentence vector and emits a translation. This process is referred to as the encoder-decoder architecture. NMT deals the local translation problem in the traditional phrase-based approach, in which captures

Figure 1. Sequence to sequence model

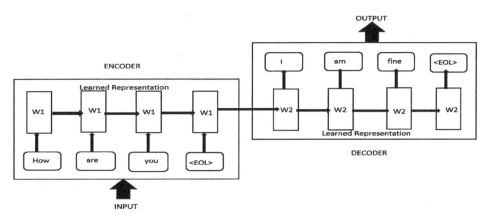

long-range dependencies in languages and produce much more fluent translations. At a high level, the NMT model consists of two recurrent neural networks. They are encoder RNN (Recurrent Neural Network) and decoder RNN. The encoder RNN simply ingests the input source words and the decoder processes the target sentence. The encoder will not predict the output while the decoder predicts the next words. In their work, they consider a deep multi-layer RNN which is unidirectional and uses LSTM as a recurrent unit.

Embedding

For the embedding layer to work, a vocabulary must be chosen, one for each language. Initially, a vocabulary size (v) is selected. The most frequent 'v' words are considered as unique ones and all other words are converted to an "unknown" token. And then all words are given the same embedding layer. During training, the embedding weights are learned as one set per language.

Encoder-Decoder

Once the word embeddings are retrieved, they are then fed as input into the main network, which consists of two multi-layer RNNs an encoder for the source language and a decoder for the target language. Zero vectors are used as the starting states of encoder RNN.

The information of the source should also be accessed by the decoder. It is done by initializing it with the last hidden state of the encoder, encoder state. The hidden state is passed at the source word to the decoder side.

Projection

Projection layer is the final layer that converts (projects) the internal representation to the larger one. It links the hidden state to the output layer. It can help LSTM to converge faster.

Loss

The model takes an input word or character vector, and tries to guess the next "best" word, based on training examples. Categorical cross entropy is a quantitative way of measuring how good the guess is. As the model iterates over the training set, it makes less mistakes in guessing the next best word (or character).The loss is minimized by back propagation.

Gradient Computation and Optimization

One of the important steps in training RNNs is gradient clipping which is done by the global norm. The max value, max_gradient_norm, is often set to a value like 5 or 1. The last step is selecting the optimizer. The Adam optimizer is a common choice. A learning rate is also selected. The value of learning rate can is usually in the range 0.0001 to 0.001; and can be set to decrease as training progresses. Standard SGD is used along with a decreasing learning rate schedule for better performance.

MAIN FOCUS OF THE CHAPTER

Sequence to sequence model may be used to extract catch phrases. The catchphrase extraction is done by a pipelined approach as shown in Figure 2, in which the legal texts are all preprocessed. Then, word vector representations were created and finally, the model is trained using LSTM. Then, the catch phrases are extracted finally.

SOLUTIONS AND RECOMMENDATIONS

Data Set Description

The dataset used to evaluate the approach is IRLeD@FIRE-2017 (Information Retrieval in Legal Domain shared task at Forum of Information Retrieval Evaluation). The dataset consists of 100 legal documents and their corresponding gold standard

Figure 2. Overall description of process

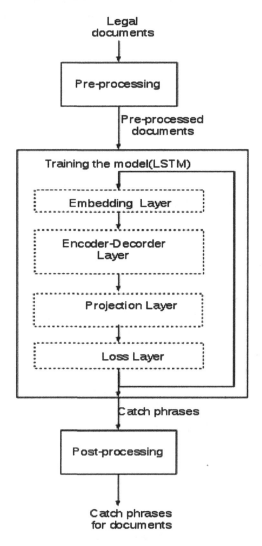

catch phrases for training and the test set consists of 300 documents whose catch phrases were to be found.

Example:
Document:

After hearing the Learned Counsel for both the parties at length, we find ourselves in agreement with the view taken by the Customs, Excise and Service Tax Appellate Tribunal (hereinafter referred to as 'CESTAT') in the impugned judgment [2006

(204) E.L.T. 61 (Tribunal)] that the product of the Appellant herein known as "Baygon Mosquito Specialist" is covered by Serial No. 37 (i.e., 'Mosquito coils, mats and other mosquito repellants') of Notification No. 9/2000-C.E. (N.T.): MANU/ CUST/0040/2000, dated 1-3-2000. Since this Notification is issued Under Section 4A of the Central Excise Act, 1944, the Revenue rightly assessed the Excise duty under the aforesaid provision. Finding no merit in any of these appeals, the same are dismissed.

Catch phrases:

Agreement, Appeal, Appellate Tribunal, Commissioner of Central Excise, Date, Duty, Excise Duty, Goods, Hearing, Information, Notification, Service, Tax, Tribunal, Valuation, Valuation of Goods.

Pre-Processing

The given data has to be prepared in a required format for giving as input for the Seq2Seq deep neural network. This network accepts set of input sequences and decode to catch phrases. Thus, the input sequences from all the given case documents are used to construct the input sequences and the corresponding catch phrases are constructed as output sequences to the network. The text should be preprocessed before giving as input to the model. The documents are preprocessed by removing the special characters and extra newlines. The unique words from the documents are extracted, which forms the vocabulary. A part of the training data is considered as development set which is used to validate the model.

Training Using LSTM

Word embeddings are obtained for all the words in the pre-processed documents in the embedding layer. The output from this layer is given to encoder-decoder layer in which vectors for the catch phrases are all trained using encoder and decoder. A multi-layered Recurrent Neural Network is used for this encoding and decoding process. In this approach, bi-directional LSTM is used as a recurrent unit. The output from the encoder-decoder layer is connected to the output layer via projection layer. This layer used the Soft-max activation function which predicts the output sequences (catch phrases). This layered approach is implemented using Neural Machine Translation model (Minh-Thang Luong et.al, 2017). The loss layer calculates the training loss which is reduced by back propagation of error and the catch phrases are extracted. A 2-layered encoder-decoder is used with 128 batch size and 0.2 dropout to build the model.

Handling Large Documents

For handling large document, the same methodology is used with a one more step of pre-processing. In addition to the removal of special characters and extra new line, the documents are split up into sentences. The catch phrases are generated for each and every sentence, as shown in Figure 3. In this figure, the given corpus containing the 100 documents (D1, D2 ..... D100) are are written into a single file master_doc_train/test_file for training/testing data respectively. Each document (D1) in the master file contains many paragraphs which may vary from m to n depending upon the number of paragraphs. Thus they are split into paragraphs which are denoted by P1,P2,P3,....Pn in master_doc_train/test_para_file. Master_catch_train/ test_para_file contains the corresponding catch phrases of paragraphs which are represented as Pc1, Pc2, Pc3,....Pcn. For training, master_doc_train/test_para_file and master_catch_train/test_para_file are given as input to the model.

After extracting the catch phrases for the individual sentences, they are combined based on the document ids as shown in Figure 4. The output of the model is the output_test file which contains the catch phrases for the test data given in the master_doc_test_para file which are represented as OP1, OP2, OP3, OP4....OPn. The output will the catch phrases directly which are to combined according to the paragraphs and given as output C1 for for first document, C2 for second document, etc.

Figure 3. Outline of pre-processing

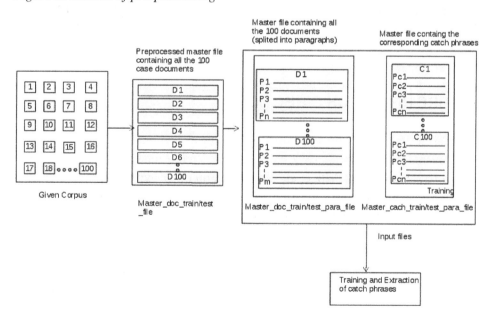

Figure 4. Outline of post processing

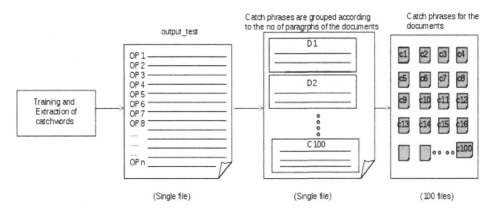

RESULTS

The performance of this approach is measured by using the metrics namely mean average precision, recall and precision@10. Precision is the fraction of relevant catch phrases retrieved to the total catch phrases retrieved. Recall is the fraction of relevant catch phrases retrieved to the total relevant catch phrases. Precision@10 is the fraction of number of relevant catch phrases until 10 retrieved to the total catch phrases retrieved. This methodology using Seq2Seq model has attained 0.787, 0.607 and 0.949 as the MAP, recall and precision@10 scores respectively. The results are shown in Table 1. The table shows that this approach performs better than the existing approaches for catch phrase extraction evaluated on IRLeD@FIRE-2017 dataset. This approach improved the precision@10 score by 66.1%, MAP score by 30.8% and recall score by 10.8% when compared with the existing approaches.

FUTURE RESEARCH DIRECTIONS

The performance may be improved further by incorporating several attention mechanisms namely Bahdanau / Normed_Bahdanau (Sutskever et.al, 2014) and Luong / Scaled Luong (Britz et.al, 2017). Several other hyper parameters such as number of layers, batch size and dropout may be fine tuned to obtain a better model. The recurrent units also may be modified in future to explore their impact in the performance.

Table 1. Comparison of existing system with proposed approach

Approaches		Precision@10	MAP	Overall Recall
Statistical method	Kulkarni et.al (Kulkarni et.al, 2017)	0.281	0.479	0.248
	Das et.al (Das et.al, 2017)	0.025	0.062	0.161
Deep learning approach	Bhargava et.al (Bhargava et.al, 2017)	0.049	0.093	0.100
Machine learning approach	Koboyatshwene et.al MAUI (Koboyatshwene et.al, 2017)	0.254	0.370	0.326
	Koboyatshwene et.al RAKE (Koboyatshwene et.al, 2017)	0.014	0.046	0.499
Proposed system		**0.942**	**0.787**	**0.607**

CONCLUSION

Catch phrases are an important tool that helps us to understand the idea of the document. Their extraction can be done many approaches namely probabilistic, machine learning and deep learning techniques. The authors have proposed a sequence to sequence model for extracting the catch phrases from the legal documents which seems to yield better results than the other methods with MAP score of 0.787.

REFERENCES

Bhargava, R., Nigwekar, S., & Sharma, Y. (2017). Catchphrase extraction from legal documents using LSTM networks. In FIRE (Working Notes). (pp. 72-73).

Bhat, A., Satish, C., D'Souza, N., & Kashyap, N. (2018). Effect of dynamic stoplist on keyword prediction in RAKE.

Britz, D., Goldie, A., Luong, M. T., & Le, Q. (2017). *Massive exploration of neural machine translation architectures.* arXiv preprint arXiv:1703.03906.

Das, S., & Barua, R. (2017). Catch phrase extraction from legal documents using deep neural network. In FIRE (Working Notes). (pp. 78-79).

Jacovi, A., Shalom, O. S., & Goldberg, Y. (2018). Understanding convolutional neural networks for text classification. *arXiv preprint arXiv:1809.08037.*

Jiang, M., Liang, Y., Feng, X., Fan, X., Pei, Z., Xue, Y., & Guan, R. (2018). Text classification based on deep belief network and softmax regression. *Neural Computing & Applications, 29*(1), 61–70. doi:10.100700521-016-2401-x

Jiang, X., Hu, Y., & Li, H. (2009, July). A ranking approach to keyphrase extraction. In *Proceedings of the 32nd international ACM SIGIR conference on Research and development in information retrieval.* (pp. 756-757). ACM.

Koboyatshwene, T., Lefoane, M., & Narasimhan, L. (2017). Machine learning approaches for catchphrase extraction in legal documents. In FIRE (Working Notes). (pp. 95-98).

Kulkarni, Y. H., Patil, R., & Shridharan, S. (2017). Detection of catchphrases and precedence in legal documents. In FIRE (Working Notes). (pp. 86-89).

Luong, M. T., Brevdo, E., & Zhao, R. (2017). Neural machine translation (seq2seq) tutorial. Retrieved from https://github. com/tensorflow/nmt

Nguyen, T. D., & Kan, M. Y. (2007, December). Keyphrase extraction in scientific publications. In *International Conference on Asian Digital Libraries* (pp. 317-326). Berlin, Germany: Springer.

Sutskever, I., Vinyals, O., & Le, Q. V. (2014). Sequence to sequence learning with neural networks. In Advances in neural information processing systems. (pp. 3104-3112).

Tran, V., Nguyen, M. L., & Satoh, K. (2018). Automatic catchphrase extraction from legal case documents via scoring using deep neural networks. *arXiv preprint arXiv:1809.05219.*

ADDITIONAL READING

Al-Ghalibi, M., Al-Azzawi, A., & Lawonn, K. (2019, March). NLP based sentiment analysis for Twitter's opinion mining and visualization. *In Eleventh International Conference on Machine Vision (ICMV 2018) (*Vol. 11041, *p.* 110412A*).* International Society for Optics and Photonics. 10.1117/12.2522679

Anta, A. F., Chiroque, L. N., Morere, P., & Santos, A. (2013). *Sentiment analysis and topic detection of Spanish tweets: A comparative study of of NLP techniques. Procesamiento del lenguaje natural, 50, 45-52.*

Badjatiya, P., Gupta, S., Gupta, M., & Varma, V. (2017, April). Deep learning for hate speech detection in tweets. *In Proceedings of the 26th International Conference on World Wide Web Companion (pp. 759-760). International World Wide Web Conferences Steering Committee.* 10.1145/3041021.3054223

Bahdanau, D., Cho, K., & Bengio, Y. (2014). *Neural machine translation by jointly learning to align and translate. arXiv preprint arXiv:1409.0473.*

Bayer, J., & Osendorfer, C. (2014). *Learning stochastic recurrent networks. arXiv preprint arXiv:1411.7610.*

Chung, J., Kastner, K., Dinh, L., Goel, K., Courville, A. C., & Bengio, Y. (2015). A recurrent latent variable model for sequential data. In Advances in neural information processing systems (pp. 2980-2988).

Fei, H., & Tan, F. (2018). Bidirectional Grid Long Short-Term Memory (BiGridLSTM): A Method to Address Context-Sensitivity and Vanishing Gradient. *Algorithms*, *11*(11), 172. doi:10.3390/a11110172

Gu, J., Wang, Z., Kuen, J., Ma, L., Shahroudy, A., Shuai, B., ... Chen, T. (2018). Recent advances in convolutional neural networks. *Pattern Recognition, 77*, 354–377. doi:10.1016/j.patcog.2017.10.013

Jianqiang, Z., Xiaolin, G., & Xuejun, Z. (2018). Deep convolution neural networks for twitter sentiment analysis. *IEEE Access: Practical Innovations, Open Solutions*, *6*, 23253–23260. doi:10.1109/ACCESS.2017.2776930

Kalchbrenner, N. E., Simonyan, K., & Espeholt, L. (2018). *U.S. Patent Application No. 16/032,971.*

Kumar, A., & Rastogi, R. (2019). Attentional Recurrent Neural Networks for Sentence Classification. In *Innovations in Infrastructure* (pp. 549–559). Singapore: Springer. doi:10.1007/978-981-13-1966-2_49

Mandal, A., Ghosh, K., Pal, A., & Ghosh, S. (2017, November). Automatic catchphrase identification from legal court case documents. In *Proceedings of the 2017 ACM on Conference on Information and Knowledge Management* (pp. 2187-2190). ACM. 10.1145/3132847.3133102

Pitsilis, G. K., Ramampiaro, H., & Langseth, H. (2018). Detecting offensive language in tweets using deep learning. *arXiv preprint arXiv:1801.04433.*

Rose, S., Engel, D., Cramer, N., & Cowley, W. (2010). Automatic keyword extraction from individual documents. *Text mining: applications and theory, 1*, 1-20.

Wehrmann, J., Becker, W. E., & Barros, R. C. (2018, April). A multi-task neural network for multilingual sentiment classification and language detection on Twitter. In *Proceedings of the 33rd Annual ACM Symposium on Applied Computing* (pp. 1805-1812). ACM. 10.1145/3167132.3167325

Wen, J., Zhou, X., Zhong, P., & Xue, Y. (2019). Convolutional Neural Network Based Text Steganalysis. *IEEE Signal Processing Letters*, *26*(3), 460–464. doi:10.1109/LSP.2019.2895286

You, R., Dai, S., Zhang, Z., Mamitsuka, H., & Zhu, S. (2018). Attentionxml: Extreme multi-label text classification with multi-label attention based recurrent neural networks. *arXiv preprint arXiv:1811.01727*.

Zhang, Y., Liu, Q., & Song, L. (2018). Sentence-state lstm for text representation. *arXiv preprint arXiv:1805.02474*.

KEY TERMS AND DEFINITIONS

Catch Phrases: The keywords that precisely describe the whole document in legal domain.

Convolutional Neural Network: A neural network with a convolutional layer which does the mathematical operation of convolution in addition to the other layers of deep neural network.

Deep Learning: A sub-field of machine learning which is based on the algorithms and layers of artificial networks.

Deep Neural Network: Neural Network with more than two layers in depth is known as deep neural network.

Information Extraction: Automated retrieval of needed information from the whole documents, databases, etc.

LSTM: Long Short Term Memory is a type of Recurrent Neural Networks (RNN) which is capable of learning long term dependencies from the sequence of terms.

Machine Learning: A field of study of algorithms and statistical methods that allows software application to predict the accurate result.

Neural Network: Fully connected network with minimum of three layers namely input layer, output layer and hidden layer.

Recurrent Neural Network: Deep neural network with recursive operation of giving the output of previous as input for next state so that the inputs and outputs are all dependent to each other.

Chapter 10

Enhanced Sentiment Classification Using Recurrent Neural Networks

Arunmozhi Mourougappane
St.Joseph's College of Engineering, India

Suresh Jaganathan
SSN College of Engineering, India

ABSTRACT

Sentiment Analysis and classification becomes a key trend in the human world in analyzing the nature and quality of the product, people's emotion, inference about products, and movies. Sentiment Analysis is the process of classification as it classifies the inference or review into positive or negative. Since the data that are labeled are very expensive and difficult to gather, it is hard. Also, the sarcastic data and homonyms are difficult to be identified. Hence the assumption of reviews will be wrong. The solution to identify the sarcastic words and the words with different meanings happens with the help of Recurrent Neural Networks.

INTRODUCTION

Sentiment Analysis has become the most promising area because of online services. Online reviews plays vital role in development of business environment, brochure, marketing and enrichment of people's life. Moreover, it helps to find subjective and objective information, review, inference, etc., Generally, the sentiment analysis is performed based on polarity. The polarity may either be a positive or a negative.

DOI: 10.4018/978-1-7998-1159-6.ch010

Beyond this, there is another type of classification technique called constructive type where the end users or the reviewers used to give some suggestions based on the usage of a product or visualization in their vision. In document level method, the process is performed dynamically with the help of user created content. In sentiment level, the classification is initially performed to identify the subjective and objective statements and finally polarity. In aspect level sentiment classification, idea and notion is analyzed. The opinion mining which is the science of using text analysis to determine the sentiment orientation of text carried out by many approaches like Lexicon- based approach, Learn based approach and Hybrid approach. The lexicon-based approach relies on a sentiment lexicons, Learning based approach is based on the ML algorithm and hybrid is based on both the sentimental approach and the learning based approach

Neural Networks consists of neurons that are connected to each other to perform highly computational tasks and to solve complex problems that are independent. Input is processed along with the activation function and the weights between different layers. Also, it does not handle with time dependent data. In order to overcome the disadvantages of neural networks such as independency, Recurrent neural Networks and Convolutional Neural Networks are used.

Recurrent Neural Networks deals with the time series data and the data that are not independent (Jian Zhang and Li, 2014). It processes sequential recognition and dynamic data. The output depends upon the previous value as well as the current input data. Different weights between the nodes and the layer are used for computation purpose. It also has memory to store the already computed values and the past histories. It can also pass the information sequentially in a selective manner. But the ability is only to perform one element at a time. The input size varies according to the specific application. Applications such as image classification, sentiment analysis, machine translation and image captioning are working under neural networks. The different classification of RNN includes the processing fixed size data, capturing images and giving out the text as a result, input and output as a text, language translation and classification based on a video.

Training Recurrent Neural Network is a highly difficult task. Training process involves Forward Pass, Backward Pass and Backpropagation. In forward pass, the sum is evaluated from initial node and in backward pass, Backpropagation is performed to minimize the squared error. In RNN, Backpropagation is performed by unfolding them into general feed-forward networks. Since RNN consists of memory to hold past values, it requires LSTM to process the data. Long Short Term Memory consists of four gates: Input Gate, Forget Gate, Memory Gate and Output Gate. These gates are said to be analog as it is very useful in differentiation during computation. Moreover, these cells allow selecting the data that needs to be remembered and the things that are not needed.

Normal Artificial Neural Networks are trained using Backpropagation. But RNN is trained using Backpropagation Through Time (BPTT). The difference is that, in BPTT, the gradient at each step depends upon the previous time step. This is when the normal neural network becomes the feed-forward delay neural networks. After considering the previous and current time series, normal Backpropagation is performed.

The impediment is that there is no longtime dependency support (Rodrigo Moraes and Neto, 2013). So RNN is elongated to bidirectional and deep bidirectional RNNs. The concept of BRNN is to divide the units or nodes of a normal RNN into forward state and negative state. In BRNN, future elements and neuron values are also taken into the sequence. In deep BRNN, number of bidirectional hidden layers is increased with time so that they become multilayer feed forward networks.

RELATED WORK

Emma Haddi and Shi, (2013) analyzed regarding the role of text preprocessing in order to reduce the noise and irrelevant features in the text to improve the accuracy of classification. The preprocessing involves irrelevant feature removal, text cleaning, stop words removal, tokenizing, stemming, and selection of features. It also involves techniques for filtering such as chi-square, information gain, mutual exclusion. With preprocessing the accuracy achieved is about 83 percent and after filtering process it is almost about 90 percent. But sarcastic words cannot be identified.

Kumar Ravi and Gautam (2015) analyzed the online and semi-online reviews and it is classified based on subjectivity. It involves collection of dataset, preprocessing and finally classification. For online learning, Probabilistic Neural Network is used and for semi-online PCAELM and ECAELM techniques are used. Finally, when compared with SVM, accuracy of classification using RNN is higher.

Yanping Yin (2015) deals with the automation of classification of textual reviews. Also, ANN and SVM is compared where ANN works well in unbalanced dataset For training, feed forward neural network and non-linear kernel is used for ANN and SVM respectively.

Wenge et al. (2014) proposed a method for learning word vectors and to increase the accuracy of detecting polarity by analyzing the structure and relationship between the words. Here, RNN is used for structured prediction for unlabeled dataset to get weights between input layer and the output layer. On analyzing the performance, the value is increased starting from one. At some particular point of time, the value starts decreasing and that point is noted. The combination of SDRNN+Dual RNN has the best performance.

Zharmagambetov and Pak (2015) deals with Movie reviews are based on deep learning techniques. This paper deals with algorithm Word2Vec which is used to represent the words with the help of vectors through which the semantic relationship between words are preserved as basic linear algebra operations. Most methods use n-gram, tf-idf and bag-of-words. Both positive and negative emotions are built using SVM, Nave Bayes, etc. Here, the extensive feature analysis is performed. The technique used here is CBOW and Skipgram Architecture (Harshali and Patil, 2015). Algorithm used is word2vec model and random forest for message classification. Preprocessing step is used for main features extraction. Distributed word vectors are applied to sentiment Analysis that accepts each sentence of large un-annotated corpus. This model trains by using deep RNN. Vector Representations of words finds the distance between words and finding semantic similar words. Cluster such semantic words are performed by k-means and random forest classifier for identifying positive, negative and neutral. There exists some limitations in this model. Since this model uses only simple k-means, limited number of clusters are formed and Semantic features requires additional information to predict.

Zhi et al. proposed a method to improve the performance in unsupervised model using the supervised model based on: Importance of a term in documents (ITD) and Importance of a term in expressing Sentiments (ITS) (Zhi-Hong Deng and Yu ., 2014). The issue in supervised learning is the representation of documents while the core problems of the documents representations are to weight terms.

For ITD, TF, IDF and Normalization factors are used for term weighting. One main approach is to weight terms by employing methods of feature selection to reduce high dimensionality of term. Brief descriptions about statistical functions are given in this paper and it is based on SVM. Results are based on ten-fold cross validation. IG produces lower accuracy in Cornell movie review set. B25 perform well in Amazon product review as well as in Stanford movie review dataset. ITD (4)*OR performs for best accuracy of 88.5 percent in movie dataset and 88.7 percent for product review.

Walaa Medhat Ahmed Hassan (2014)deals with sentiment analysis generally involves two different techniques such as Machine Learning approach and Lexicon-Based Approach. Machine Learning approach is further classified into Supervised and Unsupervised learning approach. Lexicon-Based Approach is divided into Dictionary-based and corpus-based approach. The initial step in sentiment analysis and classification involves feature selection and extraction. They are bag of words, word vectors, Chi square and Mutual Information. But it is difficult to identify ironic and sarcastic information from these sentences. Machine learning algorithms generally solve the classification problem for its simplicity and domain adaptability. But Lexicon based algorithms are computationally efficient. Overall, any method will be efficient if context and user preference is considered.

Abu et al., performed sentimental analysis and feature extraction from Twitter. Tweets are short in length but these tweets are expressing something. People may express positive, negative or neutral feelings and their thoughts. The authors applied a technique called "unigram model" which is used for emotion analysis of tweets. The authors proposed a method called "multiclass classification of human emotion" based on five classes (happiness, sadness, surprise, disgust, neutral) for emotion. The bag word model is used to transform a document into an unsorted list of words. And for feature extraction, unigram model with POS tags were used. This is the most popular model for sentimental analysis feature extraction.

The sequences of probabilities are computed initially where the method called chain rule decomposition is applied. Preprocessing is done to remove hash tags and special symbols which is used for mentioning username. The sequence of repeating characters that should be converted into short form and also abbreviations such as lol, asap and so on. Each word should be represented using POS tags in NLTK. Naïve Bayes is used for text classification To improve accuracy, Laplace smoothing is performed in analyzing emoticons, In 4-way classification the average accuracy it becomes 81% for unigram and 79.5% for unigram with POS tagging. In 5-way classification the average accuracy it becomes 66% for unigram and 64.8% for unigram with POS tagging.

Imane et al., performed sentiment analysis by gathering the public opinion and analyzing the data collected to track the people's behavior in interactive and real time nature. In this approach, the authors use the sentiment analysis for analyzing the people's behavior on big event. The dynamic dictionary of word's polarity, based on hash tags to the related topic is constructed. The dataset used is tweets related to US Election 2016. Next classification is based on positive dictionary, negative dictionary and neutral dictionary. Finally the prediction on data is done. Initially, the process is performed on very small set of positive and negative hash tags related to a given subject, then classifying the posts into several classes balancing the sentiment weight using new metrics such as uppercase words and the repetition of two consecutive letter in the word.

PROPOSED SYSTEM

The Figure 1 explains about the working of the proposed system. The ACLIMDB consists of labeled dataset for training and testing. The dataset consists of positive, negative and unclassified dataset. Tokenization acts as the first process which forms the meaningful sematic relation between statements. Also, the regular expressions are processed. Since the input for RNN must be a vector, the string dataset is converted into vector called one hot vector which is used in predictive modeling. In one hot

Figure 1. System Overview

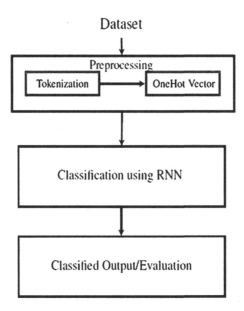

vector, the index position is renamed as 1 and all the other bits are 0. Hence, the vocabulary size is the total number of bits for each word. Initially, the dataset is preprocessed to clean text, noise removal, and regular expression removal. After preprocessing, the output is given to one hot vector where the string is converted into vectors for further processing (Yan Zhao and Li, 2014).

In Classification-Method 1, forward pass and Backpropagation is performed and only the final output is taken into account. On taking this output, this cannot be compared with any of the values. So accuracy falls below the expected rate.

Classification module involves two different methods – Many-to-one and Many-to-many. Both the classification methods involve forward pass, Backpropagation and weight updating. In forward pass, the process is initiated from the input node and the weighted sums of inputs are calculated. Backpropagation is performed in order to minimize the squared error and finally the weight is updated with the help of the error value.

Figure 2 explains about classification - method 1. The values of hidden layers are computed with the help of the previous value and the current input. If the sequence of data is less than the certain limit, the values are padded and the weight is computed. Backpropagation is performed once for all the sequences. Weight is updated at the final point.

Figure 2. Classification-Method 1

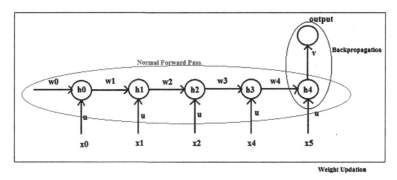

In classification-method 2, when RNN being unfolded for each and every individual input, the output is obtained at each feed-forward network is explained in the Figure 3. In order to classify the text or a review, word vectors are needed. A dictionary of positive and negative words is created. One hot vector for the dictionary is created and weight vectors are created

The final output of the text is compared with the feature weight vector that is obtained hen processing the set of dictionary words and finally the text is classified. Table 1 refers to the set of dictionary words and its one hot vector.

Figure 3. Classification-method 2

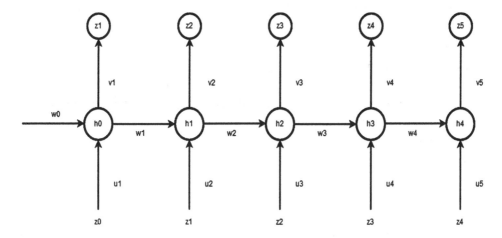

Table 1. One hot vector for dictionary of words

Vocabulary	One Hot Vector	Feature Weight Vector									
Good	1 0 0 0 0 0 0 0 0 0	For 5 features									
fine	0 1 0 0 0 0 0 0 0 0										
best	0 0 1 0 0 0 0 0 0 0										
happy	0 0 0 1 0 0 0 0 0 0										
nice	0 0 0 0 1 0 0 0 0 0										
bad	0 0 0 0 0 1 0 0 0 0										
sad	0 0 0 0 0 0 1 0 0 0										
not	0 0 0 0 0 0 0 1 0 0										
waste	0 0 0 0 0 0 0 0 1 0										
horrible	0 0 0 0 0 0 0 0 0 1										

$$\begin{bmatrix} w1 & w2 & w3 & w4 & w5 & w6 & w7 & w8 & w9 & w10 \\ w1 & w2 & w3 & w4 & w5 & w6 & w7 & w8 & w9 & w10 \\ w1 & w2 & w3 & w4 & w5 & w6 & w7 & w8 & w9 & w10 \\ w1 & w2 & w3 & w4 & w5 & w6 & w7 & w8 & w9 & w10 \\ w1 & w2 & w3 & w4 & w5 & w6 & w7 & w8 & w9 & w10 \end{bmatrix}$$

EXPERIMENT RESULT AND ANALYSIS

The dataset used here is IMDB movie review dataset. The ACLIMDB movie review dataset consists of training dataset and testing dataset. Those dataset contains positive and negative dataset. The dataset is almost 12500 reviews. The dataset includes both sarcastic reviews and words with different meanings. Since the concept of one hot vector is used, the dimensionality is very high and hence it is difficult for computation. In order to reduce the dimensionality, the concept of grouping is introduced. Consider the following sequences:

1. Very good
2. Good Music Director
3. An Unimaginable Bad story

The Table 2 explains about the Classification using Recurrent Neural Networks based on one hot vector which is followed by the computation along with the weight matrix.

$$\begin{bmatrix} 0 0 1 0 0 \end{bmatrix}_{1\times 5} \begin{bmatrix} 0.688 & -1.816 & 0.152 & -1.826 & 1.590 & 1.477 & 1.57 & -1.06 & -0.67 & 0.25 \\ -0.228 & -0.494 & -4.07 & -1.459 & 0.851 & -0.582 & 1.80 & 1.60 & 1.115 & 1.25 \\ 1.832 & 0.941 & -0.085 & -0.062 & -0.795 & 0.391 & 1.573 & 1.077 & -1.900 & 0.43 \\ -1.638 & 1.320 & -0.10 & -0.867 & -0.99 & 0.268 & -1.042 & 0.364 & -1.096 & 0.36 \\ 0.763 & 0.098 & 1.824 & 0.894 & -0.706 & -0.679 & 1.167 & -1.622 & -1.165 & 0.21 \end{bmatrix}_{5\times 10}$$

CONCLUSION

The dataset is tokenized into words which are then transformed into binary values. Each string is converted into one hot vector of size of tokens. The one hot vector of each word is fed as the input to the Recurrent Neural Network in order to perform classification. Classification is based on two different methods. Method 1 involves many to one method which has a drawback of comparison. There is no possibility

Table 2. Grouping of data

Dataset Type	Total Datasets Processed	One Hot Vector Without Grouping	One Hot Vector with Grouping
Positive	5000	68261	65951
Negative	5000	66012	63588
Unsup	5000	59765	57549

Table 3. Classification of data

Instances	Original One Hot Vector	Padded One Hot Vector	Classification
1	10 01	00010 (w3) 00001 (w4)	1
2	100 010 001	00100 (w2) 00010 (w3) 00001 (w4)	1
3	1000 0100 0010 0001	01000 (w1) 00100 (w2) 00010 (w3) 00001 (w4)	0

of comparing the values to predict the sentiment of the statement which has only final value. To overcome the above-mentioned drawback, Method 2 is used. Here, many to many method is used. It is possible to compare the values because it has value for each and every unit. Feature word vector is generated based on the set of vocabulary words which is finally used in comparison to predict the sentiment. Even in the method 2, prediction for the sentiment is not classified exactly as needed and to improve this, LSTM can be added as the future work.

REFERENCES

Aliza Sarlan Chayanit Nadam, S. B. (2014). Twitter sentiment analysis. IEEE Xplore, doi:. doi:10.1109/ICIMU.2014.7066632:212–1218

Chaudhuri, A. (2016). *Sentiment analysis of customer reviews using robust hierarchical bidirectional recurrent neural network*. Research Gate. doi:10.1007/978-3-319-33625-1_23

Emma Haddi, X. L., & Shi, Y. (2013). The role of text pre-processing in sentiment analysis. Procedia Computer Science. *Sciverse ScienceDirect, 17*, 26–32.

Guo, J. (2013). *Backpropagation through time* (pp. 1–9).

Harshali, P., & Patil, D. M. A. (2015). Sentiment analysis for social media: a survey. *IEEE Xplore, DOI, 5*. doi:10.1109/ICISSEC.2015.7371033:1–4

Isel Grau Gonzalo Npoles, I. B., & Garca, M. M. (2013). Backpropagation through time algorithm for training recurrent neural networks using variable length instances. 17, 1. 15–24.

Jian Zhang, D. Q., & Li, Z. (2014). An improved recurrent neural network language model with context vector features. In *Proceedings International Conference on Computing, Communication and Automation*. doi:– 831.10.1109/ICSESS.2014.6933694:828

Jian Zhang, D. Q., & Li, Z. (2014). An improved recurrent neural network language model with context vector features. In *Proceedings International Conference on Computing, Communication and Automation*. doi: – 831.10.1109/ICSESS.2014.6933694:828

Kumar Ravi, V. R., & Gautam, C. (2015). Online and semi-online sentiment classification. In *Proceedings International Conference on Computing, Communication and Automation*, doi: – 943.10.1109/CCAA.2015.7148531:938

Rodrigo Moraes, J. F. V., & Neto, W. P. (2013). Document-level sentiment classification: an empirical comparison between SVM and ANN. Expert Systems with Applications. *Elsevier ScienceDirect*, *40*, 621–623.

Ruales, J. (n.d.). *Recurrent neural networks for sentiment analysis*. pp. 1–5.

Walaa Medhat Ahmed Hassan, H. K. (2014). Sentiment analysis algorithms and applications: A survey. *Elsevier ScienceDirect*, *5*, 1093–1113.

Wenge Rong Baolin Peng, C. L., & Xiong, Z. (2014). Semi-supervised dual recurrent neural network for sentiment analysis. Expert systems with applications. *Elsevier ScienceDirect*, *41*, 3506–3513.

Yadhav, S. K. (2015). Sentiment analysis and classification: A survey. *International Journal of Advance Research in Computer Science and Management Studies, 3*(3), 113–121, 83, 84.

Yan Zhao, S. D., & Li, L. (2014). Sentiment analysis on news comments based on supervised learning method. *International Journal of Multimedia and Ubiquitous Engineering*, *9*(7), 333–346. doi:10.14257/ijmue.2014.9.7.28

Yanping Yin, Z. J. (2015). Document sentiment classification based on the word embedding. In *Proceedings International Conference on Mechatronics, Materials, Chemistry and Computer Engineering, 2*. 456–461.

Zharmagambetov, A. S., & Pak, A. A. (2015). Sentiment analysis of a document using deep learning approach and decision trees. In *Proceedings International Conference on Electronics Computer and Computation*. – 4.10.1109/ICECCO.2015.7416902

Zhi-Hong Deng, K. H. L., & Yu, H. L. (2014). A study of supervised term weighting scheme for sentiment analysis. *Elsevier ScienceDirect*, *41*(7), 3506–3513.

Chapter 11

Natural Language Processing–Based Information Extraction and Abstraction for Lease Documents

Sumathi S.
St.Joseph's College of Engineering, India

Rajkumar S.
HCL Technologies Ltd., India

Indumathi S.
Jerusalem College of Engineering, India

ABSTRACT

Lease abstraction is the method of compartmentalization of key data from a lease document. Lease document for a property contains key business, money, and legal data about a property. A lease abstract report contains details concerning the property location and basic lease details, price schedules, key events, terms and conditions, automobile parking arrangements, and landowner and tenant obligations. Abstracting a true estate contract into electronic type facilitates easy access to key data, exchanging the tedious method of reading the whole contents of the contract every time. Language process may be used for data extraction and abstraction of knowledge from lease documents.

DOI: 10.4018/978-1-7998-1159-6.ch011

INTRODUCTION

Text Classification

Text classification is that the method of assignment tags or classes to text consistent with its content. It's one amongst the elemental tasks in language process (NLP) with broad applications like sentiment analysis, topic labeling, spam detection, and intent detection (Esuli & Sebastiani,2013). Unstructured data in the form of text is everywhere: emails, chats, web pages, social media, support tickets, survey responses, and more. Text can be an extremely rich source of information, but extracting insights from it can be hard and time-consuming due to its unstructured nature. Businesses are turning to text classification for structuring text in a fast and cost-efficient way to enhance decision-making and automate processes. With the help of text classification it's able to classify between the documents whether it is lease documents for any office or for house.

Topic Modeling

Topic modeling could be a kind of statistical modeling for locating the abstract "topics" that occur in an exceedingly assortment of documents. Latent Dirichlet Allocation (LDA) (Blei, Ng, & Jordan, 2003) is associate degree example of topic model and is employed to classify text in an exceedingly document to a selected topic.

It builds a subject per document model and words per topic model, sculptured as Dirichlet distributions. It is used to discover the topics that occur in the document

Information Extraction

Information Extraction (Hakkani-Tür, Ji, & Grishman, 2007) refers to the machine-controlled extraction of structured data like entities, relationships between entities, and attributes describing entities from unstructured sources. This enables a lot of richer styles of queries on the luxuriant unstructured sources than potential with keyword searches alone. When structured and unstructured data co-exist, information extraction makes it possible to integrate the two types of sources and pose queries spanning them.

The extraction of structure from creaking, unstructured sources may be a difficult task that has engaged a veritable community of researchers for over 20 years currently. With roots in the Natural Language Processing (NLP) community, the topic of structure extraction now engages many different communities spanning machine learning, information retrieval, database, web, and document analysis. Early extraction tasks were concentrated around the identification of named entities, like people and company names and relationship among them from natural language text. With the help of information extraction important details in the lease agreements will be retrieved.

Data Abstraction

Whether abstracts are needed for a single building or an entire portfolio, Complete Legal Outsourcing's lease abstraction process is scaled to meet all client needs. Lease abstraction relates to abstraction of vital and relevant information from a lease document that has been signed by the owner and also the Tenant (Sengupta, 2018).

In easy terms, we can define abstraction as the process of making things simple and precise. The abstraction team at Complete Legal Outsourcing has the expertise to abstract leases into any desired format, including direct input into accounting software or Microsoft Excel/Word.

A lease abstract could be an outline of specific and crucial info from an in depth lease document and makes helpful information obtainable to review the key points simply. The lease abstract acts as a condensed version of the initial lease document. The abstract summarizes vital info from the lease and tells the reviewer wherever to appear for careful info.

- **Basic Information:** Lease and provide quick access to the identity of the Landlord and Tenant, description of premises, square footage, term of the lease, commencement and lease expiration date
- **Financial Information:** Rent, renewal rent, security deposits, late fees and interest, real estate taxes, common area maintenance (CAM) costs and percentage rents
- **Options:** Tenant or Landlord could also significantly alter the value of the assets.
- **Retail Leases:** Gross sales, break points, sales reporting an, tenant's obligation to join a marketing fund, signage restrictions, radius restrictions
- **Miscellaneous:** Monthly parking fees and storage fees

MAIN FOCUS OF THIS CHAPTER

In recent years, a considerable amount of text processing approaches are proposed and implemented by the researchers to examine the text datasets. The recent works on lease document abstraction is done by using neural networks. The process involved in Natural language processing based information extraction and abstractions for Lease Documents are

1. Text Classification
2. Topic Modeling
3. Information Extraction
4. Data Abstraction

These processes are explained in coming sub divisions.

TEXT CLASSIFICATION

Text classification (a.k.a. text categorization or text tagging) is the task of assigning a set of predefined categories to free-text. Text classifiers are often accustomed organize, structure, and categories just about something.

For example, new articles can be organized by topics, support tickets can be organized by urgency, chat conversations can be organized by language, brand mentions can be organized by sentiment, and so on .As an example, take a look at the following text below: "The user interface is quite straightforward and easy to use." A classifier will take this text as associate degree input, analyze its content, then and mechanically assign relevant tags, like UI and straightforward To Use that represent this text as in figure 1.

How Does Text Classification Work?

Text classification will be exhausted in totally different ways: manual and automatic classification. In the former, a human annotator interprets the content of text and categorizes it accordingly. This methodology sometimes will offer quality results however it's long and valuable.

The latter applies machine learning, natural language processing, and other techniques to automatically classify text in a faster and more cost-effective way.

Figure 1. Text Classification model

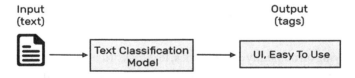

There are many approaches to automatic text classification, which can be grouped into three different types of systems:

1. Rule-based systems
2. Machine Learning based systems
3. Hybrid systems

Rule-Based Systems

Rule-based approaches (Pazzani & Billsus, 2007) classify text into organized teams by employing a set of handcrafted linguistic rules. These rules instruct the system to use semantically relevant elements of a text to identify relevant categories based on its content. Each rule consists of an antecedent or pattern and a predicted category.

Say that you want to classify news articles into 2 groups, namely, Sports and Politics. First, you'll have to be compelled to outline **2** lists of words that characterize every cluster (e.g. Words related to sports such as football, basketball, LeBron James, etc., and words related to politics such as Donald Trump, Hillary Clinton, Putin, etc.). Next, when you want to classify a new incoming text, you'll need to count the number of sport-related words that appear in the text and do the same for politics-related words. If the number of sport-related word appearances is greater than the number of politics-related word count, then the text is classified as sports and vice versa.

For example, this rule-based system will classify the headline "When is LeBron James' first game with the Lakers?" as Sports because it counted 1 sport-related term (Lebron James) and it didn't count any politics-related terms.

Rule-based systems are human comprehensible and can be improved over time. But this approach has some disadvantages. For starters, these systems need deep data of the domain.

They are also time-consuming, since generating rules for a complex system can be quite challenging and usually requires a lot of analysis and testing. Rule-based systems are also difficult to maintain and don't scale well given that adding new rules can affect the results of the pre-existing rules.

Machine Learning Based Systems

Instead of relying on manually crafted rules, text classification with machine learning learns to make classifications based on past observations (Sebastiani, 2002).

By victimization pre-labeled examples as coaching information, a machine learning algorithm can learn the different associations between pieces of text and that a particular output (i.e. Tags) is anticipated for a selected input (i.e. text).

The first step towards training a classifier with machine learning as in Figure 2 is feature extraction: a method is used to transform each text into a numerical representation in the form of a vector. One of the most frequently used approaches is bag of words, where a vector represents the frequency of a word in a predefined dictionary of words.

For example, if we have defined our dictionary to have the following words, and we wanted to vectorize the text "This is awesome", we would have the following vector representation of that text:(1,1,0,0,1,0,0). Then, the machine learning algorithm is fed with training data that consists of pairs of feature sets (vectors for each text example) and tags (e.g. sports, politics) to produce a classification model

Once it's trained with enough training samples, the machine learning model can begin to make accurate predictions. The same feature extractor as in Figure 3 is used to transform unseen text to feature sets which can be fed into the classification model to get predictions on tags (e.g. sports, politics):

Text classification with machine learning is sometimes way more correct than human-crafted rule systems, particularly on advanced classification tasks.

Also, classifiers with machine learning square measure easier to take care of and you'll be able to continually tag new examples to be told new tasks.

Text Classification Algorithms

Some of the most popular machine learning algorithms for creating text classification models includes the Naive Bayes family of algorithms, support vector machines, and deep learning.

Figure 2. Training process in text classification

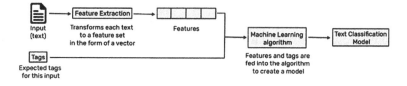

Figure 3. Prediction processes in text classification

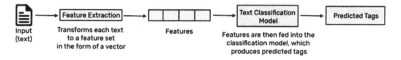

Naive Bayes

Naive Bayes is a family of statistical algorithms we can make use of when doing text classification. One of the members of that family is Multinomial Naive Bayes (MNB) (Rish, 2001). One of its main advantages is that you can get really good results when data available is not much (~ a couple of thousand tagged samples) and computational resources are scarce.

All you need to know is that Naive Bayes is based on Bayes Theorem, which helps us compute the conditional probabilities of occurrence of two events based on the probabilities of occurrence of each individual event. This means that any vector that represents a text will have to contain information about the probabilities of appearance of the words of the text within the texts of a given class in order that the algorithmic program will reckon the probability of that text's happiness to the class.

Support Vector Machines

Support Vector Machines (SVM) is simply one out of the many algorithms we will make a choice from once doing text classification.

Like Naive Bayes, SVM doesn't need much training data to start providing accurate results. Although it needs more computational resources than Naive Bayes, SVM can achieve more accurate results.

In short, SVM takes care of drawing a "line" or hyper plane that divides a space into two subspaces: one subspace that contains vectors that belong to a group and another subspace that contains vectors that do not belong to that group. Those vectors are representations of your training texts and a group is a tag you have tagged with.

Deep Learning

Deep learning is a set of algorithms and techniques inspired by how the human brain works. Text classification has benefited from the recent resurgence of deep learning architectures due to their potential to reach high accuracy with less need of engineered features. The two main deep learning architectures used in text classification are Convolutional Neural Networks (CNN) and Recurrent Neural Networks (RNN).

On the one hand, deep learning algorithms require much more training data than traditional machine learning algorithms, i.e. at least millions of tagged examples. On the other hand, traditional machine learning algorithms such as SVM and NB reach a certain threshold where adding more training data doesn't improve their accuracy. In contrast, deep learning classifiers continue to get better the more data you feed them with.

Figure 4. Deep Learning vs. Traditional Machine Learning algorithms

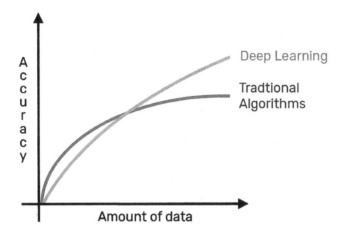

Deep learning algorithms such as Word2Vec or GloVe are also used in order to obtain better vector representations for words and improve the accuracy of classifiers trained with traditional machine learning algorithms. Figure 4 shows the comparison between Deep Learning Algorithm vs Traditional Machine Learning algorithms

Hybrid Systems

Hybrids systems combine a base classifier trained with machine learning and a rule-based system, which is used to further improve the results. These hybrid systems can be easily fine-tuned by adding specific rules for those conflicting tags that haven't been correctly modeled by the base classifier.

Metrics and Evaluation

Cross-validation is a common method to evaluate the performance of a text classifier. It consists in splitting the training dataset randomly into equal-length sets of examples (e.g. 4 sets with 25% of the data). For each set, a text classifier is trained with the remaining samples (e.g. 75% of the samples). Next, the classifiers make predictions on their respective sets and the results are compared against the human-annotated tags. This allows finding when a prediction was right (true positives and true negatives) and when it made a mistake (false positives, false negatives).

With these results, you can build performance metrics that are useful for a quick assessment on how well a classifier works:

- **Accuracy:** The percentage of texts that were predicted with the correct tag.
- **Precision:** The percentage of examples the classifier got right out of the total number of examples that it predicted for a given tag.
- **Recall:** The percentage of examples the classifier predicted for a given tag out of the total number of examples it should have predicted for that given tag.
- **F1 Score:** The harmonic mean of exactitude and recall.

Importance of Text Classification

According to IBM, it is estimated that around 80% of all information is unstructured, with text being one of the most common types of unstructured data. Because of the messy nature of text, analysing, understanding, organizing, and sorting through text data is hard and time-consuming so most companies fail to extract value from that.

This is wherever text classification with machine learning steps in. By using text classifiers, companies can structure business information such as email, legal documents, web pages, chat conversations, and social media messages in a fast and cost-effective way. This allows companies to save time when analyzing text data, help inform business decisions, and automate business processes.

Text classification can also be used in a broad range of contexts such as classifying short texts (e.g. as tweets, headlines or tweets) or organizing much larger documents (e.g. customer reviews, media articles or legal contracts).

TOPIC MODELING

Analytics trade is all concerning getting the "Information" from the info. With the growing quantity of information in recent years, that too principally unstructured, it's troublesome to get the relevant and desired info. But, technology has developed some powerful ways which may be wont to mine through the info and fetch the knowledge that we have a tendency of trying to find. One such technique in the field of text mining is Topic Modeling (Ding, Ishwar, Rohban, & Saligrama, 2013). As the name suggests, it is a process to automatically identify topics present in a text object and to derive hidden patterns exhibited by a text corpus. Thus, assisting better decision making.

Topic Modelling is totally different from rule-based text mining approaches that use regular expressions or wordbook primarily based keyword looking out techniques.

It is associate degree unsupervised approach used for locating and observant the bunch of words (called "topics") in massive clusters of texts.

Topics are outlined as "a continuance pattern of co-occurring terms during a corpus". A good topic model ought to lead to – "health", "doctor", "patient", "hospital" for a topic – Healthcare, and "farm", "crops", "wheat" for a topic – "Farming".

Topic Models are terribly helpful for the aim for document clump, organizing large blocks of textual data, information retrieval from unstructured text and feature selection.

For Example – big apple Times are victimization topic models to spice up their user – article recommendation engines.

Various professionals are victimization topic models for achievement industries wherever they aim to extract latent options of job descriptions and map them to right candidates. They are getting used to arrange massive datasets of emails, client reviews, and user social media profiles. Figure 5 shows the complete process of Topic Modeling

Latent Dirichlet Allocation for Topic Modeling

There square measure several approaches for getting topics from a text like – Term Frequency and Inverse Document Frequency (Blei, Ng, & Jordan, 2002). Latent Dirichlet Allocation is that the most well-liked topic modeling technique and during this article, we are going to discuss constant.

LDA assumes documents square measure made from a combination of topics. Those topics then generate words supported their chance distribution.

Figure 5. Complete process of topic modeling

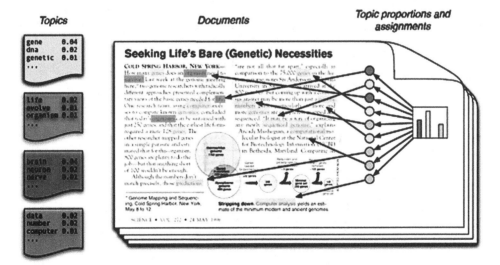

Given a dataset of documents, LDA backtracks and tries to work out what topics would produce those documents within the 1st place.

LDA is a matrix factorization technique. In vector house, any corpus (collection of documents) may be pictured as a document-term matrix. The following matrix shows a corpus of N documents D1, D2, D3 … Dn and vocabulary size of M words W1,W2 .. Wn.

The value of i,j cell provides the frequency count of word Wj in Document Di as in Figure 6.

LDA converts this Document-Term Matrix into two lower dimensional matrices – M1 and M2.M1 is a document-topics matrix and M2 is a topic – terms matrix with dimensions (N, K) and (K, M) respectively, where N is the number of documents, K is the number of topics and M is the vocabulary size.

Notice that these two matrices already provides topic word and document topic distributions, However, these distribution needs to be improved, which is the main aim of LDA. LDA makes use of sampling techniques in order to improve these matrices. It iterates through every word "w" for every document "d" and tries to regulate this topic – word assignment with a replacement assignment.

A new topic "k" could be assigned to word "w" with a chance P that is a product of 2 possibilities p1 and p2. For every topic, 2 possibilities p1 and p2 square measure calculated.

P1: p(topic t / document d) = the proportion of words in document d that are currently assigned to topic t.

P2: p(word w / topic t) = the proportion of assignments to topic t over all documents that come back from this word w.

Figure 6. Frequency count of word Wj in Document Di

	W1	W2	W3	Wn
D1	0	2	1	3
D2	1	4	0	0
D3	0	2	3	1
Dn	1	1	3	0

Figure 7. Topic word and document Topic distributions

	K1	K2	K3	K
D1	1	0	0	1
D2	1	1	0	0
D3	1	0	0	1
Dn	1	0	1	0

	W1	W2	W3	Wm
K1	0	1	1	1
K2	1	1	1	0
K3	1	0	0	1
K	1	1	0	0

The current topic – word assignment is updated with a replacement topic with the chance, product of p1 and p2 . In this step, the model assumes that each one the present word – topic assignments except this word square measure correct. This is primarily the chance that topic t generated word w, therefore it is sensible to regulate this word's topic with new chance.

After variety of iterations, a gradual state is achieved wherever the document topic and topic term distributions square measure fairly smart. This is the convergence point of LDA.

Parameters of LDA

Alpha and Beta Hyper parameters – alpha represents document-topic density and Beta represents topic-word density. Higher the worth of alpha, documents square measure composed of additional topics and lowers the worth of alpha, documents contain fewer topics.

On the opposite hand, higher the beta, topics are composed of a large number of words in the corpus, and with the lower value of beta, they are composed of few words.

Number of Topics – range of topics to be extracted from the corpus.

Researchers have developed approaches to get associate degree best range of topics by victimization Kullback Leibler Divergence Score (Moreno, Ho, & Vasconcelos, 2004).

Number of Topic Terms – range of terms composed in a very single topic.

It is generally decided according to the requirement. If the problem statement talks about extracting themes or concepts, it is recommended to choose a higher number, if problem statement talks about extracting features or terms, a low number is recommended.

Number of Iterations / passes – Maximum number of iterations allowed to LDA algorithm for convergence.

Information Extraction from Lease Document

Once you've got known, extracted, and cleaned the content required for your use case, future step is to possess associate degree understanding of that content. In many use cases, the content with the most important information is written down in a natural language (such as English, German, Spanish, Chinese, etc.) and not conveniently tagged. To extract information from this content you will need to rely on some levels of text mining, text extraction, or presumably full-up natural language processing (NLP) techniques.

Typical full-text extraction for Internet content includes:

- Extracting entities – like firms, people, greenback amounts, key initiatives, etc.
- Categorizing content – positive or negative (e.g.sentiment analysis), by perform, intention or purpose, or by trade or alternative classes for analytics and trending.
- Clustering content – to spot main topics of discourse and/or to get new topics.
- Fact extraction – to fill databases with structured info for analysis, visual image, trending, or alerts
- Relationship extraction – to fill out graph databases to explore real-world relationships

Information extraction follows the following 7 steps as in Figure 8

STEP 1: The Basics

Figure 8. Steps in Information Extraction

The input to linguistic communication process is going to be a straightforward stream of Unicode characters (typically UTF-8).

Basic process are going to be needed to convert this character stream into a sequence of lexical things (words, phrases, and grammar markers) which might then be wont to higher perceive the content.

The basics include: Structure extraction, Identify and mark sentence, phrase, and paragraph boundaries, Language identification, Tokenization, Acronym normalization and tagging, Lemmatization / Stemming, de-compounding, Entity extraction, phrase extraction.

STEP 2: Decide on Macro versus Micro Understanding
STEP 3: Decide if what you wish is possible (Within an inexpensive Cost)
STEP 4: Understand the Whole Document (Macro Understanding)
STEP 5: Extracting Facts, Entities, and Relationships (Micro Understanding)
STEP 6: Maintain Provenance / Traceability
STEP 7: Human-Aided Processes

Methods of Extraction

Data extraction can be done on 2 dimensions: hand-coded or learning-based and rule-based or applied mathematics.

Hand-Coded or Learning-Based

A hand-coded system requires human experts to define rules or regular expressions or program snippets for performing the extraction. That person needs to be a domain expert and a programmer, and possess descent linguistic understanding to be able to develop robust extraction rules. In contrast, learning-based systems require manually labeled unstructured examples to train machine learning models of extraction.

Even in the learning-based systems, domain expertise is needed in identifying and labelling examples that will be representative of the actual deployment setting. It is also necessary to possess an understanding of machine learning to be able to choose between various model alternatives and also to define features that will be robust on unseen data. The nature of the extraction task and also the quantity of noise within the unstructured knowledge ought to be wont to decide between a hand-coded and a learning-based system.

Rule-Based or Statistical

Rule-based extraction methods are driven by hard predicates, whereas statistical methods make decisions based on a weighted sum of predicate firings. Rule-based methods are easier to interpret and develop, whereas statistical methods are more robust to noise in the unstructured data.

Therefore, rule-based systems are additional helpful in closed domains wherever human involvement is each essential and out there. In open-ended domains like truth extraction from speech transcripts, or opinion extraction from Blogs, the soft logic of statistical ways is more acceptable.

Output of Extraction Systems

There are 2 primary modes during which an extraction system is deployed. First, the goal is to identify all mentions of the structured information in the unstructured text. Second, wherever the goal is to populate info of structured entities. In this case, the end user does not care about the unstructured text after the structured entities are extracted from it. The core extraction techniques stay a similar regardless of the shape of the output.

Data Abstraction From Lease Documents

A lease contains vital information just like the date of commencement, total area that is to be leased, term of the lease, subletting options, the rental amount, provisions of holdover, etc. which are crucial to all leases. However, most of the content of a lease isn't relevant and isn't required on a commonplace. The content of a lease will vary from number of pages to many pages as per the wants of the owner and also the Tenant, and to flip through hundreds of pages trying to find the precise info are often a tedious and a time intense task. Thus abstraction reveals solely the specified info crucial to the business and hides the gratuitous information.

The process of abstraction, steps in here that provides a certain outline of the vital and relevant info from the lease documents so all the vital info is offered at one's fingertips leading to saving precious operating hours.

A helpful lease abstract is one that's short and straightforward. Ideally, abstract function as a road map that helps in navigating the lease document. The contents of leases vary as they're supported the precise details that the lease document contains. Some vital things that seem in most abstracts square measure the tenants' and landlord's names, lease term, square footage, address, base rent, rent escalations and percentage rent. Preparing a decent and helpful lease abstract desires specific skills. Commercial leases typically contain normal clauses, like alterations, damage, late charge, default, destruction and estoppel. Each clause has precise details that require to be extracted from the lease document to grant form to the contents of the abstract. Understanding industrial leases is a vital thus on perceiving what info is crucial and desires to be extracted.

It is conjointly value mentioning that everyone the monetary knowledge of the lease deal are documented within the abstract, that makes it advantageous for property investors or lenders. Providing a lease abstract instead of a full lease text conjointly saves time and cash for those that ought to perform due diligence on the property for a possible sale or acquisition. Commercial property transactions became terribly complicated and need elaborated business leases with clauses that cowl numerous details.

Many offshore service suppliers offer contract-and-lease-abstraction-services to the shoppers based mostly across the world. The data thus abstracted is done so as per the client's instructions so as to fulfill their requirements. At times, a tailor created answer is provided therefore on make sure that the consumer needs are met. The reason business leases are abstracted is to help a leasing agent, lease administrator, and maintenance or property manager locate frequently referenced items in the lease without the need to refer to the original lease document. Commercial leases sometimes embody an oversized degree of legal language that produces it tough to quickly notice crucial lease knowledge. The author simplifies the language so it will be understood by common plenty World Health Organization don't have a legal background.

Lease abstraction method is a necessary part for effective knowledge management. The abstraction method makes it terribly straightforward for the busy executives as they will look at the abundant required info by flipping through one or two of pagers rather that reading the entire lease. Whether the consumer demand pertains to a lease abstracts to be ready for one building or a jailer lease administration method for the complete portfolio, Complete Legal Outsourcing's lease abstracting, and administration services will be scaled to satisfy all desires. Complete Legal Outsourcing maintains a regular lease abstraction method, ensuring consistency, accuracy and uniformity.

As we all are aware that the concept of outsourcing is not new. Outsourcing is taken into account as a very important tool for business growth within the epoch. The offshore service suppliers have down the art of abstraction and are currently with success job to the companies set across the world. Abstraction is most well-liked by the companies conjointly because it saves time and cash as abstraction if done in-house proves costly when put next to offshore service suppliers.

CONCLUSION

Lease documentation incorporates a direct impact on the cost of in running a business. The costs associated with leases and supporting documents are rent, renewal rent, security deposits, late fees and interest, taxes and GST, maintenance costs, percentage rents for retail and critical components that affect the transaction. Abstraction will provide an organization with the cost data required to budget and forecast property expenses and ensure the appropriate funding is available. In this chapter four level process such as text classification to differentiate the types of lease documents, Topic modeling to find the best topic from multiple documents, information extraction to identify the important information from the lease documents and abstraction of data to identify the data such as basic information, financial information, retail and miscellaneous such as monthly parking fees and storage fees.

REFERENCES

Blei, D. M., Ng, A. Y., & Jordan, M. I. (2002). Latent dirichlet allocation. In Advances in neural information processing systems (pp. 601-608).

Blei, D. M., Ng, A. Y., & Jordan, M. I. (2003). Latent dirichlet allocation. *Journal of Machine Learning Research*, *3*(Jan), 993–1022.

Ding, W., Ishwar, P., Rohban, M. H., & Saligrama, V. (2013). Necessary and sufficient conditions for novel word detection in separable topic models. arXiv preprint arXiv:1310.7994.

Esuli, A., & Sebastiani, F. (2013). Improving text classification accuracy by training label cleaning. *ACM Transactions on Information Systems*, *31*(4), 19. doi:10.1145/2516889

Hakkani-Tür, D., Ji, H., & Grishman, R. (2007). Using information extraction to improve cross-lingual document retrieval. MuLTI-SOuRcE, MuLTILINguAL INfORMATION ExTRAcTION ANd SuMMARIzATION, 7.

Moreno, P. J., Ho, P. P., & Vasconcelos, N. (2004). A Kullback-Leibler divergence-based kernel for SVM classification in multimedia applications. In Advances in Neural Information Processing Systems (pp. 1385-1392).

Pazzani, M. J., & Billsus, D. (2007). Content-based recommendation systems. In *The adaptive web* (pp. 325–341). Berlin, Germany: Springer. doi:10.1007/978-3-540-72079-9_10

Rish, I. (2001, August). An empirical study of the naive Bayes classifier. In IJCAI 2001 workshop on empirical methods in artificial intelligence, 3(22), pp. 41-46.

Sebastiani, F. (2002). Machine learning in automated text categorization. *ACM computing surveys (CSUR), 34*(1), 1-47.

Sengupta, S., Mohamedrasheed, A. K., Lakshminarasimhan, C., Kapur, M., George, J., Srivastava, M., & Swamy, S. (2018). U.S. Patent No. 9,946,924. Washington, DC: U.S. Patent and Trademark Office.

Chapter 12
Neural Network Applications in Hate Speech Detection

Brian Tuan Khieu
San Jose State University, USA

Melody Moh
ⓘ https://orcid.org/0000-0002-8313-6645
San Jose State University, USA

ABSTRACT

This chapter presents a literature survey of the current state of hate speech detection models with a focus on neural network applications in the area. The growth and freedom of social media has facilitated the dissemination of positive and negative ideas. Proponents of hate speech are one of the key abusers of the privileges allotted by social media, and the companies behind these networks have a vested interest in identifying such speech. Manual moderation is too cumbersome and slow to deal with the torrent of content generation on these social media sites, which is why many have turned to machine learning. Neural network applications in this area have been very promising and yielded positive results. However, there are newly discovered and unaddressed problems with the current state of hate speech detection. Authors' survey identifies the key techniques and methods used in identifying hate speech, and they discuss promising new directions for the field as well as newly identified issues.

DOI: 10.4018/978-1-7998-1159-6.ch012

INTRODUCTION

With the spread of social networking websites, it has become easier than ever to broadcast one's opinions on whichever topic one may choose. While the quick dissemination of information through such sites can elicit much good, in irresponsible or scheming hands, such power can bring about great division and anguish. One such example of the harm that can come about is the birth of echo chambers on the internet; misguided or misinformed people can find themselves trapped in a vicious cycle of ingraining more and more radical and polarizing sentiments. Hate speech and its prevalence in online social networks have proven to be an ongoing problem on such sites. While manual user flaggings of comments or posts can help, the process can be abused to silence opinions one disagrees with. With the constant stream of content generation, simply employing an army of moderators will not solve the issue either. Thus, there is a need for an effective and automated system for identifying hate speech.

One way to identify hate speech is to use a lexical-based approach where certain negative words are always flagged to indicate a need for further inspection. Certain words are statistically identified to appear in manually identified hate speech more than others, and they are subsequently added to a ruleset to follow. Unfortunately, such approaches are somewhat naive and ill-equipped to handle slang and symbolism. Although, these lexical-based approaches are sometimes used in conjunction with other methods to form a more robust solution.

The more generally accepted method of identifying hate speech is the use of machine learning and deep learning algorithms. This approach more readily handles slang and symbolism since the models will be trained upon a dataset that includes such words and phrases.

Machine learning and deep learning models built for hate speech detection can fall into one of two categories, word-based and character-based models. Word-based models rely on extracting features from n-grams of different tokenized word combinations while character-based models do so from n-grams of characters. Word-based models can also utilize lexical-based techniques and factor in a word's sentiment or connotation.

One of the earliest machine learning techniques leveraged to identify hate speech is logistic regression. Logistic regression involves using the sigmoid function to squash values between 0 and 1 in order to map observations to a number of discrete classes. Since the values are forced to be between 0 and 1, the output is composed of probabilities instead of continuous values like linear regression does.

While logistic regression is somewhat effective at identifying hate speech detection, researchers have been eager to apply deep learning methods to the problem. Another early attempt at solving the issue using deep learning incorporated a Multilayer

Perceptron Network. A Multilayer Perceptron is a composed of several layers of nodes where each node is connected to every node in the preceding layer. This approach did not significantly outperform the logistic regression model and did struggle somewhat to effectively identify hate speech. This most likely is the result of the lack of memory of the network; past events are not taken into consideration when determining the current event's significance. In the area of hate speech detection and natural language processing, forgoing the effect past words have on current and future words leads to a loss of meaning and context. Long Short-Term Networks are a subset of Recurrent Neural Networks and both retain memory of past events through use of an internal state. Specifically for Long Short-Term Networks, they use a combination of input and output gates to properly discard, retain, and pass on old information. This makes them more appropriate for addressing the issue of hate speech detection since past words can properly give current words context and meaning. Recurrent Neural Networks themselves have an issue with retaining information from long ago in the past which is why Gated Recurrent Units were developed to address the issue. Gated Recurrent Units are often paired with Convolutional Neural Networks, networks that apply convolutions and pooling operations incoming data. The purpose is to have the Convolutional Neural Networks extract key features from the input data while having the Gated Recurrent Units retain past information to give context. Both Long Short-Term Memory and the combination of Convolutional Neural Networks and Gated Recurrent Units identify hate speech comparably well to one another. However, it's important to note that the training time for the combination is significantly less than that of the Long Short-Term Memory.

While many researchers are tackling the hate speech detection problem, most fail to take into account the existence of adversarial examples. Current state of the art hate speech detection models only consider naive examples that originate from entities that do not attempt to avoid detection. However, the real world is filled with adversaries who wish to spread hate speech on a platform while going undetected. There are three easy and effective attacks for the adversaries to utilize; they are word modifications, whitespace manipulation, and benign word insertion. Word modifications are simple changes to the hate speech text, and they include simple typos or deterministic LEETSPEAK where letters are exchanged for numbers. Whitespace manipulation revolves around the removal or insertion of spaces within a given text to throw off word-based models. Finally, benign word insertion is the addition of normal or positive words not normally associated with hate speech, such as "love", in order to fool the model. These attacks require little to no training for the average person to use, and it was found that the combination of whitespace removal and benign word insertion zeroed out the F-1 scores for many of the state of the art models.

In this book chapter, we would first establish the current state of hate speech detection and the common features and approaches used between different models. The sections will cover the various statistical based and semantic features commonly found. Then, we will describe the various lexical models used. Afterwards, we would detail the different deep learning applications to hate speech detection. Then, we would cover the promising avenue of hate speech detection, context aware models. Consequently, we would highlight the vulnerabilities the approaches possess versus easy to execute attacks. Next, we will cover some preliminary work addressing these newly found vulnerabilities. Finally, we would conclude our study with a summary and identify areas for future work regarding this subject matter.

BACKGROUND INFORMATION

Armed with the power of anonymity, many groups and individuals abuse social media tools in order to proliferate messages advocating for violence and suppression of another people. Such language and its spread across online social networks (OSNs) presents several issues to the managers of such networks, but there is an inherent issue with rooting out such speech. The definition and classification of hate speech has not reached a universal consensus. Merriam-Webster designates hate speech as language "expressing hatred of a particular group of people" while the European Union defined it as speech that "spread, incite, promote or justify racial hatred, xenophobia, antisemitism or other forms of hatred based on intolerance". There is a notable distinction between the two definitions above; the latter places an emphasis on hateful "calls to action" while the former does not. This difference, the "call to action", typically is the borderline between merely offensive speech and hateful speech in the eyes of OSN moderators and admins. Even with this boundary, the problem of classifying hate speech remains a troublesome one since declaring whether one has crossed the border is still murky. Regardless, the identification of hate speech a persistent problem for OSN moderators, and due to the sheer volume of generated content on said networks, manual moderation is infeasible.

Several approaches towards detecting such language have been proposed and recently developed in order to combat the rise of hate speech. With the spread of social networking websites, it has become easier than ever to broadcast one's opinions on whichever topic one may choose. While the quick dissemination of information through such sites can elicit much good, in irresponsible or scheming hands, such power can bring about great division and anguish. One such example of the harm that can come about is the birth of echo chambers on the internet; misguided or misinformed people can find themselves trapped in a vicious cycle of ingraining more and more radical and polarizing sentiments.

Hate speech and its prevalence in online social networks have proven to be an ongoing problem on social media sites such as Facebook and Youtube. While manual user flaggings of comments or posts can help, the process can be abused to silence opinions one disagrees with. With the constant stream of content generation, simply employing an army of moderators will not solve the issue either. Thus, there is a need for an effective and automated system for identifying hate speech.

CURRENT METHODS AND FEATURES

Methods

One method of identifying hate speech is to use a rule-based approach where certain negative words are always flagged to indicate a need for further inspection. Certain words are statistically identified to appear in manually identified hate speech more than others, and they are subsequently added to a ruleset to follow. Classification of hate speech is determined by the construction of a dictionary compiling all "hate" words or through a binary classification of "benign" or "hate" types. Unfortunately, such approaches are somewhat naive and ill-equipped to handle slang and symbolism. It should be noted that some of these rule-based approaches are used in conjunction with other methods to form a more robust solution.

The more generally accepted method of identifying hate speech is the use of machine learning and deep learning algorithms. This approach more readily handles slang and symbolism since the models will be trained upon a dataset that includes such words and phrases. Machine learning and deep learning models built for hate speech detection can fall into one of two categories, word-based and character-based models. Word-based models rely on extracting features from n-grams of different tokenized word combinations while character-based models do so from n-grams of characters. Word-based models can also utilize rule-based techniques and factor in a word's sentiment or connotation.

Definition

There is no agreed upon standard for hate speech detection, several papers contain significant departures from one another in terms of definitions, classes, features, and architecture used. This complicates the problem of hate speech detection while underlining how it remains an actively worked upon challenge.

In the case of definitions, there is no consensus upon what hate speech actually is. The generic idea consists of language expressing a large degree of hatred of a people, but it becomes tricky differentiating it from offensive speech. As noted before, the European Union draws the line at the "call to action", speech is not considered hateful until it advocates for the suppression or violence against others. For those who utilize this distinction for the categorization of speech, the problem turns into a ternary classification situation with benign, hate, and offensive speech labels (Davidson, Warmslay, Macy, & Weber 2017). Not everyone abides by this definition however, and in those instances, the line between hate speech and offensive speech blurs. In other cases, hate speech is divided not by the severity or by the existence of a "call to action" but rather the areas for attack such as racism and sexism (Wuclzyn, Thain, & Dixon, 2017) Thus, different hate speech detection models do not necessarily compare directly to one another due to the variations in definitions and classes used. It follows that with different classes or labels used, these models use quite different datasets as well. With these variations, the direct evaluation and comparison of different hate speech detection models is difficult.

Features

There is a common thread of features used in addressing hate speech detection. The most commonly used features consist of Term Frequency Inverse Document Frequency (TF-IDF), bag of words vectors, n-grams of characters or words, Global Vectors for Word Representation (GloVe),. From each of these features, the statistical properties and makeup of hate speech can be determined. Nobata et al. (2016) found that these statistical based features are more effective in classifying speech than semantic features such as polarity and sentiment. This may be due to how sentiment based features can be mixed within both benign and hate speech. Benign speech can contain words that register negatively in sentiment while hateful material can contain words that register positively. Contrastingly, statistical based features make class associations based on the appearance of a combination of words or characters within a test class. Despite this issue, sentiment-based features are still commonly paired with statistical based features as seen in Gao and Huang (2018).

TF-IDF

TF-IDF or Term Frequency Inverse Document Frequency is a numerical statistic that reflects the importance of a word or term in a given document. This statistic is primarily based upon the frequency with which a term appears within a given document; if the term appears frequently, it presumably holds more importance than terms that do not. Notably, the second portion of the term, Inverse Document Frequency, reflects that the weight of the frequency of occurrence is inversely proportional to the amount of times the term appears in other documents. In short, a term may appear quite frequently while holding no real significance, and one such example is a common word "the". This statistic has been used in many hate speech detection models, ones that are primarily lexical based (Ruwandika & Weerasinghe 2018; Davidson, Warmslay, Macy, & Weber 2017; Badjatiya, Gupta, Gupta, & Varma 2017).

Bag of Words

Bag of Words is a representation of text using frequencies with an assortment of words. This is a surface level feature that reflects the statistical makeup of a given piece of text. It has been used in several works, primarily lexical based models but also some neural network based models (Ruwandika & Weerasinghe 2018; Badjatiya, Gupta, Gupta, & Varma 2017).

N-Grams

In a broad sense, n-grams refer to continuous sequences of n items from a document or given piece of data. Specifically for hate speech detection, these sequences consist of letters or words. N-grams are utilized by many different hate speech detection models, but in the case of neural networks, they are typically used to learn word embeddings (Wuclzyn, Thain, & Dixon, 2017; Nobata et al., 2016; Badjatiya, Gupta, Gupta, & Varma, 2017). Character based n-grams are suited for handling typos due to majority of n-grams being preserved even with typos. On the other hand, word-based n-grams are better at capturing implicit hate as well as less computationally intensive to generate. Word based n-grams look to be more popular overall than character-based n-grams for hate speech detection models.

GloVe or Word Embeddings

This type of feature consists of representing terms or more usually words as vectors. These vectors are numerical representations of words or terms in a vector space and are used to denote whether certain words are closely associated with one another or not. Word embeddings are primarily used by neural network hate speech detection models since a neural network is usually required to create them in the first place. Several pre-trained embeddings are available and used by several papers for their neural networks (Gao & Huang 2018; Badjatiya, Gupta, Gupta, & Varma 2017; Zhang, Robinson, & Tepper 2018). Of note is that these embeddings rely heavily on proper tokenization, and any variations in spelling will cause a new vector to be created instead of modifying the original term's vector.

Semantic Features

While statistic based and surface level features have been used to great effect, models incorporating these as well as semantic features have shown performance improvements (Nobata et al. 2016). Semantic features typically revolve around the positive and negative connotations of words or polarity. Some of these rely upon a pre-built lexicon dictionary to judge whether a given word is good or bad. It follows that semantic features are useful in aiding hate speech detection because by nature hate speech should contain more words with negative polarities than benign text. Gao and Huang (2018) showcase the usefulness of semantic features by making chiefly utilizing both the polarity and a lexicon dictionary in their hate speech detection model along with other statistical based features. Of note is that semantic features can overlap with one another while coming from different classes. As an example, hate speech can contain many words with a positive polarity while expressing a passionate fervor for the condemnation of another group of people. Meanwhile, benign text that consists of complaints for ordinary problems will contain many words with negative polarities. This "cross contamination" signifies that semantic features are not usually linearly separable by class; to our knowledge, no hate speech detection model uses only semantic features. Semantic features are quite useful in supplementing statistical feature-based models but not that useful on their own.

LEXICAL BASED MODELS

Lexical based models revolve around the usage of simple surface level features such as character and word n-grams to predict the class of a text. These surface level features have shown to be quite effective in this prediction problem (Wuclzyn, Thain & Dixon 2017 and Nobata et al. 2016). Also, these models can leverage sentiment-based features. Some of the most popular classification models for this type consist of Naive Bayes, Logistic Regression, Random Forest, and Support Vector Machines (SVM).

Ruwandika and Weerasinghe (2018) experimented with supervised and unsupervised learning techniques and a variety of different features for hate speech detection. The researchers focused on binary classification. Amongst the methods, naive bayes, logistic regression, svm, decision tree, and k-means, naive bayes achieved the highest F-1 score when using tf-idf features. Ruwandika and Weerasinghe (2018) also noted the ineffectiveness of K-means clustering in this problem space; it ranked the worst in performance in nearly every scenario.

Similarly, Wuclzyn, Thain, and Dixon (2017) treated the hate speech detection problem as a binary classification problem. However, the authors chose to focus only on a few methods chiefly logistic regression and with character and word n-grams as features. Of note is that the authors found that hate speech or attacks were clustered together in time. The authors concluded that this may be due to how hate begets hate and causes a chain reaction of hateful comments to be unleashed.

Contrasting to the previous two works, Davidson, Warmslay, Macy, and Weber (2017) used TF-IDF and a specifically built sentiment lexicon as features for a logistic regression model. Also, the authors treated the hate speech detection problem as a ternary classification model with hate, offensive, and benign labels. After testing several different methods such as SVM, Naive Bayes, and Random Forest, the authors chose to use logistic regression with L2 regularization as their final model. They found that their model tended to misclassify tweets as less hateful or offensive than humans did. They attribute this to how their dataset contains few tweets that cross the "hate" class threshold for humans (Davidson, Warmslay, Macy, & Weber 2017). Also, the authors identified certain words such as profanity may be used in both hateful and offensive language while others such as racial slurs are more associated wit just hate speech.

Contrastingly, Watanabe, Bouazizi, and Ohtsuki (2018) used unigrams along with extracted patterns to develop dictionaries. They used these dictionaries paired with sentiment, semantic and polarity features with a machine learning algorithm, "J48graft" to classify speech into binary and ternary classifications. The researchers made the distinction between hate speech and offensive speech; the ternary classifier used "hateful", "offensive", and "clean" labels similarly to Davidson, Warmslay, Macy, and Weber (2017). The authors found that extracted patterns yielded promising results in the area of hate speech detection and recommended further work to incorporate them when building models (Watanabe, Bouazizi, & Ohtsuki 2018).

NEURAL NETWORK HATE SPEECH DETECTION MODELS

Neural Network based methods use neural networks to learn abstract feature representations of test hate speech data through several stacked layers. Input features consist of task-specific embeddings learned using FastText, CNNs and LSTMs and other forms of feature encoding. The goal of these neural network-based approaches is to learn new abstract feature representations from simple input text. Some of the popular methods used in this category consist of Convolutional Neural Networks (CNNs), Recurrent Neural Networks (RNNs), and Long Short-Term Memory (LSTM) networks. For the most part, this approach relies upon character or word n-gram one hot encodings.

Wuclzyn, Thain, and Dixon (2017) used a multilayer perceptron (MLP) models, a type of artificial neural network, in addition to logistic regression models to handle the binary classification problem. They noted that the MLP models were better at detecting implicit hate speech as opposed to the logistic regression models.

Badjatiya, Gupta, Gupta, and Varma (2017) treated the hate speech detection issue as a binary classification problem and used a variety of deep neural networks to attempt to address it. Amongst the various features, tf-idf, bag of words vectors and embeddings learned, and models, FastText, CNNs, and LSTMs, LSTMs using random embeddings and Gradient Boosting Decision Trees (GDBT) performed the best. The authors reasoned that this may be due to the inherent nature of LSTMs. LSTMs are a subset of RNNs and both retain memory of past events through use of an internal state. However, LSTMs do not suffer from an issue that RNNs do that prevents them from propagating information far into the future. The authors noted that the random embeddings version outperformed the pre-trained versions which may be due to the need for backpropagation for the associated GDBTs to learn embeddings for the task (Badjatiya, Gupta, Gupta, & Varma 2017).

Contrastingly, Zhang, Robinson, and Tepper (2018) used a combination approach of CNN and RNN combination architecture to classify hate speech. Specifically, a Gated Recurrent Unit (GRU), a type of RNN, was used in conjunction with a CNN. Recurrent Neural Networks suffer from the vanishing gradient problem which prevents the propagation of information into the distant future. Gated Recurrent Units were developed to address the issue and are often paired with Convolutional Neural Networks, networks that apply convolution and pooling operations. In this case, the purpose is to have the CNNs extract co-occurring word n-grams as patterns while having the Gated Recurrent Units retain past pattern information to give context. The authors concluded that while both LSTM networks and the combination of CNNs and GRUs can identify hate speech comparably well to one another, the training time for the combination is significantly less than that of the LSTMs (Zhang, Robinson, & Tepper 2018).

CONTEXT AWARE HATE SPEECH DETECTION

A new type of approach to hate speech detection involves the leveraging of context as a semantic feature. Hate groups often attempt to avoid detection by the use of words with hidden meaning. In addition, current events give background information that can turn seemingly innocuous text into hate speech once considering the context. There is relatively a small amount of work done in this niche area compared to the generic version of hate speech, but some papers have identified it grondahl et al. as an area for future work.

To our best knowledge, only one significant work has been published in the area of context aware hate speech detection. Gao and Huang (2018) define context as any information not included within the original text itself. In addition to typical word and character n-grams, Gao and Huang (2018)utilized lexicon derived features such as polarity and emotion as well as context features consisting of usernames and article titles. The authors created a corpus of Fox News comments that were annotated according to strict guidelines; this included context features and is purported to be the first of its kind.

Gao and Huang (2018) tested both logistic regression and bi-directional LSTM models while treating hate speech detection as a binary classification problem. They found that in both models' cases, there was an improvement in F-1 score by using the additional context information. The authors noted the pros of both model approaches. Logistic regression makes good use of character n-grams which helps with capitalizations and misspellings while LSTMs can capture the hidden and subtle meanings of implicit hate speech. To maximize usage of both models strengths, the authors combined the two into an ensemble model which yielded significant performance increases over the use of a single model.

EVADING HATE SPEECH DETECTION

Evasion Schemes

Unfortunately, sources of hate can undertake actions to morph their text to evade detection thus complicating the problem. The inherent goal of morphing text is to introduce enough noise so that detection models cannot correctly classify phrases and passages as "hateful" while also maintaining the meaning and readability of the original message. Prior work has shown that simple modifications such as the removal of whitespace can decimate the accuracy of state-of-the-art models and that there is a need for some method of defense against these evasion schemes.

Grondahl et al. (2018) utilized new hate speech detection models from four papers as the basis for testing new evasion schemes. (Zhang, Robinson, & Tepper 2018, Badjatiya, Gupta, Gupta, & Varma 2017, Davidson, Warmslay, Macy, & Weber 2017, and Wuclzyn, Thain, & Dixon 2017). While the five models used from performed well on their own datasets, Grondahl et al. (2018) noted that performance dropped once each model trained upon all datasets (Zhang, Robinson, & Tepper 2018, Badjatiya, Gupta, Gupta, & Varma 2017, Davidson, Warmslay, Macy, & Weber 2017, and Wuclzyn, Thain, & Dixon 2017). Grondahl et al. (2018) noted that hate speech detection models fail to take into account the existence of adversarial examples. Current state of the art hate speech detection models only consider naive examples that originate from entities that do not attempt to avoid detection.

However, the real world is filled with adversaries who wish to spread hate speech on a platform while going undetected.

Grondahl et al. (2018) created six different evasion schemes to morph text; these schemes reliably diminished the effective of each detection model while preserving the meaning of the original text. The six attacks proposed fall into one of three categories: word modifications, whitespace manipulation, and benign word insertion. Word modifications are simple changes to the hate speech text, and they include simple typos or deterministic LEETSPEAK where letters are exchanged for numbers. Whitespace manipulation revolves around the removal or insertion of spaces within a given text to throw off word-based models. Finally, benign word insertion is the addition of normal or positive words not normally associated with hate speech, such as "love", in order to fool the model. These attacks require essentially no training for the average person to use, and Grondahl et al. (2018) found that the combination of whitespace removal and benign word insertion zeroed out the F-1 scores for many of the state-of-the-art models. The following passages detail the attacks addressed in this chapter along with our newly proposed attack.

The typo attack used in Grondahl et al. (2018) consists of a single swapping of letters within the middle of a word. This was done to more effectively trick spell checkers while also maintaining readability and the original meaning of the text. The preservation of readability and meaning must be taken into account for the creation of any lexical attack; fooling detection models can be done easily if the new text loses all meaning. In this case, the evasion scheme relies on previous cognitive research that determined single character swaps have the least impact on retaining readability.

Whitespace removal converts a given piece of text into one single chunk of characters. This attack greatly hinders the effectiveness of word-based models due to their reliance on proper tokenization of words. Word-based models rely on word-embeddings; if fed improperly tokenized data, these models fail to leverage these embeddings. In this case, such models treat text with removed whitespace as new words with no particular associations thereby allowing adversaries to evade detection. Conversely, character-based models better handle this issue; removing whitespace does cause issues in terms of the separation of words, but the majority n-gram character combinations remain the same.

Benign word insertion attacks, more specifically the word "love", involve the random placement of a positive or neutral word into a text. Grondahl et al. (2018) notes that this attack affected both word-based and character-based models comparably. The effectiveness of this evasion schemes comes from an asymmetric problem regarding the insertion of material. Inserting hateful material into a benign or positive piece of text results in the creation of hateful material while the reverse, inserting positive material into hateful material, does not yield positive material. However, detection models do not take this into account and thus significantly decrease in performance when faced with the evasion scheme.

In summary, hate speech detection models are not well equipped to handle adversarial examples originating from entities that wish to evade detection. These attacks are effective and easy to apply to text. There is a need for researchers to address the threat these evasion schemes pose due to the low barrier of execution.

Preliminary Work

A key issue with addressing lexical evasion schemes for hate speech detection models is the problem of detecting and classifying whether sample text has been morphed and which evasion scheme has been applied. Thus, there is a need to categorize which evasion scheme has been applied to a text before using attempting to reverse the text morphing. To our knowledge, this problem has not been addressed in any other published work.

We chose to use the following Out of Box models:

1.   Multinomial Naive Bayes
2.   AdaBoost
3.   Random Forest
4.   Logistic Regression
5.   K-Nearest Neighbors
6.   Stochastic Gradient Descent
7.   Support Vector Machines (One vs All)

Our workflow in testing these models is as follows. First, we chose to conduct feature engineering in order to create features for these models to use. Then, we did feature selection to pick the best features from those we created. Afterwards, we applied gridsearch to several models to tune our hyperparameters/

The rest of this section is laid out in the following subsections: Feature Engineering, Feature Selection, Hyperparameter Tuning, and Results.

Feature Engineering

Given that our dataset only contained input text and the attack classification label, that prompted our work in feature engineering. Feature engineering is the creation of new features through the usage of domain knowledge.

Our efforts yielded six new features, word count, character count, average word length, number of numerics, number of spaces, and number of special characters. We also utilized a variation of tf-idf which we name Char tf-idf; our version utilized character n-grams ranging from two to three letters. Tf-idf is a numerical statistic that signifies how important a term is based on its frequency of appearance while inversely proportional to how many other documents it appears in.

Feature Selection

In order to reduce complexity of our models, we conducted feature selection to pick the best features out of the ones we created. We used recursive feature elimination (RFE) in order to accomplish this. RFE involves recursively dropping the weakest feature for a model and retraining on the remaining ones.

The consistent best features found through RFE were character count, average word length, and number of spaces. We determined that these ones were most likely picked due to the significant changes these features undergo when an evasion scheme such as whitespace removal is applied. Once applied, we discovered a significant .03 boost in F-1 scores across the board.

Hyperparameter Tuning

In order to boost the results of our models, we applied hyperparameter tuning to the selected models. We achieved this through the usage of gridsearch, a method of hyperparameter tuning that iterates through different combinations of hyperparameters. An example of the hyperparameters we allowed gridsearch to adjust is the following for SVM:

- Alpha
- Max Iterations
- Learning Rate
- Random State

The tuning completed by gridsearch yielded a bump of 0.02 points in F-1 score when completed.

Results

Table 1 displays our results from testing every model. We applied 5-fold cross validation when testing and used one of three sets of features for models to train upon. The three feature sets consist of Char tf-idf, Engineered, and Engineered RFE. Engineered signifies all six features were used while Engineered RFE denotes that only character count, average word length, and number of spaces were used as features.

Table 1. Macro averaged precision, recall, f-1 scores of model, feature type combinations for lexical evasion scheme classification

Model, Dataset	Macro Averaged Metric		
	Precision	Recall	F-1
LR Char, W	0.96	0.96	0.96
Random Forest, Char Tfidf	0.40	0.39	0.40
Random Forest, Engineered	0.73	0.73	0.68
AdaBoost, Char Tfidf	0.44	0.00	0.00
AdaBoost, Engineered	0.48	0.40	0.25
Naive Bayes, Char Tfidf	0.95	0.95	0.95
SGD, Char Tfidf	0.96	0.96	0.96
SVM, Char Tfidf	0.99	0.92	0.95
Logistic Regression, Engineered	0.42	0.43	0.40
Logistic Regression, Engineered RFE	0.42	0.42	0.41
Logistic Regression, Char Tfidf	0.98	0.98	0.98
KNN, Engineered	0.41	0.40	0.40

Overall, our engineered features performed poorly with most achieving a F-1 score of 0.42. This may be due to a lack of ability for our features to capture the statistical makeup of the text itself. Meanwhile, the models that used Char tf-idf as a feature yielded extremely strong results with logistic regression managing to reach a 0.98 F-1 score. We attribute this high performance to the ability of Char tf-idf to capture the important character n-grams that are frequently modified in significant ways when an evasion scheme is applied.

Our best performing models consist of Random Forest, Stochastic Gradient Descent, and Logistic Regression. These models achieved strong results which we consider to be a result of these models' ability to leverage changes in statistical information and makeup when comparing different attacks.

CONCLUSION AND FUTURE WORK DIRECTIONS

Hate speech detection remains an unsolved problem, and due to the large variations in definitions and classification problem treatment, there are some difficulties in directly comparing new solutions to one another. Nearly all the models covered in this chapter use some feature that reflects the statistical makeup of text. Some supplement them with semantic features, but none use only semantic features. Several papers treated hate speech detection as a binary classification problem while others treated it as a ternary or multiclass problem. This creates issues in direct comparisons of efficacy because classification type conversion favors the model that does not undergo it.

Context aware hate speech detection is a potential new avenue for the future of hate speech detection since little work has been done in the area. Due to the F-1 score improvements made, the addition of context features and ensemble character based and neural network based models were suggested as potential improvements over current hate speech detection schemes.

Current hate speech detection models also face a new issue, dealing with adversaries attempting to avoid detection. The existence of these adversaries has been overlooked in the formulation of hate speech detection models, and the evasion methods that can be deployed not only significantly reduce performance but also are very easy to execute. Context aware hate speech detection may be able to help address this issue, but the problem warrants future discussion and research.

REFERENCES

Badjatiya, P., Gupta, S., Gupta, M., & Varma, V. (2017). Deep learning for hate speech detection in tweets. In *Proceedings of the 26th International Conference on World Wide Web Companion - WWW 17 Companion.* 10.1145/3041021.3054223

Davidson, T., Warmslay, D., Macy, M., & Weber, I. (2017). Automated hate speech detection and the problem of offensive language. In *Proceedings of the 11th Conference on Web and Social Media.* 512-515.

Gao, L., & Huang, R. (2017). Detecting online hate speech using context aware models. RANLP 2017 - Recent advances in natural language processing meet deep learning. doi:10.26615/978-954-452-049-6_036

Grondahl, T., Pajola, L., Juuti, M., & Conti, M. & Asokan, N (2018). All you need is" love": Evading hate-speech detection. *Proceedings of the 11th ACM Workshop on Artificial Intelligence and Security.* 2-12. doi:10.1145/3270101.3270103

Nobata, C., Tetreault, J., Thomas, A., Mehdad, Y., & Chang, Y. (2016). Abusive language detection in online user content. In Proceedings WWW. doi:10.1145/2872427.2883062

Ruwandika, N., & Weerasinghe, A. (2018). Identification of hate speech in social media. In *2018 18th International Conference on Advances in ICT for Emerging Regions (ICTer).* doi:10.1109/icter.2018.8615517

Schofield, A., & Davidson, T. (2017). Identifying hate speech in social media. XRDS: Crossroads. *The ACM Magazine for Students*, *24*(2), 56–59. doi:10.1145/3155212

Watanabe, H., Bouazizi, M., & Ohtsuki, T. (2018). Hate speech on Twitter: A pragmatic approach to collect hateful and offensive expressions and perform hate speech detection. *IEEE access: Practical innovations, open solutions*, *6*, 13825–13835. doi:10.1109/ACCESS.2018.2806394

Wulczyn, E., Thain, N., & Dixon, L. (2017). Ex machina: Personal attacks seen at scale. *Proceedings of the 26th International Conference on World Wide Web - WWW 17*. doi:10.1145/3038912.3052591

Zhang, Z., Robinson, D., & Tepper, J. (2018). Detecting hate speech on Twitter using a convolution-GRU based deep neural network. The Semantic Web Lecture Notes in Computer Science, 745-760. doi:10.1007/978-3-319-93417-4_48

KEY TERMS AND DEFINITIONS

Bag of Words: A representation of text using frequencies with an assortment of words.

Context: Any information not present within the original text such as current events.

Convolution Neural Network: A type of deep neural networks that uses convolution and pooling layers to typically classify imagery.

Hate Speech: Language expressing hatred of a type of people with varying degrees of a call to action.

Long Short Term Memory: A type of recurrent neural network that process sequential data while also retaining information deep in the past.

Recurrent Neural Network: A type of neural network where nodes are connected in a temporal sequence to retain information from the past.

Term Frequency Inverse Document Frequency: A statistic that reflects how important a word is based on how frequently it appears in a document while inversely proportional to how often in appears in other documents.

Word Embeddings: Vector representation of terms that reflect the distance between different terms. These are primarily used and generated by neural network text models.

Compilation of References

Achananuparp, P., Hu, X., Zhou, X., & Zhang, X. (2008). Utilizing sentence similarity and question type similarity to response to similar questions in knowledge-sharing community. In *Proceedings of QAWeb Workshop*. pp. 41-52.

Adamczak, R., Porollo, A., & Meller, J. (2004). Accurate prediction of solvent accessibility using neural networks–based regression. *Proteins*, *56*(4), 753–767. doi:10.1002/prot.20176 PMID:15281128

Alain, G., & Bengio, Y. (2013). What regularized auto-encoders learn from the data generating distribution. In *ICLR'2013*, arXiv:1211.4246.

Al-Ayyoub, M., Nuseir, A., Alsmearat, K., Jararweh, Y., & Gupta, B. (2018). Deep learning for Arabic NLP: A survey. *Journal of Computational Science*, *26*, 522–531. doi:10.1016/j. jocs.2017.11.011

Al-Bdour, G. (2017). Comparative study between deep learning frameworks using multiple benchmark datasets. (Doctoral dissertation, Master's thesis, Jordan University of Science and Technology).

alexeyo26. (n.d.). News - Cognitive Toolkit - CNTK. Retrieved from https://docs.microsoft.com/en-us/cognitive-toolkit/news

Alipanahi, B., Delong, A., Weirauch, M. T., & Frey, B. J. (2015). Predicting the sequence specificities of DNA-and RNA-binding proteins by deep learning. *Nature Biotechnology*, *33*(8), 831–838. doi:10.1038/nbt.3300 PMID:26213851

Aliza Sarlan Chayanit Nadam, S. B. (2014). Twitter sentiment analysis. IEEE Xplore, doi:. doi:10.1109/ICIMU.2014.7066632:212–1218

Al-Rfou, R., Alain, G., Almahairi, A., Angermueller, C., Bahdanau, D., Ballas, N., & Bengio, Y. (2016). Theano: A Python framework for fast computation of mathematical expressions. arXiv preprint arXiv:1605.02688.

Arel, I., Rose, D. C., & Karnowski, T. P. (2010). Deep machine learning-a new frontier in artificial intelligence research. *IEEE Computational Intelligence Magazine*, *5*(4), 13–18. doi:10.1109/MCI.2010.938364

Arnold, L., Rebecchi, S., Chevallier, S., & Paugam Moisy, H. (2011). An introduction to deep learning. In Proceedings ESANN, pp. 477–488.

Arsa, D. M. S., Jati, G., Mantau, A. J., & Wasito, I. (2016). Dimensionality reduction using deep belief network in big data case study: Hyperspectral image classification. In *2016 International Workshop on Big Data and Information Security (IWBIS)*, pp. 71–76. 10.1109/IWBIS.2016.7872892

Arulkumaran, K., Deisenroth, M. P., Brundage, M., & Bharath, A. A. (2017). Deep reinforcement learning: A brief survey. *IEEE Signal Processing Magazine*, *34*(6), 26–38. doi:10.1109/MSP.2017.2743240

Badjatiya, P., Gupta, S., Gupta, M., & Varma, V. (2017). Deep learning for hate speech detection in tweets. In *Proceedings of the 26th International Conference on World Wide Web Companion - WWW 17 Companion*. 10.1145/3041021.3054223

Bahrampour, S., Ramakrishnan, N., Schott, L., & Shah, M. (2015). Comparative study of deep learning software frameworks. arXiv preprint arXiv:1511.06435.

Barabasi, A.-L. (2016). Network science. *Cambridge University Press*, 2016.

Barry, J. (2016). Sentiment analysis of online reviews using bag-of-words and LSTM approaches. Google Tech Report. A. Suresh Babu and P. N. V. S.

Bengio, Y. (2009). Learning deep architectures for AI, *Foundations and trendsR in Machine Learning*, 2, 1, pp. 1–127.

Bengio, Y. (2009). Learning deep architectures for AI. Foundations and trends® in Machine Learning, 2(1), 1-127.

Bengio, Y., Yao, L., Alain, G., & Vincent, P. (2013c). Generalized denoising autoencoders as generative models. In NIPS'2013.

Bengio, Y., Courville, A., & Vincent, P. (2013). Representation learning: A review and new perspectives. *IEEE Pattern Analysis and Machine Intelligence*, *35*(8), 1798–1828. doi:10.1109/TPAMI.2013.50 PMID:23787338

Bhargava, R., Nigwekar, S., & Sharma, Y. (2017). Catchphrase extraction from legal documents using LSTM networks. In FIRE (Working Notes). (pp. 72-73).

Bhat, A., Satish, C., D'Souza, N., & Kashyap, N. (2018). Effect of dynamic stoplist on keyword prediction in RAKE.

Bizzoni, Y., & Ghanimifard, M. (2018). Bigrams and BiLSTMs Two neural networks for sequential metaphor detection. In *Proceedings of the Workshop on Figurative Language Processing*, pp. 91–101. 10.18653/v1/W18-0911

Blei, D. M., Ng, A. Y., & Jordan, M. I. (2002). Latent dirichlet allocation. In Advances in neural information processing systems (pp. 601-608).

Blei, D. M., Ng, A. Y., & Jordan, M. I. (2003). Latent dirichlet allocation. *Journal of Machine Learning Research*, *3*(Jan), 993–1022.

Bonarini, A., Lazaric, A., Montrone, F., & Restelli, M. (2009). Reinforcement distribution in fuzzy Q-learning. Fuzzy Sets and Systems. *Special Issue: Fuzzy Sets in Interdisciplinary Perception and Intelligence*, *160*(10), 1420–1443.

Bottou, L. (2015). *Multilayer neural networks*. Deep Learning Summer School.

Britz, D., Goldie, A., Luong, M. T., & Le, Q. (2017). *Massive exploration of neural machine translation architectures.* arXiv preprint arXiv:1703.03906.

Brownlee, J. (2017). Deep learning for natural language processing. Machine learning mastery. Edition: v1.1

Brownlee, J. (2016). *Master machine learning algorithms: Discover how they work and implement them from scratch.* Jason Brownlee.

Buduma, N., & Locascio, N. (2017). *Fundamentals of deep learning: Designing next-generation machine intelligence algorithms.* O'Reilly Media.

Building deep neural networks in the Cloud with Azure GPU VMs, MXNet, and Microsoft R Server.

Caffe2. (2017). A new lightweight, modular, and scalable deep learning framework. Retrieved from *https://caffe2.ai/*

Case studies: TensorFlow. (n.d.). Retrieved from https://www.tensorflow.org/about/case-studies

Causevic, D. (2017, Nov. 29). Getting started with TensorFlow: A machine learning tutorial. Retrieved from https://www.toptal.com/machine-learning/tensorflow-machine-learning-tutorial

Chaudhuri, A. (2016). *Sentiment analysis of customer reviews using robust hierarchical bidirectional recurrent neural network.* Research Gate. doi:10.1007/978-3-319-33625-1_23

Chelba, C., Norouzi, M., & Bengio, S. (2017, June 20). N-gram language modelling using recurrent neural network estimation. arXiv:1703.10724v2 [cs.CL]. Google Tech Report

Chicco, D., Sadowski, P., & Baldi, P. (2014, September). Deep autoencoder neural networks for gene ontology annotation predictions. In *Proceedings of the 5th ACM conference on bioinformatics, computational biology, and health informatics* (pp. 533-540). ACM. 10.1145/2649387.2649442

Chintala, S. (n.d.). Convnet benchmarks. Retrieved from https://github.com/soumith/convnetbenchmarks

Cho, K., Van Merriënboer, B., Gulcehre, C., Bahdanau, D., Bougares, F., Schwenk, H., & Bengio, Y. (2014). Learning phrase representations using RNN encoder-decoder for statistical machine translation. arXiv preprint arXiv:1406.1078.

Chollet, F. (2015). *Keras.* Retrieved from http://keras. io

Chortaras, A., Stamou, G., & Stafylopatis, A. (2005, September). Learning ontology alignments using recursive neural networks. In *Proceedings International Conference on Artificial Neural Networks* (pp. 811-816). Berlin, Germany: Springer.

Chung, J., Gulcehre, C., Cho, K., & Bengio, Y. (2014). Empirical evaluation of gated recurrent neural networks on sequence modeling. *NIPS'2014 Deep Learning workshop*, arXiv 1412.3555.

Cole, R. A., Yan, Y., & Bailey, T. (2001). The influence of bigram constraints on word recognition by humans: Implications for computer speech recognition. ARPA HLT meeting.

Collobert, R., Kavukcuoglu, K., & Farabet, C. (2011). Torch7: A matlab-like environment for machine learning. In BigLearn, NIPS workshop (No. CONF).

Collobert, R., Weston, J., Bottou, L., Karlen, M., Kavukcuoglu, K., & Kuksa, P. (2011). Natural language processing (almost) from scratch. *Journal of Machine Learning Research*, 2493–2537.

Complete Visual Networking Index (VNI). (2016). Forecast, Cisco, San Jose, CA, June.

Copeland, B. M. (2016). The difference between AI, machine learning, and deep learning?. The Official NVIDIA Blog. Np, 29.

Costa, A. L. (2001). *Developing minds: A resource book for teaching thinking* (3rd ed.). Alexandria, VA: Association for Supervision and Curriculum Development.

Das, S., & Barua, R. (2017). Catch phrase extraction from legal documents using deep neural network. In FIRE (Working Notes). (pp. 78-79).

Davidson, T., Warmslay, D., Macy, M., & Weber, I. (2017). Automated hate speech detection and the problem of offensive language. In *Proceedings of the 11th Conference on Web and Social Media.* 512-515.

Deep learning for java. (2017). Open-source, distributed, deep learning library for the JVM.

Deep learning. (2017). For data scientists who need to deliver. Retrieved from *https://skymind.ai/*

Dehghan, A., Masood, S. Z., Shu, G., & Ortiz, E. (2017). View independent vehicle make, model and color recognition using convolutional neural network. arXiv preprint arXiv:1702.01721.

Deng, L. (2014). A tutorial survey of architectures, algorithms, and applications for deep learning. APSIPA Transactions on Signal and Information Processing, 3.

Deng, L., Hinton, G., & Kingsbury, B. (2013, May). New types of deep neural network learning for speech recognition and related applications: An overview. In *Proceedings 2013 IEEE International Conference on Acoustics, Speech, and Signal Processing (ICASSP),* (pp. 8599-8603). IEEE.

Deng, L. (2013). Recent advances in deep learning for speech research at Microsoft. In *Proceedings of ICASSP, 2013*, pp. 8604–8608.

Ding, W., Ishwar, P., Rohban, M. H., & Saligrama, V. (2013). Necessary and sufficient conditions for novel word detection in separable topic models. arXiv preprint arXiv:1310.7994.

Doya, K. (1993). Bifurcations of recurrent neural networks in gradient descent learning. *IEEE Transactions on Neural Networks*, *1*, 75–80.

Ehrig, M., & Sure, Y. (2004, May). Ontology mapping–an integrated approach. In *European semantic web symposium* (pp. 76-91). Berlin, Germany: Springer. 10.1007/978-3-540-25956-5_6

Emma Haddi, X. L., & Shi, Y. (2013). The role of text pre-processing in sentiment analysis. Procedia Computer Science. *Sciverse ScienceDirect*, *17*, 26–32.

Esuli, A., & Sebastiani, F. (2013). Improving text classification accuracy by training label cleaning. *ACM Transactions on Information Systems*, *31*(4), 19. doi:10.1145/2516889

Fadlullah, Z. M., Tang, F., Mao, B., Kato, N., Akashi, O., Inoue, T., & Mizutani, K. (2017). State-of-the-art deep learning: Evolving machine intelligence toward tomorrow's intelligent network traffic control systems. *IEEE Communications Surveys and Tutorials*, *19*(4), 2432–2455. doi:10.1109/COMST.2017.2707140

Fausett, L. (1994). *Fundamentals of neural networks: architectures, algorithms, and applications.* Prentice-Hall.

Faust, O., Hagiwara, Y., Hong, T. J., Lih, O. S., & Acharya, U. R. (2018). Deep learning for healthcare applications based on physiological signals: A review. *Computer Methods and Programs in Biomedicine*, *161*, 1–13. doi:10.1016/j.cmpb.2018.04.005 PMID:29852952

Fjodor van Veen from Asimov Institute compiled a wonderful cheatsheet on NN topologies.

G. team. Google. (n.d.). Retrieved from https://www.tensorflow.org/

Gao, L., & Huang, R. (2017). Detecting online hate speech using context aware models. RANLP 2017 - Recent advances in natural language processing meet deep learning. doi:10.26615/978-954-452-049-6_036

Ge, L. L., Wu, Y. H., Hua, B., Chen, Z. M., & Chen, L. (2017). Image registration based on SOFM neural network clustering. In *Proceedings 2017 36th Chinese Control Conference (CCC)*, pp. 6016–6020, July.

Géron, A. (2018). Neural networks and deep learning.

Gheisari, M., Wang, G., & Md, Z. A. B. (2017). A survey on deep learning in big data. *IEEE Computer Society. 2017 IEEE International Conference on Computational Science and Engineering (CSE) and IEEE International Conference on Embedded and Ubiquitous Computing (EUC).* doi:10.1109/CSE-EUC.2017.215

Glauner, P. O. (2015). Comparison of training methods for deep neural networks. arXiv preprint arXiv:1504.06825.

Goldsborough, P. (2016). A tour of tensorflow. arXiv preprint arXiv:1610.01178.

Goldstein, J., Mittal, V., Carbonell, J., & Kantrowitz, M. (2000). Multidocument summarization by sentence extraction. In *Proceedings of the 2000 NAACLANLP Workshop on Automatic summarization-Vol. 4*, pp. 40–48. ACL. 10.3115/1117575.1117580

Goodfellow, I., Bengio, Y., & Courville, A. (2016). *Deep learning*. Book in preparation for MIT Press Online.

Goodfellow, I., Bengio, Y., & Courville, A. (2018). *Deep learning*. MIT Press.

Grondahl, T., Pajola, L., Juuti, M., & Conti, M. & Asokan, N (2018). All you need is" love": Evading hate-speech detection. *Proceedings of the 11th ACM Workshop on Artificial Intelligence and Security*. 2-12. doi:10.1145/3270101.3270103

Guo, J. (2013). *Backpropagation through time* (pp. 1–9).

Gupta, S., Davidson, J., Levine, S., Sukthankar, R., & Malik, J. (2017). Cognitive mapping and planning for visual navigation. In *Proc. CVPR*, 2017, pp. 1252-1264.

Hakkani-Tür, D., Ji, H., & Grishman, R. (2007). Using information extraction to improve cross-lingual document retrieval. MuLTI-SOuRcE, MuLTILINguAL INfORMATION ExTRAcTION ANd SuMMARIzATION, 7.

Han, L., Kashyap, A., Finin, T., Mayfield, J., & Weese, J. (2013). UMBC EBIQUITY-CORE: Semantic Textual Similarity Systems, Second Joint Conference on Lexical and Computational Semantics (*SEM), *Proceedings of the Main Conference and the Shared Task*, Atlanta, GA. Association for Computational Linguistic, vol. 1, pp. 44-52.

Hariri, B. B., Abolhassani, H., & Sayyadi, H. (2006). A neural-networks-based approach for ontology alignment. In Proceedings SCIS & ISIS 2006 (pp. 1248-1252). Japan Society for Fuzzy Theory and Intelligent Informatics.

Harris, D. (2014, June 2). A startup called Skymind launches, pushing open source deep learning. Retrieved from GigaOM.com.

Harshali, P., & Patil, D. M. A. (2015). Sentiment analysis for social media: a survey. *IEEE Xplore, DOI, 5*. doi:10.1109/ICISSEC.2015.7371033:1–4

Hassan, S. & Mihalcea, R. (2009). Cross-lingual semantic relatedness using encyclopedic knowledge. In Proceedings EMNLP, pp. 1192–1201.

Hatcher, W. G., & Yu, W. (2018). A survey of deep learning: Platforms, applications and emerging research trends. *IEEE transactions.* pp. 2169-3536.

Hatcher, W. G., Booz, J., McGiff, J., Lu, C., & Yu, W. (2017). Edge computing-based machine learning mobile malware detection. In National Cyber Summit.

He, K., Zhang, X., Ren, S. & Sun, J. (2016). Deep residual learning for image recognition. In *Proceedings of CVPR, 2016*, pp. 770–778.

Hinton, G. E. (2009). Deep belief networks. *Scholarpedia, 4*(5), 5947. doi:10.4249cholarpedia.5947

Hinton, G., Deng, L., Yu, D., Dahl, G., Mohamed, A., Jaitly, N., ... Kingsbury, B. (2012). Deep neural networks for acoustic modeling in speech recognition: The shared views of four research groups [Nov]. *IEEE Signal Processing Magazine, 29*(6), 82–97. doi:10.1109/MSP.2012.2205597

Hu, M., & Liu, B. (2004). Mining and summarizing customer reviews. In Proceedings KDD, pp. 168–177. doi:10.1145/1014052.1014073

Huang, H.-H., & Kuo, Y.-H. (2010). Cross-lingual document representation and semantic similarity measure: A fuzzy set and rough set-based approach. *IEEE Transactions on Fuzzy Systems, 18*(6), 1098–1111. doi:10.1109/TFUZZ.2010.2065811

Huhns, M. N., & Singh, M. P. (1997). Ontologies for agents. *IEEE Internet Computing, 1*(6), 81–83. doi:10.1109/4236.643942

Isel Grau Gonzalo Npoles, I. B., & Garca, M. M. (2013). Backpropagation through time algorithm for training recurrent neural networks using variable length instances. 17, 1. 15–24.

Islam, A., & Inkpen, D. (2008). Semantic text similarity using corpus-based word similarity and string similarity. *ACM Transactions on Knowledge Discovery from Data*, 178–190.

Jacovi, A., Shalom, O. S., & Goldberg, Y. (2018). Understanding convolutional neural networks for text classification. *arXiv preprint arXiv:1809.08037.*

Jermyn, M., Desroches, J., Mercier, J., Tremblay, M.-A., St-Arnaud, K., Guiot, M.-C., ... Leblond, F. (2016). Neural networks improve brain cancer detection with Raman spectroscopy in the presence of operating room light artifacts. *Journal of Biomedical Optics, 21*(9). doi:10.1117/1. JBO.21.9.094002 PMID:27604560

Jeyalakshmi, C., Revathi, A., & Yenkataramani, Y. (2016). Integrated models and features-based speaker independent emotion recognition. *International Journal of Telemedicine and Clinical Practices, 1*(3), 277–291. doi:10.1504/IJTMCP.2016.077920

Jia, Y., Shelhamer, E., Donahue, J., Karayev, S., Long, J., Girshick, R., . . . Darrell, T. (2014). Caffe: Convolutional architecture for fast feature embedding. *arXiv preprint arXiv:1408.5093.*

Jian Zhang, D. Q., & Li, Z. (2014). An improved recurrent neural network language model with context vector features. In *Proceedings International Conference on Computing, Communication and Automation.* doi:– 831.10.1109/ICSESS.2014.6933694:828

Jiang, M., Liang, Y., Feng, X., Fan, X., Pei, Z., Xue, Y., & Guan, R. (2018). Text classification based on deep belief network and softmax regression. *Neural Computing & Applications, 29*(1), 61–70. doi:10.100700521-016-2401-x

Jiang, X., Hu, Y., & Li, H. (2009, July). A ranking approach to keyphrase extraction. In *Proceedings of the 32nd international ACM SIGIR conference on Research and development in information retrieval.* (pp. 756-757). ACM.

Jia, Y., Shelhamer, E., Donahue, J., Karayev, S., Long, J., Girshick, R., & Darrell, T. (2014, November). Caffe: Convolutional architecture for fast feature embedding. In *Proceedings of the 22nd ACM international conference on Multimedia* (pp. 675-678). ACM. 10.1145/2647868.2654889

Johnson, J., & Karpathy, A. (2015). *Convolutional neural networks for visual recognition. Convolutional neural networks for visual recognition* (p. 94305). Stanford, CA: Stanford University.

Keras. (2017). The python deep learning library. Retrieved from https://keras.io/

King, J. L. (1983). Centralized versus decentralized computing: Organizational considerations and management options. *ACM Computing Surveys, 15*(4), 319–349. doi:10.1145/289.290

Koboyatshwene, T., Lefoane, M., & Narasimhan, L. (2017). Machine learning approaches for catchphrase extraction in legal documents. In FIRE (Working Notes). (pp. 95-98).

Koolagudi, S. G., Sharma, K., & Rao, K. S. (2012, August). Speaker recognition in emotional environment. In *International Conference on Eco-friendly Computing and Communication Systems* (pp. 117-124). Berlin, Germany: Springer.

Kotsiantis, S. B., Zaharakis, I., & Pintelas, P. (2007). Supervised machine learning: A review of classification techniques. Emerging artificial intelligence applications in computer engineering, 160, 3-24.

Kovalev, V., Kalinovsky, A., & Kovalev, S. (2016). Deep learning with theano, torch, caffe, tensorflow, and deeplearning4j: Which one is the best in speed and accuracy?

Krizhevsky, A., Sutskever, I., & Hinton, G. E. (2012). ImageNet classification with deep convolutional neural networks. In Proceedings Advances in neural information processing systems (pp. 1097-1105). NIPS.

Kulkarni, Y. H., Patil, R., & Shridharan, S. (2017). Detection of catchphrases and precedence in legal documents. In FIRE (Working Notes). (pp. 86-89).

Kumar Ravi, V. R., & Gautam, C. (2015). Online and semi-online sentiment classification. In *Proceedings International Conference on Computing, Communication and Automation*, doi: – 943.10.1109/CCAA.2015.7148531:938

Kumar, P. (2010). Comparing neural network approach with Ngram approach for text categorization. *International Journal on Computer Science and Engineering, 2*(1). pp. 80-83.

Kumar, V., & Garg, M. L. (2017, November). Deep learning in predictive analytics: A survey. In *Proceedings International Conference on Emerging Trends in Computing and Communication Technologies (ICETCCT),* (pp. 1-6). IEEE. 10.1109/ICETCCT.2017.8280331

Lan, S., He, Z., Chen, W., & Chen, L. (2018, July). Hand gesture recognition using convolutional neural networks. In *2018 USNC-URSI Radio Science Meeting (Joint with AP-S Symposium)* (pp. 147-148). IEEE. 10.1109/USNC-URSI.2018.8602809

LeCun, Y., Bengio, Y., & Hinton, G. (2015). Deep learning. *Nature 521.*

LeCun, Y., Bengio, Y., & Hinton, G. (2015). Deep learning. *Nature, 521*(7553), 436.

LeCun, Y., Bengio, Y., & Hinton, G. (2015). Deep learning. *Nature, 521*(7553), 436–444. doi:10.1038/nature14539 PMID:26017442

Lee, C. C., Mower, E., Busso, C., Lee, S., & Narayanan, S. (2011). Emotion recognition using a hierarchical binary decision tree approach. *Speech communication, 53*(9-10), 1162–1171. doi:10.1016/j.specom.2011.06.004

Levine, S., Finn, C., Darrell, T., & Abbeel, P. (2016). End-to-end training of deep visuomotor policies. *Journal of Machine Learning Research, 17*(39), 1–40.

Li, B., Liu, T., & Zhao, Z., Wang, P., & Du, X. (2017). Neural bag-of-Ngrams. In *Proceedings of the Thirty-First AAAI Conference on Artificial Intelligence.* pp. 3067-3074.

Lin, M., Chen, Q., & Yan, S. (2014). Network in network. In *Proceedings of ICLR.*

Liu, W., Wang, Z., Liu, X., Zeng, N., & Liu, Y. (2016). A survey of deep neural network architectures and their applications. *Neurocomputing,* (December). doi:10.1016/j.neucom.2016.12.038

Li, Y., McLean, D., Bandar, Z., O'Shea, J., & Crockett, K. (2006). Sentence similarity based on semantic nets and corpus statistics. *IEEE Transactions on Knowledge and Data Engineering, 18*(18), 1138–1149. doi:10.1109/TKDE.2006.130

Long, J., Shelhamer, E., & Darrell, T. (2015). Fully convolution networks for semantic segmentation. In *Proceedings of CVPR-2015*, pp. 3431–3440.

Luo, T., & Nagarajan, S. G. (2018). Distributed anomaly detection using autoencoder neural networks in WSN for IoT. IEEE.

Luong, M. T., Brevdo, E., & Zhao, R. (2017). Neural machine translation (seq2seq) tutorial. Retrieved from https://github. com/tensorflow/nmt

Maas, A. L., Daly, R. E., Pham, P. T., Huang, D., Ng, A. Y., & Potts, C. (2011, June). Learning word vectors for sentiment analysis. In *Proceedings of the 49th Annual Meeting of the Association for Computational Linguistics: Human language technologies-Vol. 1* (pp. 142-150). Association for Computational Linguistics.

Marquardt, D., & Doclo, S. (2017). Noise power spectral density estimation for binaural noise reduction exploiting direction of arrival estimates. In *2017 IEEE Workshop on Applications of Signal Processing to Audio and Acoustics (WASPAA)*, pp. 234–238, October. 10.1109/WASPAA.2017.8170030

Martinez-Gil, J., & Aldana-Montes, J. F. (2011). Evaluation of two heuristic approaches to solve the ontology meta-matching problem. *Knowledge and Information Systems, 26*(2), 225–247. doi:10.100710115-009-0277-0

Microsoft. (n.d.). The Microsoft cognitive toolkit. Retrieved from https://docs.microsoft.com/en-us/cognitive-toolkit/cntk-evaluationoverview

Mikolov, T., Chen, K., Corrado, G., & Dean, J. (2013, Sept. 7). Efficient estimation of word representations in vector space. arXiv:1301.3781v3 [cs.CL]. Google Tech Report

Moreno, P. J., Ho, P. P., & Vasconcelos, N. (2004). A Kullback-Leibler divergence-based kernel for SVM classification in multimedia applications. In Advances in Neural Information Processing Systems (pp. 1385-1392).

MXNet - Deep learning framework of choice at AWS - All things distributed. Retrieved from www.allthingsdistributed.com

Narayanan, A., Toubiana, V., Barocas, S., Nissenbaum, H., & Boneh, D. (2012). A critical look at decentralized personal data architectures. arXiv preprint arXiv:1202.4503.

Nguyen, T. D., & Kan, M. Y. (2007, December). Keyphrase extraction in scientific publications. In *International Conference on Asian Digital Libraries* (pp. 317-326). Berlin, Germany: Springer.

Nguyen, N. D., Nguyen, T., & Nahavandi, S. (2017). System design perspective for human-level agents using deep reinforcement learning: A survey. *IEEE Access: Practical Innovations, Open Solutions*, 5, 27091–27102. doi:10.1109/ACCESS.2017.2777827

Nielsen, M. A. (2015). *Neural networks and deep learning* (Vol. 25). USA: Determination Press.

Nobata, C., Tetreault, J., Thomas, A., Mehdad, Y., & Chang, Y. (2016). Abusive language detection in online user content. In Proceedings WWW. doi:10.1145/2872427.2883062

Novet, J. (2014, June 2). Skymind launches with open-source, plug-and-play deep learning features for your app.

Oliva, J., Serrano, J. I., Dolores del Castillo, M., & Iglesias, Á. (2011). SyMSS: A syntax-based measure for short-text semantic similarity. *Data & Knowledge Engineering*, 70(4), 390–405. doi:10.1016/j.datak.2011.01.002

Palaniappan, S., & Krishnamurthi, I. (2015). Register linear based model for question classification using costa level questions, *WSEAS Transactions on Computers, 14,* pp. 369-381.

Patterson, J., & Gibson, A. (2017). *Deep learning: A practitioner's approach*. O'Reilly Media.

Pazzani, M. J., & Billsus, D. (2007). Content-based recommendation systems. In *The adaptive web* (pp. 325–341). Berlin, Germany: Springer. doi:10.1007/978-3-540-72079-9_10

Pelletier, F. J. (1994). The principle of semantic compositionality. *Topoi*, 13(1), 11–24. doi:10.1007/BF00763644

Pfeiffer, M., Schaeuble, M., Nieto, J., Siegwart, R., & Cadena, C. (2017). From perception to decision: A data-driven approach to end-to-end motion planning for autonomous ground robots. In *Proc. ICRA*, 2017, pp. 1527–1533.

Pick, R. A. (2015). Shepherd or servant: Centralization and decentralization in information technology governance. *International Journal of Management & Information Systems*, 19(2), 61–68.

Pulido, J. R. G., Ruiz, M. A. G., Herrera, R., Cabello, E., Legrand, S., & Elliman, D. (2006). Ontology languages for the semantic web: A never completely updated review. *Knowledge-based systems*, *19*(7), 489–497. doi:10.1016/j.knosys.2006.04.013

Rao, K. S., Kumar, T. P., Anusha, K., Leela, B., Bhavana, I., & Gowtham, S. V. S. K. (2012). Emotion recognition from speech. *International Journal of Computer Science and Information Technologies*, *3*(2), 3603–3607.

Revathi, A., & Jeyalakshmi, C. (2018). Emotions recognition: different sets of features and models. *International Journal of Speech Technology, 1-10*.

Rish, I. (2001, August). An empirical study of the naive Bayes classifier. In IJCAI 2001 workshop on empirical methods in artificial intelligence, 3(22), pp. 41-46.

Ritze, D., & Paulheim, H. (2011, October). Towards an automatic parameterization of ontology matching tools based on example mappings. In *Proc. 6th ISWC ontology matching workshop (OM)*, Bonn, Germany. (pp. 37-48).

Rodrigo Moraes, J. F. V., & Neto, W. P. (2013). Document-level sentiment classification: an empirical comparison between SVM and ANN. Expert Systems with Applications. *Elsevier ScienceDirect*, *40*, 621–623.

Ruales, J. (n.d.). *Recurrent neural networks for sentiment analysis*. pp. 1–5.

Russakovsky, O., Deng, J., Su, H., Krause, J., Satheesh, S., Ma, S., ... Fei-Fei, L. (2015). ImageNet large scale visual recognition challenge. *International Journal of Computer Vision*, *115*(3), 211–252. doi:10.100711263-015-0816-y

Ruwandika, N., & Weerasinghe, A. (2018). Identification of hate speech in social media. In *2018 18th International Conference on Advances in ICT for Emerging Regions (ICTer)*. doi:10.1109/icter.2018.8615517

Sapra, A., Panwar, N., & Panwar, S. (2013). Emotion recognition from speech. *International Journal of Emerging Technology and Advanced Engineering*, *3*(2), 341–345.

Scanzio, S., Cumani, S., Gemello, R., Mana, F., & Laface, P. (2010). Parallel implementation of Artificial Neural Network training for speech recognition. *Pattern Recognition Letters*, *31*(11), 1302–1309. doi:10.1016/j.patrec.2010.02.003

Schmidhuber, J. (2015). Deep learning in neural networks: An overview. *Neural Networks*, *61*, 85–117. doi:10.1016/j.neunet.2014.09.003 PMID:25462637

Schofield, A., & Davidson, T. (2017). Identifying hate speech in social media. XRDS: Crossroads. *The ACM Magazine for Students*, *24*(2), 56–59. doi:10.1145/3155212

Sebastiani, F. (2002). Machine learning in automated text categorization. *ACM computing surveys (CSUR)*, *34*(1), 1-47.

Sengupta, S., Mohamedrasheed, A. K., Lakshminarasimhan, C., Kapur, M., George, J., Srivastava, M., & Swamy, S. (2018). U.S. Patent No. 9,946,924. Washington, DC: U.S. Patent and Trademark Office.

Sermanet, P., Eigen, D., Zhang, X., Mathieu, M., Fergus, R., & LeCun, Y. (2014). OverFeat: Integrated recognition, localization and detection using convolutional networks. In *Proceeding ICLR.*

Shaikh, F. (2017). *Why are GPUs necessary for training deep learning models?* Analytics Vidhya.

Shalev-Shwartz, S., Shammah, S., & Shashua, A. (2016). Safe, multi-agent, reinforcement learning for autonomous driving. In *Proc. NIPS Workshop Learn. Inference Control Multi-Agent Syst., 2016.* pp. 563-575.

Shi, S., Wang, Q., Xu, P., & Chu, X. (2016). Benchmarking state-of-the-art deep learning software tools. *ArXiv e-prints, Aug. 2016.*

Shi, S., Wang, Q., Xu, P., & Chu, X. (2016, November). Benchmarking state-of-the-art deep learning software tools. In *2016 7th International Conference on Cloud Computing and Big Data (CCBD),* (pp. 99-104). IEEE. 10.1109/CCBD.2016.029

Silver, D., Huang, A., Maddison, C. J., Guez, A., Sifre, L., van den Driessche, G., ... Hassabis, D. (2016). Mastering the game of Go with deep neural networks and tree search. [EP –, Jan]. *Nature, 529*(7587), 484–489. doi:10.1038/nature16961 PMID:26819042

Simonyan, K., & Zisserman, A. (2014). Two-stream convolution networks for action recognition in videos. In *Proceedings of NIPS-2014,* pp. 568–576.

Simonyan, K., & Zisserman, A. (2015). Very deep convolutional networks for large-scale image recognition. In ICLR.

Simonyan, K., & Zisserman, A. (2015). Very deep convolutional networks for large-scale image recognition. In *Proceedings of ICLR.*

Skymind intelligence layer community edition. (n.d.). Retrieved from deeplearning4j.org.

Skymind's Deeplearning4j, the Eclipse Foundation, and scientific computing in the JVM. *Jaxenter.*

Sridevi, U. K., Shanthi, P., & Nagaveni, N. (2018). Deep model framework for ontology-based document clustering. In M. Habib (Ed.), *Handbook of research on investigations in artificial life research and development* (pp. 424–435). Hershey, PA: IGI Global. doi:10.4018/978-1-5225-5396-0.ch019

Sutskever, I., Vinyals, O., & Le, Q. V. (2014). Sequence to sequence learning with neural networks. In Advances in neural information processing systems. (pp. 3104-3112).

Sze, V., Chen, Y. H., Yang, T. J., & Emer, J. S. (2017). Efficient processing of deep neural networks: A tutorial and survey. *Proceedings of the IEEE, 105*(12), 2295-2329.

Szegedy, C. (2015). Going deeper with convolutions, *in Proceedings of CVPR,* 2015, pp. 1–9.

Szegedy, C., Liu, W., Jia, Y., Sermanet, P., Reed, S., Anguelov, D., . . . Rabinovich, A. (2014a). Going deeper with convolutions. Technical report, arXiv:1409.4842

The Microsoft cognitive toolkit. (2017). Retrieved from https://docs.microsoft.com/en-us/cognitive-toolkit/

Theano. (2017). Retrieved from http://deeplearning.net/software/theano/

Thompson, J., Jain, A., LeCun, Y., & Bregler, C. (2014). Joint training of a convolutional network and a graphical model for human pose estimation. In NIPS'2014.

Torch. (2017). A scientific computing framework for Luajit. Retrieved from http://torch.ch/

Towards data science. (n.d.). Retrieved from https://towardsdatascience.com/

Tran, V., Nguyen, M. L., & Satoh, K. (2018). Automatic catchphrase extraction from legal case documents via scoring using deep neural networks. *arXiv preprint arXiv:1809.05219.*

Tsai, C.-F. (2012). Bag-of-words representation in image annotation: A review article. *ISRN Artificial Intelligence, 2012,* 1–19. doi:10.5402/2012/376804

Umbrich, J., Gutierrez, C., Hogan, A., Karnstedt, M., & Parreira, J. X. (2013, May). The ACE theorem for querying the web of data. In Proceedings *WWW* (pp. 133–134). Companion Volume.

Valduriez, P. (2011, August). Principles of distributed data management in 2020? In *Proceedings International Conference on Database and Expert Systems Applications* (pp. 1-11). Berlin, Germany: Springer. 10.1007/978-3-642-23088-2_1

van den Oord, A. (2016). WaveNet: A generative model for raw audio. [Online]. Available: Bengio, Yoshua, Courville, Aaron, Vincent, Pascal. (2013). Representation learning: A review and new perspectives. *IEEE Transactions on Pattern Analysis and Machine Intelligence, 35*(8), 1798–1828.

Walaa Medhat Ahmed Hassan, H. K. (2014). Sentiment analysis algorithms and applications: A survey. *Elsevier ScienceDirect, 5,* 1093–1113.

Wang, D., Khosla, A., Gargeya, R., Irshad, H., & Beck, A. H. (2016). Deep learning for identifying metastatic breast cancer. arXiv preprint arXiv:1606.05718.

Watanabe, H., Bouazizi, M., & Ohtsuki, T. (2018). Hate speech on Twitter: A pragmatic approach to collect hateful and offensive expressions and perform hate speech detection. *IEEE access: Practical innovations, open solutions, 6,* 13825–13835. doi:10.1109/ACCESS.2018.2806394

Wenge Rong Baolin Peng, C. L., & Xiong, Z. (2014). Semi-supervised dual recurrent neural network for sentiment analysis. Expert systems with applications. *Elsevier ScienceDirect, 41,* 3506–3513.

Wiemer-Hastings, P. (2004). All parts are not created equal: SIAM-LSA, *Proceedings of 26th Annual Conference of the Cognitive Science Society,* pp. 22-41.

Woodhouse, J. (2016, January). Big, big, big data: Higher and higher resolution video surveillance. [Online]. Available at http://technology.ihs.com

Wulczyn, E., Thain, N., & Dixon, L. (2017). Ex machina: Personal attacks seen at scale. *Proceedings of the 26th International Conference on World Wide Web - WWW 17*. doi:10.1145/3038912.3052591

Wu, S., Falk, T. H., & Chan, W. Y. (2011). Automatic speech emotion recognition using modulation spectral features. *Speech communication, 53*(5), 768–785. doi:10.1016/j.specom.2010.08.013

Xiong, H. Y., Alipanahi, B., Lee, L. J., Bretschneider, H., Merico, D., Yuen, R. K. C., ... Frey, B. J. (2015). The human splicing code reveals new insights into the genetic determinants of disease. *Science, 347*(6218), 1254806. doi:10.1126cience.1254806 PMID:25525159

Yadhav, S. K. (2015). Sentiment analysis and classification: A survey. *International Journal of Advance Research in Computer Science and Management Studies, 3*(3), 113–121, 83, 84.

Yan Zhao, S. D., & Li, L. (2014). Sentiment analysis on news comments based on supervised learning method. *International Journal of Multimedia and Ubiquitous Engineering, 9*(7), 333–346. doi:10.14257/ijmue.2014.9.7.28

Yanping Yin, Z. J. (2015). Document sentiment classification based on the word embedding. In *Proceedings International Conference on Mechatronics, Materials, Chemistry and Computer Engineering, 2.* 456–461.

Yeshwanth, C., Sooraj, P. S. A., Sudhakaran, V., & Raveendran, V. (2017). Estimation of intersection traffic density on decentralized architectures with deep networks. In *2017 International Smart Cities Conference (ISC2)*, pp. 1–6, Sept.

Yeung, C. M. A., Liccardi, I., Lu, K., Seneviratne, O., & Berners-Lee, T. (2009, January). Decentralization: The future of online social networking. In *W3C Workshop on the Future of Social Networking Position Papers* (Vol. 2, pp. 2-7).

Youngy, T., Hazarikaz, D., Poria, S., & Cambria, E. (2018, November). Recent trends in deep learning based natural language processing. arXiv:1708.02709v8 [cs.CL]. Google Tech Report

Yu, D., Eversole, A., Seltzer, M., Yao, K., Huang, Z., Guenter, B., & Droppo, J. (2014). An introduction to computational networks and the computational network toolkit. Microsoft Technical Report MSR-TR-2014–112.

Yu, F. R., & He, Y. (n.d.). Deep reinforcement learning for wireless networks.

Yu, D., Yao, K., & Zhang, Y. (2015). The computational network toolkit [best of the web]. *IEEE Signal Processing Magazine, 32*(6), 123–126. doi:10.1109/MSP.2015.2462371

Zeng, H., Edwards, M. D., Liu, G., & Gifford, D. K. (2016). Convolutional neural network architectures for predicting DNA–protein binding. *Bioinformatics (Oxford, England), 32*(12), i121–i127. doi:10.1093/bioinformatics/btw255 PMID:27307608

Zhang, T., Kahn, G., Levine, S., & Abbeel, P. (2016). Learning deep control policies for autonomous aerial vehicles with MPC-guided policy search. In *Proc. ICRA, 2016*, pp. 528–535.

Zhang, X., Pan, X., & Wang, S. (2017). Fuzzy DBN with rule-based knowledge representation and high interpretability. In *2017 12th International Conference on Intelligent Systems and Knowledge Engineering (ISKE)*, pp. 1–7.

Zhang, Z., Cui, P., & Zhu, W. (2018). Deep learning on graphs: A survey. *arXiv:1812.04202v1 [cs.LG] 11 Dec 2018*.

Zhang, Z., Robinson, D., & Tepper, J. (2018). Detecting hate speech on Twitter using a convolution-GRU based deep neural network. The Semantic Web Lecture Notes in Computer Science, 745-760. doi:10.1007/978-3-319-93417-4_48

Zhang, G. P. (2000). Neural networks for classification: A survey. *IEEE Transactions on Systems, Man and Cybernetics. Part C, Applications and Reviews*, *30*(4), 451–462. doi:10.1109/5326.897072

Zhang, Y., Jin, R., & Zhou, Z.-H. (2012). Understanding bag-of-words model: A statistical framework. In *ECCV Workshop on Statistical Learning in Computer Vision*, Prague, Czech Republic

Zharmagambetov, A. S., & Pak, A. A. (2015). Sentiment analysis of a document using deep learning approach and decision trees. In *Proceedings International Conference on Electronics Computer and Computation*. – 4.10.1109/ICECCO.2015.7416902

Zhi-Hong Deng, K. H. L., & Yu, H. L. (2014). A study of supervised term weighting scheme for sentiment analysis. *Elsevier ScienceDirect*, *41*(7), 3506–3513.

Zhou, J., & Troyanskaya, O. G. (2015). Predicting effects of noncoding variants with deep learning-based sequence model. *Nature Methods*, *12*(10), 931–934. doi:10.1038/nmeth.3547 PMID:26301843

About the Contributors

Sumathi S. obtained her B.E. degree in Computer science and Engineering from GCE, Tirunelveli in 2000, and Master's degree from Sathyabama University with distinction in 2009. She received her Doctorate from Anna University in January 2017. She is currently working as Associate Professor in St. Joseph's College of Engineering in the department of Information Technology, Chennai. She has 15 years of teaching experience. She has published 12 papers in journal and International conferences. From 2000 to 2002, she worked as an embedded software engineer and completed several projects for NIOT-Chennai. She is passionate towards innovative projects and has guided many students in the field of Networks, Artificial intelligence etc. She has also mentored students in competitions such as Smart India Hackathon and Nokia Technology Day. She has been invited as session chair for many international conferences. Her student's project has been nominated for CTS best project and also for INAE award. She is an active Doctoral Committee member through which she has provided guidance to those carrying out research.

Janani M. obtained her B.TECH degree in Information Technology from Prince Shri Venkateshwara Padmavathy Engineering College with Distinction in 2009 and Master's degree from Anna University in 2011. She is currently working as Assistant Professor in St.Joseph's College of Engineering in the department of Information Technology, Chennai. She has 8 years of teaching experience. She has published a paper in an International conference in the field of Natural Language Processing. She is passionate towards innovative projects and has guided many students in the field of Networks, NLP, Multimedia, IOT, etc.

* * *

Bhanu Chander, a research scholar at Pondicherry University, India, graduated from Acharya Nagarjuna University, A.P, in the year of 2013. A post-graduate degree from Central University of Rajasthan, Rajasthan in the year of 2016. Presently his main interesting areas include Wireless Sensor Networks, Machine Learning, Deep Learning, Neural networks, Cryptography, and Computer networks.

Anjali Daisy is a Research scholar in School of Management, SASTRA Deemed University, Thanjavur, Tamilnadu, India. She has done her undergraduation in the field of computer science and post graduation in the field of Management studies. She has done her MBA in PSG Institute of Management, Coimbatore. She has worked as a HR Executive in PEPSICO India Pvt Ltd. She has published many research articles in Scopus and ESCI indexed journals. Her Research area is in the field of "Emotional Intelligence". She has published articles about the neurobiology of emotions.

Chitra A. Dhawale is currently working as a professor and Head, P.G. Department of Computer Application, P.R. Pote College of Engineering and Management, Amravati. She worked as a professor at Symbiosis International University, Pune. She is a senior member of the IACSIT, Member of International Association of Engineers (IAENG), Hong Kong and Life Member of ISTE, New Delhi. Her research interest includes image and video processing, multi-biometric, cloud security. She is guiding research scholars in computer science from S.G.B. Amravati and R.T.M. Nagpur University. She has published more than 60 research papers in reputed international journals and IEEE, Springer, Elsevier, ACM conferences proceedings and 04 book chapters in IGI Global Publications. She worked on the organizing and program committees of various National and International Conferences, chaired sessions and delivered invited talk in various faculty development programs, orientation, refresher courses, national and international conferences. She is a motivational speaker. Till now she has conducted several workshops on "Effective Research Methodology", "Research Writing Skills", "Placement Preparation", "100 techniques for speed mathematics", "Interview Techniques", "Spiritual thoughts" etc. She has been reviewing books from various prestigious publication and also reviewer for international journals. As a part of social contribution, she is executive member of NGO "AADHAR Foundation", Amravati.

Kritika Dhawale is studying in B.Tech (ECE) at Indian Institute of Information Technology, Nagpur, She is having keen interest in Deep Learning. She completed course on machine learning from IIT Chennai, presented paper at International Conference and currently doing internship.

S. Indumathi obtained her B.E degree in Electronics and Communication Engineering from Thangavelu engineering college, Chennai and Master's degree from Anna University with first class in 2010. She is currently working as Assistant

Professor in Jerusalem College of Engineering in the department of Information Technology, Chennai. She has 13 years of teaching experience. She has published papers in International journals and also has published many papers in international and national conference. She is passionate towards innovative projects and has guided many students in the field of Networks, Artificial intelligence, etc.

Suresh Jaganathan is an Associate Professor in the Department of Computer Science and Engineering has more than 22 years of teaching experience. He received his PhD in Computer Science from Jawaharlal Nehru Technological University, Hyderabad, M.E. Software Engineering from Anna University and B.E Computer Science & Engineering, from Mepco Schlenk Engineering College, Madurai Kamarajar University. He has more than 26 publications in International Journals and Conferences of which four are Refereed SCI Indexed journals. Apart from this, to his credit he has filed 2 Patents and written a book on "Cloud Computing: A Practical Approach for Learning and Implementation", published by Pearson Publications. He is recognized reviewer for the following journals, 1. Elsevier Journal of "Computers in Biology and Medicine", ISSN:0010-4825, 2. Elsevier Journal of "Network and Computer Applications", ISSN: 1084-8045 and 3. IET "Computer Vision", ISSN: 1751-9632. His areas of interest are Distributed Computing, Multimedia Streaming, Big Data Analytics & Machine learning.

S. Kayalvizhi, Junior Research Fellow in Department of Computer science and Engineering. She completed her B.E. in computer science engineering from RMD Engineering College and M.E. in computer science engineering from SSN College of Engineering. Area of interest are machine learning, natural language processing and deep learning.

Brian Khieu is a Computer Science master's student at San Jose State University, and he received his bachelor's in Computer Science and Engineering from the University of California Davis. Currently, he is working on his master's thesis which comprises of defending hate speech detection models against adversaries and lexical evasion schemes. His research interests are in information flow, inference control, blockchain applications, and natural language processing. He has several years of IT experience providing support and maintenance for a network of health clinics in the Salinas area.In his free time, he enjoys planting trees and tending to his various garden plants.

Melody Moh obtained her MS and Ph.D., both in computer science, from Univ. of California - Davis. She joined San Jose State University in 1993, and has been a Professor since Aug 2003. Her research interests include cloud computing, mobile, wireless networking, security/privacy for cloud and network systems, and machine learning applications. She has received over 500K dollars of research grants from both NSF and industry, has published over 150 refereed papers in international journals, conferences and as book chapters, and has consulted for various companies. Her conference papers have earned the Honorary Paper Award at ACM IMCOM 2018 and the Best Paper Runner-Up award at ACMSE 2019.

Arunmozhi Mourougappane had received her B.Tech Degree in Computer Science and Engineering from SMVEC, Pondicherry University, India in 2015 and M.E in Computer Science and Engineering from SSN College of Engineering, Anna University in 2017. In 2017, she joined as Assistant Professor in the Department of Information Technology at St. Joseph's College of Engineering, Chennai. Her current research area includes Deep Learning, Big Data.

Pathur Nisha S has completed her Master's degree in Computer Science and Engineering and completed her Doctorate in Information and Communication Engineering in Anna University.She has published many papers in national and international conference and journals.Her current research area includes Big Data, Data Mining.

Shanthi Palaniappan has obtained her Doctorate degree and has 15 years of teaching experience. She has published more national and international journals papers. She has research interest in the areas of information retrieval, NLP, semantic similarity, question classification and question answering. Currently, she is doing research on Deep learning.

Priyanka Pranav Patel received her Bachelor degree in Information Technology in the year 2006 with First Class. During 2005-2008 she has worked as a software engineer in one of the reputed Software engineering Solution Company.in 2009 she was hired as the assistant professor at A.D. Patel engineering institute. She got Master degree in Computer science & Engineering from Chandubhai S Patel Institute of Technology, CHARUSAT in 2013 and is currently working as Assistant Professor at CHARUSAT University, Gujarat. Her area of interest is in Image and Video Processing, Programing in C, Object-oriented programming, Software Engineering, Machine learning, deep learning. She writes and presents many research work on computer vision, image processing, machine learning, and deep learning.

A. Revathi has obtained B.E (ECE), M.E (Communication Systems), and Ph.D (Speech Processing) from National Institute of Technology, Tiruchirappalli, Tamilnadu, India in 1988, 1993 and 2009 respectively. She has been serving on the faculty of Electronics and Communication Engineering for 30 years and she is currently working as a Professor in the Department of ECE, SASTRA Deemed University, Thanjavur, India. She has published 25 papers in Reputed International journals and presented papers in more than 30 International Conferences. Her areas of interest include Speech processing, Signal processing, Image processing, Biometrics & Security, Communication Systems, Embedded Systems and Computer Networks.

Rajkumar S. is working as a Senior Technical Lead in Engineering and R&D Services, HCL Technologies Ltd., India. He has done his Big Data Analytics (BDA) from Indian Institute of Management, Bangalore (IIMB) and he is pursuing an M. Tech in Data Analytics specialization from BITS Pilani. He has over 15 years of rich industry experience in Automating the complex jobs using NLP / Machine Learning / RPA with Python/Java/Hive/Spark/.net/MSSQL/MYSQL in the field of Data Mining /Text processing.

N. Sasikaladevi working as a faculty at SASTRA Deemed University since 2014. She authored a book titled in "Programming in C#.NET" published by Prentice Hall of India. She has presented papers in IEEE, Springer and Elsevier conferences. She published papers in various reputed journals. She received young professional award from CSI, India. She got young scientist award and woman scientist award from Department of Science and Technology, Government of India. Her research interest includes curve based cryptography, quantum cryptography and network security.

U.K Sridevi has over 18 years of experience in teaching. Her research interests include information retrieval, data mining and data analytics. Information extraction concepts related to NLP, Linear Regression, Semantic similarity, Question Classification and Question Answering are carried in the research. She has published many papers in national and international conference and journals.

Amit Thakkar has received his B.E Degree in I.T. from Gujarat University in 2002 and Master Degree from Dharmsinh Desai University, Gujarat, India in 2007. He has finished his PhD in the area of Multi Relational Classification from-KadiSarvaVishwaVidyalaya (KSV), Gandhinagar, India in 2016. He is working as an Associate Professor in the Department of Information Technology in Faculty of Engineering and Technology, CHARUSAT University, Changa, Gujarat Since 2002. He has published more than 50 research papers in the field of Machine Learning & Data Mining. He has also published 3 books in the area of Data Mining. His current research interest includes Machine Learning, Multi Relational Data Mining, Relational Classification and Big Data Analytics.He has guided more than 30 M.Tech Dissertation in the area of Machine Learning, Data Analytics and Image

Processing. He is currently guiding 3 M.Tech and 7 Ph.D Research Scholars. He has delivered many expert talks at various STTP and Workshops. He has also severed as a member of Technical Committee at Various National and International Journals/ Conferences. He is also a Team Lead for I-Doc project a joint consultancy work between CHARUSAT and CELTIC System Pvt. Ltd, Vadodara. He has received N NVidia Titan X GPU from NVidia for research work in the area of deep learning. He has also received grant of 6.36 lakhs for development of computer vision and pattern recognition lab from AICTE.

D. Thenmozhi, Associate Professor in the Department of Computer Science has 24 years of teaching and research experience. She received her B.E degree in Computer Science Engineering from Madras University, and M.E in Computer Science and Engineering from Anna University. She completed her PhD in Natural Language Processing from Anna University, India. Her area of interest includes Natural Language Processing, Information Retrieval, Artificial Intelligence, Data Mining, Machine Learning and Deep Learning. She has published 37 research papers in the International Journals and Conferences.

Index

Ensure Quality Research is Introduced to the Academic Community

Become an IGI Global Reviewer for Authored Book Projects

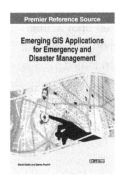

Premier Reference Source

Emerging GIS Applications for Emergency and Disaster Management

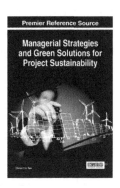

Premier Reference Source

Managerial Strategies and Green Solutions for Project Sustainability

Premier Reference Source

Comparative Approaches to Using R and Python for Statistical Data Analysis

Premier Reference Source

Solutions for High-Touch Communications in a High-Tech World

The overall success of an authored book project is dependent on quality and timely reviews.

In this competitive age of scholarly publishing, constructive and timely feedback significantly expedites the turnaround time of manuscripts from submission to acceptance, allowing the publication and discovery of forward-thinking research at a much more expeditious rate. Several IGI Global authored book projects are currently seeking highly-qualified experts in the field to fill vacancies on their respective editorial review boards:

Applications and Inquiries may be sent to:
development@igi-global.com

Applicants must have a doctorate (or an equivalent degree) as well as publishing and reviewing experience. Reviewers are asked to complete the open-ended evaluation questions with as much detail as possible in a timely, collegial, and constructive manner. All reviewers' tenures run for one-year terms on the editorial review boards and are expected to complete at least three reviews per term. Upon successful completion of this term, reviewers can be considered for an additional term.

If you have a colleague that may be interested in this opportunity, we encourage you to share this information with them.

IGI Global Proudly Partners With eContent Pro International

Receive a 25% Discount on all Editorial Services

Editorial Services

IGI Global expects all final manuscripts submitted for publication to be in their final form. This means they must be reviewed, revised, and professionally copy edited prior to their final submission. Not only does this support with accelerating the publication process, but it also ensures that the highest quality scholarly work can be disseminated.

English Language Copy Editing

Let eContent Pro International's expert copy editors perform edits on your manuscript to resolve spelling, punctuaion, grammar, syntax, flow, formatting issues and more.

Scientific and Scholarly Editing

Allow colleagues in your research area to examine the content of your manuscript and provide you with valuable feedback and suggestions before submission.

Figure, Table, Chart & Equation Conversions

Do you have poor quality figures? Do you need visual elements in your manuscript created or converted? A design expert can help!

Translation

Need your documjent translated into English? eContent Pro International's expert translators are fluent in English and more than 40 different languages.

Email: customerservice@econtentpro.com   www.igi-global.com/editorial-service-partners